BERGLUND CENTER FOR INTERNET STUDIES

INTERFACE

THE JOURNAL OF EDUCATION, COMMUNITY, AND VALUES
Volume 13

Published by
Berglund Center for Internet Studies
bcis.pacificu.edu

Printed in the United States of America
Volume 13
ISBN 978-0-983453-3-4 (paperback)
Interface (Forest Grove, Oregon)
ISSN 1940-915X

Berglund Center for Internet Studies
Pacific University
2043 College Way, Forest Grove, OR 97116
http://bcis.pacificu.edu

Published by Staff of Pacific University Oregon's
Berglund Center for Internet Studies,
Forest Grove, Oregon, USA

Jerry Greenfeld, Managing Editor
Matthew Yasuoka, Copy Editor/Publisher
Justin Redona, Assisting Copy Editor/Publisher

The online version of Interface was produced by:
Matthew Yasuoka, Copy Editor, Publisher
Justin Redona, Assisting Copy Editor/Publisher
Brianna Castellini, Assisting Copy Editor/Publisher
Kristina Nagai, HTML Editor
Josh Siva, Systems Operators

http://bcis.pacificu.edu/interface/

Acknowledgements

The publication of this annual issue of our journal, *Interface*, Volume 13, marks our thirteenth year of regular production as an e-journal. Through the generosity of James and Mary Berglund, alumni of Pacific University, the Berglund Center has been able to facilitate the research of topics pertaining to the Internet and its effects on our community.

We are also grateful to this year's Berglund Center student staff, as well as the staff members who have preceded them, thank you all for your hard work!

Also, we'd like to thank our writers and editors, who have spent many hours ensuring the quality and usefulness of the information contained in our journal. We are especially grateful to Jerry Greenfeld, member of our advisory board and guiding hand, without his support this journal would not have been possible.

And let's not forget the tireless efforts of our present Program Coordinator, Nicole Nowlin. It was due to her efforts that our staff was able to produce and design what we know as the thirteenth volume of *Interface.*

We would also like to extend a warm welcome to our new director, Andy Soria, who brings an exciting vision and purpose to the Center.

And thank you to everyone else who has made the Berglund Center and *Interface* possible.

The Interface Team
Pacific University, Oregon
April, 2014

Introduction

Interface, the electronic journal of the Berglund Center for Internet Studies, Pacific University Oregon, is written and produced for those interested in the impact of the Internet on the world around them. The Internet has influenced many aspects of our lives, which include the way we work, communicate, teach, and learn. The utility of the Internet grows exponentially as people realize the ever-expanding range of its abilities.

In *Interface*, we study all of these phenomena, utilizing the flexibility of an electronic journal, which can be useful to all audiences, unlike the rigidly determined form of traditional journals. At the Berglund Center we not only publish the results of our authors' research and thought, but also have the great pleasure of encouraging such productivity through grants and scholarships.

In 2013, the Berglund Center for Internet Studies entered a period of great change. We completed six fascinating Roundtables, all available for viewing online, gathered the articles in this edition of *Interface* from all walks of study, and saw the retirement of our esteemed Program Coordinator, Theresa Floyd. In July, we left the College of Arts & Sciences to come under the growing umbrella of Pacific University's new College of Business. As we march into a near year and a new Berglund Center, we dedicate this volume to those who brought us this far – our founders, the Berglund's, as well as their daughter Julie, who serves currently on our Advisory Board; Jeffrey Barlow, Professor Emeritus and retired Director of the Center; and Theresa Floyd, retired Program Coordinator.

This is the final volume of *Interface* in its current iteration. As the Berglund Center undergoes a transition of leadership and direction, *Interface* too will be reborn for special issues over the course of the next year. We thank our loyal contributors and readers, the student and faculty fellows, and the staff who have worked so hard to grow *Interface* to its current evolution. Please look for previous editions of *Interface* and other publications by the Berglund Center for Internet Studies on Amazon and Barnes & Noble.

We hope you enjoy this volume and look forward to presenting new work to you in the near future.

Nicole Nowlin
Program Co-ordinator

Contents

HEALTH CARE

DIGITAL NARRATIVE PROJECTS

SOCIAL SCIENCES

ENGLISH

BOOK REVIEWS

EDITORIAL

DIRECTOR'S MESSAGE

APPENDICES

LAW

Volume 13

Challenges in Cyberspace

by Leonard D. DuBoff*

The World Wide Web has provided incredible communication opportunities. By merely posting an item on a computer in your home or office, you can have it transmitted around the globe. There are, however, numerous challenges presented by this modern process.

Many creative people feel that anything found on the Web is available for them to use and exploit in any way they desire. Indeed, a prominent law professor, Lawrence Lessig, cofounder of Creative Commons, espouses the theory that free use of others' materials fosters creativity. [1] Unfortunately, this belief is not consistent with the law in many countries. It presents a clash of rights between the creators of a work and those who wish to freely use it.

One of the ways in which this collision of rights may occur is when a scholar finds an interesting article written by somebody else, reproduces that article on his or her own website and provides hyperlinks for particular portions of that article. For example, if a teaching technique is discussed, a link may be inserted so as to showcase an example of that teaching technique by directing the reader to another website when the name of the technique is clicked. Similarly, a link may be used to provide a more expanded explanation of a particular concept. Links may also be used for the purpose of having pictorial illustrations of materials discussed.

This situation, in which hyperlinks are added to somebody else's article, should be distinguished from the common practice of adding links to one's own work. Just as scholars legally add footnotes referencing the works of other scholars to books or articles they themselves have written, in most instances, adding a hyperlink directing the reader to another's website for purposes of citation or providing a more detailed explanation is not a problem according to case law.

The situation discussed here is different. A scholar copying someone else's article to his or her own website and then adding hyperlinks to that article appears more analogous to a person republishing another author's book after adding footnotes to it.

Is this use of another's article without permission legal? Is the addition of hyperlinks for the purpose of explanation or illustration legal? These are the kind of questions that are now being presented by the expanded opportunities available in cyberspace.

Focusing on the law of the United States, since that is the jurisdiction in which the Berglund Center is located, we begin the analysis by reviewing US copyright law. Section 106 of that statute sets forth "the bundle of rights" that are provided to the copyright owner in this country. Among those rights are the right to make reproductions of the copyrighted work and the right to create derivative works. When the researcher reproduces an article found on the web without first obtaining permission from the copyright owner, the researcher may be creating an unauthorized copy of the protected work in violation of one of the copyright owner's exclusive rights. Unless there is some exception available for this unauthorized reproduction, the copying would be an unlawful infringement.

One of the most common exceptions available, the "fair use doctrine," is found in section 118 of the statute. This section of the law provides that a use that might otherwise be deemed infringing and unlawful will be a permitted "fair use" in certain circumstances. The law provides that at least four factors must be considered in order to determine whether the use is "fair."

First, the nature of the use must be evaluated. If the use is "productive," such as writing a book review using quotes from the book, the use is likely to be fair. If, on the other hand, the work is merely reproduced in order to satisfy a need for that work, it is likely not. Second, the character of the work must be considered. Using a quotation from a reference book of quotable quotations would likely be permitted while reproducing a workbook, which is a consumable, would probably not. Third, the extent of copying should be evaluated. Copying a little bit is likely permissible, while reproducing the entire work, or the most important part of a work, is probably not. Finally, the effect that the copying has on the copyright owner's market must be considered. If the creator of the work is deprived of a sale, then there is likely an infringement.

In addition to the problem presented by an unauthorized reproduction, the researcher must determine whether adding hyperlinks for purposes of explanation or illumination is legal.

Since the copyright law provides the copyright owner with the exclusive right to create derivative works, it is important to consider how the law defines "derivative work."

The copyright law defines a "derivative work" as follows: "a work based upon one or more preexisting works, such as a translation, musical arrangement, dramatization, fictionalization, motion picture version, sound recording, art reproduction, abridgment, condensation, or any other form in which a work may be recast, transformed, or adapted. A work consisting of editorial revisions, annotations, elaborations, or other modifications which, as a whole, represent an original work of authorship, is a "derivative work". 17 USC § 101.

It is, therefore, apparent that the addition of hyperlinks to add definitions, examples, illustrations, and the like would be the creation of a derivative work and likely an infringement.

Thus, the creative scholar who finds an interesting article on the Web and decides to adopt that work without first obtaining permission is likely infringing the rights of the work's copyright owner in two ways. Even if the copy were considered "fair use," the researcher would still have to overcome another obstacle, since the addition of hyperlinks to the article is likely to be considered the creation of a derivative work, thus compounding the infringing activity. The scholar would be well advised to seek permission before engaging in these activities since the consequences of infringing another's copyright-protected work can be serious.

While the World Wide Web provides a great many opportunities, it also presents a host of challenges. Balancing the rights of those who create copyrightable work with the rights of those who desire to exploit materials they find online is a modern challenge. Scholars are now responsible not only for developing innovative projects, but also for determining whether their innovations are legal in order to protect themselves from liability.

Acknowledgements

*Thanks to Rudolph Lopez III, clerk with The DuBoff Law Group, LLC, for his assistance with this article.

Notes

[1] Lessig, Lawrence. (2004) *Free Culture: How Big Media Uses Technology and the Law to Lock Down Culture and Control Creativity*. New York, NY: The Penguin Press. Retrieved from http://www.free-culture.cc/freeculture.pdf

EDUCATION

Volume 13

"Hole in the Wall" Education and its Benefits to Society

by Taylor N. Farris

In the realm of today's technology, the TED organization has the power and mobility necessary to spread the buzz about any number of topics dealing with Technology, Entertainment, or Design. The nonprofit company, which began in 1984, aims to spread ideas across the globe and provide insight and inspiration in nearly every aspect of life. [1] These inspirational, educational perspectives have given a new depth to the concept of lifelong learning for many, and have spawned numerous creative and innovative environments. In recent years, the group's TED Talks have been particularly insightful, and have spurred the coveted TED prize—a $1 million grant in support of "one wish to change the world." Previous noteworthy winners include Jamie Oliver for his quest to provide a nutritional revolution, Bill Clinton for a healthcare system in Rwanda, and Bono's push for American activism in Africa. [2] The 2013 winner of the TED prize is a man by the name of Sugata Mitra [LINK TO http://en.wikipedia.org/wiki/Sugata_Mitra], who may be less famous but certainly possesses no less ambition or success. As an educational researcher, Dr. Mitra has long studied different learning styles and methods, but has received most notable praise for his groundbreaking "Hole in The Wall" experiments.

Dr. Mitra, Chief Scientist Emeritus at NIIT and Professor of Educational Technology at the School of Education, Communication and Language Sciences at Newcastle University, England, was constantly struck by the notion that the children living in the nearby slum may never have the opportunity to experience technology-based learning. At the same time, Mitra was being constantly approached by wealthy families making interesting claims. He stated that: "[I] had…lots of parents, rich people, who had computers, and who used to tell me, "You know, my son, I think he's gifted, because he does wonderful things with computers. And my daughter -- oh, surely she is extra-intelligent." And so on. So I suddenly figured that, how come all the rich people are having these extraordinarily gifted children? What did the poor do wrong?" [3] For his own curiosity, Mitra made a hole in the boundary wall separating his office from the slum, and put an English-based computer through it in the hopes of attracting nearby children.

Sure enough, kids flocked to the device, eager to learn more about it. They asked Mitra what it was, and how to use it—questions which he shrugged off before leaving the children to their own devices. After eight hours, Mitra returned to find the children browsing the internet and teaching their peers how to do the same. However, Mitra and his team were skeptical; perhaps a passerby had shown the kids little tips and tricks. Instead of discounting the findings, Mitra traveled to a remote village approximately 300 miles from New Delhi, where he put another computer and returned home. He came back a few months later to find children from all around the village playing games. Mitra laughed:

When they saw me, they said, "We want a faster processor and a better mouse." So I said, "How on Earth do you know all this?" And they said something very interesting to me. In an irritated voice, they said, "You've given us a machine that works only in English, so we had to teach ourselves English in order to use it." That's the first time, as a teacher, that I had heard the word[s] 'teach ourselves' said so casually. [3] Mitra has since repeated the experiment over 20 times in India, and has implemented over 100 permanent setups in Cambodia, Egypt, and South Africa. The experiments, called the Hole in the Wall experiments, are backed by such organizations as NIIT, the International Finance Corporation, and the Ministry of External Affairs from the Government of India. [4] His goal of providing access to education through individual manipulation and exploration of technology has been echoed in each unique setup, all garnering some form of positive feedback.

With the vast amount of resources and technology available today, Mitra—along with many others—believes that the education system focuses too much on what esteemed educational philosopher Paulo Freire considers the "banking model;" teachers are the almighty depositors, whose purpose is to fill the children, or the depositories, with information. [5] The most valuable lessons we learn generally come from things we do ourselves through a process of trial and error, but by "teaching" our kids that the most socially accepted form of education happens because of someone else's intelligence, we are doing them an immense disservice. The Hole in the Wall model seeks to allow children to study both individually or in large groups, and learn of their own accord despite their location or socioeconomic status. The November 2006 issue of the British Journal of Educational Technology points out that "[i]t enables contact and exposure to a large number of school children, particularly to those who are unable to attend regular school." [6]

The philosopher Plato famously wrote in Book VII of the Republic, "Knowledge which is acquired under compulsion has no hold on the mind. Therefore do not use compulsion, but let early education be rather a sort of amusement." This is exactly the philosophy Mitra considers throughout his ongoing Hole in The Wall trials. By giving children the means to advance their learning, but not necessarily the constructs, they are free to explore boundaries in a safe, healthy environment. A follow-up article in the British Journal of Educational Technology commends this belief; "A child is curious by nature; he or she has a natural instinct to make sense of the world around him. The need to explore on their own is a strong motivating aspect that provides the necessary impetus to go ahead with learning." [7] Because the technology itself has so much potential, children find themselves propelled to explore countless new concepts besides the basic click and browse techniques we typically see. For example, during the Hole in the Wall experiment in Madantusi, both boys and girls were exposed to a computer without internet access; they not only learned how to manipulate and utilize the keyboard and CD-ROM drive, but also managed to acquire the English language—the children were observed using over 200 words to describe their interactions with the technology, and their methods of teaching one another. [9] Creating an interactive environment to foster development of new linguistic skills is incredibly beneficial to a child's overall educational success. According to the American Speech-Language-Hearing Association, advantages for bilingual children include a better ability to learn new words, the ability to use information in new ways, good listening skills, and improved problem-solving skills. [8] Overall, the potential for children to develop different pathways of learning is nearly infinite.

In one example, Mitra visited the South Indian, Tamil-speaking village of Kallikuppam to install a computer with complex articles about DNA replication written entirely in English. As with previous experiments, Mitra assembled the system, told any approaching children that he was unaware of how to use the machine, before leaving for months at a time. Upon his return, he assumed that the childrens' literacy rates couldn't have improved, and that he'd finally thwarted his own research. However, though the children first admitted to learning nothing, their definition of "nothing" differs very much from ours; Mitra recalls "a little girl…she raised her hand, and she says…in broken Tamil and English, she said, 'Well, apart from the fact that improper replication of the DNA molecule causes disease, we haven't understood anything else.'" [3]

This statement gives a sliver of truth to what French journalist and Nobel Prize winner Anatole France once said: "[t]he whole art of teaching is only the art of awakening the natural curiosity of young minds for the purpose of satisfying it afterwards." The children were so driven and motivated to continue learning that they overshot their anticipated levels of education, and surpassed all expectations.

This raises a crucial question for education today: what are we doing wrong? Why aren't schools producing this sort of excitement or enthusiasm for learning? Mitra himself answers this question carefully; Schools as we know them now, they're obsolete. I'm not saying they're broken. It's quite fashionable to say that the education system's broken. It's not broken. It's wonderfully constructed. It's just that we don't need it anymore. It's outdated. [3] In fact, Mitra's experiments have spawned a new spectrum of educational theory, called "minimally invasive education," or MIE. Indeed, one of the hypotheses from the original experiments sought to prove that "[i]f given appropriate access, connectivity and content, groups of children can learn to operate and use computers and the Internet to achieve a specified set of the objectives of primary education, with none or minimal intervention from adults." [9] Perhaps with the growth of this minimally invasive school of thought, schools could produce the same eager-to-learn results.

Though the concept seems almost overly radical, many other nontraditional forms of education exist that provide excellent alternatives for a child's educational well-being. For example, the K-12 Summerhill boarding school in England seeks to challenge the concept of forcing a child to absorb information in what could easily be called minimally invasive education. Here, the small population of pupils sleep in age-arranged housing units and are allowed to clean, dress, and play as they please; "lessons are optional…children can go to them or stay away from them—for years if they want to. There is a timetable—but only for the teachers." [10] Though many critics frown on this new form of learning, the founders of the school show little concern for their opposition. "When my first wife and I began the school [in 1921], we had one main idea: to make the school fit the child—instead of making the child fit the school," recalls founder A.S. Neill in his book Summerhill School: A New View of Childhood. [10] Even in the 1920's, educational advocates realized that a child's love of independent thinking and learning would be a key factor in their overall educational success.

Mitra's revolutionary Hole in the Wall project has catalyzed a reconsideration of not only technology's role in education, but also of the way our children learn in standard school settings today. By giving kids access to information, but not forcing it upon them—essentially leading our horses to water, but not demanding they drink it—an innate curiosity and overwhelming desire for self-betterment begins to flourish. Though the concept seems highly unusual, it begs a necessary question: how are our schools truly preparing our children to learn? By putting children through a schooling system, we are giving them information through a medium—a teacher—and expecting them to absorb it; however, there seems to be something to be said about the sheer power of letting children explore and absorb at their own rate. Just ask Arun Chavan, who experienced the Hole in the Wall at age 12 and is now is now on track for a PhD in Evolutionary Biology from Yale University. "Sugata Mitra's Hole if the Wall idea is quite radical, I think," he explains in an interview with TED. "But it's too important to be ignored. I like how he dares to imagine (and also hopes for) a completely different future of education than most of us do." [11]

Notes

[1] TED. (2013a). About US. Retrieved from http://www.ted.com/pages/about.

[2] TED (2013b). TED Prize Winners: Sugata Mitra. Retrived from http://www.ted.com/talks/sugata_mitra_build_a_school_in_the_cloud.html#349794

[3] Mitra, Sugata. (2013). Build a School in the Cloud. TED Talks. Retrieved from http://www.ted.com/talks/sugata_mitra_build_a_school_in_the_cloud.html#349794

[4] Hole in the Wall Education & Learning. (2013). *HiWEL*. Retrieved from http://www.hole-in-the-wall.com/

[5] Freire, Paulo. (2012). The Banking Concept of Education. In Ed. A. S. Canestrani (eds.) *Educational Foundations: An Anthology of Critical Readings* (103-116, 3rd ed). Los Angeles: SAGE Publications.

[6] Dangwal, R., Swati, J., & Preeti, K. Impact of Minimally Invasive Education on children: an Indian perspective. *British Journal of Educational Technology* 37 (2) (2006): 295-298. doi/10.1111/j.1467-8535.2005.00514.x/

[7] Dangwal, R. & Preeti, K. "Learning through teaching: Peer-mediated instruction in minimally invasive education." British Journal of Educational Technology 40.1 (2009), 5-22. Wiley Online Library. Web. 22 Apr. 2013. <http://onlinelibrary.wiley.com/doi/10.1111/j.1467-8535.2008.00863.x/full>.

[8] "The Advantages of Being Bilingual." (n.d.) American Speech-Language-Hearing Association. Retrieved from http://www.asha.org/about/news/tipsheets/bilingual.htm

[9] Mitra, Sugata. (2003). Minimally invasive education: a progress report on the "hole-in-the-wall" experiments. *British Journal of Educational Technology* 34 (3), 367-371. DOI: 10.1111/1467-8535.00333

[10] Neil, A. S. (2012). The Idea of Summerhill. In Ed. A. S. Canestrani (ed.), Educational Foundations: An Anthology of Critical Readings (3rd, 133-138) ed. Los Angeles: SAGE Publications.

[11] From the Hole in the Wall to Yale: A Q&A with Arun Chavan. (2013) TEDPrize.com. Retrieved from http://blog.tedprize.com/from-the-hole-in-the-wall-to-yale-a-qa-with-arun-chavan/

Pay Attention, MOOCs On The Loose!

by Justin Redona
Student Fellow, The Berglund Center for Internet Studies

During high school, I utilized a vast amount of open educational resources (OERs) available on the Internet to aid my learning of various subjects such as biology, chemistry, calculus, and literature. Whenever I had difficulty understanding a concept in any subject, the Internet made it easy to find helpful, relevant information. This recurring process led me to discover many video lectures offered on YouTube, Khan Academy, and AcademicEarth; along with countless online self-quizzes and premade digital flashcard sets. I later discovered a plethora of OERs through websites. Among them were the Open Learning Initiative at Carnegie Mellon, OpenCourseWare by MIT, and University of California College Prep. There was no doubt that online learning through OERs was happening with the advent of Web 2.0 and that students like me were probably using them to their advantage. Without giving much thought to OERs and their implications for higher education, I continued to pursue a college degree, after receiving my high school diploma, in hopes of obtaining a job or moving on to graduate school in the future. My idea of success originated after the Second World War; it was an institutionalized view that a college degree was a ticket to prosperity. [1]

Four years later, now that I am months away from earning a bachelor's degree at a small private university, I am beginning to notice how recent developments in online learning (i.e. e-learning) may alter the role of a traditional undergraduate degree in ultimately obtaining a job. Through my casual perusal of interesting TED Talks, I came across Daphne Koller's compelling talk entitled: "What we're learning from online education." [2] In it, she presents on the phenomenon of massive open online courses (MOOCs) and their implications to life-long learning and open access to education. Through Coursera, a for-profit venture established by Koller in 2012, Koller demonstrated the amazing capability of MOOCs to allow access to higher education in places where education is not readily accessible. Aside from their philanthropic potential, MOOCs may also be useful for undergraduate students by enhancing their education and supplementing their studies beyond college for the sake of acquiring meaningful knowledge. According to Rob Bencini [3], a Certified Economic Developer (CEcD) and economic futurist from North Carolina, "A college degree is no longer an absolute necessity to make intellectual contributions to the economy." It seems that MOOCs may change how prospective college students pursue higher education if some employers are seeking knowledgeable workers regardless of having a diploma. For those of us who are currently enrolled in a college or university, MOOCs raise concerns as to how we may compare to employers' expectations once we enter the job market. Of course, although this issue does depend on the type of desired job, the ultimate implication of MOOCs accessibility with no financial obligations for the student drastically changes our traditional view of higher education for students, educators, and employers. Ultimately, major tuition-free (or nearly free) MOOC platforms such as Coursera, edX, and Udacity have given students another option for higher education over costly academic institutions. This article will provide a brief introduction into the MOOC phenomenon and its implications for higher education.

What is a MOOC?

A MOOC is an online course that has a global reach (i.e., massive) and is accessible (i.e., open) to anyone with an Internet connection. It can be characterized as providing a structured means of facilitating learning between students and an expert or experts. [4] In 2008, George Siemens and Stephen Downes offered the first MOOC through the University of Manitoba's Learning Technologies Centre and Extended Education. [5] Since then, MOOC offerings have expanded and are causing a stir in higher education.

Currently, typical MOOC lectures have similar components of traditional college lecture courses, such as quizzes, assessments, and assignment deadlines, except that more people can "see" the course, take the assessments, engage in discussion with fellow classmates, and obtain statements of accomplishments. [6] [7] This traditional model of teaching, however, may change as the current state of MOOCs and online learning lack a pedagogy that ensures learning outcomes can be reached. [8] As Joseph Harris, a writing professor at Duke University recently remarked in The Chronicle of Higher Education, a MOOC cannot be viewed as "much more than a digitized textbook." [9] With many interactive technologies already in existence to supplement video presentations [10] and room for pedagogical innovation in making online learning effective, MOOC platforms will undoubtedly refine the way they disseminate knowledge to online masses. Until then, research on the effectiveness of MOOCs and the pedagogy facilitated by its major platforms is currently lacking and, therefore, invites further investigation. [11] [12] [13]

What makes MOOCs unique compared to other forms of e-learning is the lack of prerequisites, costs, formal accreditations, and defined levels of required participation. [14] [15] [16] In this sense, MOOCs can be seen as an extension of e-learning, popularizing the phenomenon, probably through effective marketing strategies, with appealing topics and prestigious professors from top-notch institutions. [17] Prior to MOOCs, elite universities, on a global scale, offered no structured form of free, online learning, disregarding OERs. And now that this method of acquiring knowledge is available, young minds that are prepping for college or eager to enter the workforce may think twice before subjecting themselves to student loans, as MOOCs pervade the higher educational landscape.

Although motivations—intrinsic and extrinsic—for subscribing to MOOCs may vary, I propose that career-oriented rationales may be the predominant basis for utilizing these resources. Research conducted by Penn's Graduate School of Education has shown that students of MOOCs, termed here "MOOC subscribers," have unexplained disparities in participation and engagement behaviors, with an average of four percent of enrollees completing their courses. [18] More research has to be done to discern actual motivations among MOOC subscribers, the frequency of MOOC subscribers with such motivations, and their varying associations with particular courses, disciplines, or platforms. [19] Certainly, this touches upon only one aspect of MOOCs that provide research opportunities. According to Sarah Pritchard, Dean of Libraries at Northwestern University, aside from the struggles of logistics, technology, pedagogical and policy issues, we should consider large research opportunities:

The timing is such that could be tested by comparing the outcomes of varied models of delivery (Coursera, 2U, edX, Udacity), the possible impact of different home institutional characteristics, and the effectiveness of MOOCs in different disciplines or levels of courses. The critical important step is – start now to gather data and test effectiveness in the traditional or "control" setting. [20]

Certainly, there is a need to perform before-and-after or cross-institutional studies to gain insights into the MOOC phenomenon and education. The demand for such research suggests that there is insufficient evidence to support any conclusions describing implications for students, employers, and academic institutions. Therefore, it seems that most considerations are based on suggestive pieces of evidence that are anecdotal or isolated to one MOOC delivered by a single MOOC platform. Large-scale research will enable critical questions surrounding the MOOC-phenomenon to be elucidated, whereby consumers of education (i.e. students) can make informed decisions about their method of higher education.

Although MOOC creators and their proponents have expressed that "MOOCs would break down economic, geographic, racial and gender barriers to higher education," [21] such a vision will not significantly materialize if retention and participation among MOOC-subscribers remains dismal. I foresee that immediate major effects of the MOOC phenomenon will be seen among an educated demographic comprised of digital natives and immigrants in developed countries. An additional study indicates that some 80% of subscribers already have an advanced degree, suggesting post-graduate-based rationales for taking a MOOC, such as fostering general curiosities, obtaining professional development, or working towards occupational promotions. [22] Furthermore, this finding does not support the philanthropic, idealistic view of what MOOCs were proposed to accomplish. Instead, the majority of current MOOC-subscribers are already well-educated, Westernized, and, most likely, financially stable. With MOOCs being offered as a free service, those 80% of subscribers are invested in expanding their skill or knowledge base in hopes of advancing their career. It seems that MOOCs will have to gain more popularity among its intended audiences, who lack access to traditional methods of higher education, in order for the idealistic vision of MOOC creators to appreciably materialize. But for now, current MOOC subscriber trends suggest this matter is secondary.

Until we see retention rates rise and the intended, underserved demographic significantly engaged, implications for higher education and degree-pursuing students will be the main focus of this article. My commentary stems from an undergraduate perspective along with current views surrounding the MOOC phenomenon; I do not have information science nor education expertise.

Implications for Undergraduate Students

MOOCs present another means of obtaining higher education at little or no cost, enhancing preexisting education, and acquiring desired career-related skills. Therefore, considerations for current undergraduates include how much they are willing to pay, what quality of education they want, and the type of knowledge or skills their desired jobs require.

Attending college is already costly. Public college tuition this year rose 4.6 percent to an average of $16,510 according to the College Board [23] and not all college students graduate within four years or make it to graduation. Likely due to money and debt, only 56 percent of US students graduate in six years, according to a study conducted by Harvard. [24] If students are not willing to pay or cannot afford a college education, then MOOCs may be the next best option to obtain a higher education. To address the problem of rising college tuition, a novel type of MOOC, offered by the online platform Education Portal, has been created in allowing students to earn low-cost, transferable credit—in some cases, paying less than $100 for three credits—that can be applied toward their degrees. [25] Some students, however, may still prefer a traditional educational setting that is face-to-face versus online.

A genuine liberal arts college experience is characterized by close relationships with professors and fellow students; the daily challenge of critical thinking; discussion-based courses; and meaningful encounters with peers from different backgrounds. [26] This form of education has its worth, as our knowledge based society requires higher order skills of critical thinking, creativity, and originality, all of which are difficult, if not impossible to teach, using the behaviorist pedagogy that most MOOCs use. [27] In this sense, there is notable value in having a college experience, even if tuition is expensive. Contrary to massive online educational settings, getting individualized attention and being mentored on a personal level may be of paramount importance to a liberal arts college experience. However, a major academic analysis by the Babson Survey Research Group provides preliminary evidence that e-learning is comparable, if not better, than traditional college instruction in terms of quality and outcomes: "more than three-quarters of academic leaders rated learning outcomes in online education as the same as or superior to face-to-face instruction." [28] Yet, some educators who are skeptical about the quality of learning online, emphasize the importance of learning in brick-and-mortar classrooms and argue that learning by doing is better. [29] If we are reducing education to "learning outcomes," then MOOCs seem to fit this model. On the other hand, if we are focusing on a holistic view of education, then attending brick-and-mortar institutions seems more suitable. Which method students choose is likely to be determined by cost. And cost reduction, in choosing MOOCs over college, is done at the expense of having quality faculty members, who are the heart of an educational process, and respond to individual learning needs of students, lead classes through enlightening discussions, and serve as student mentors. [30] For now, MOOCs and the college experience seem to be on opposite sides of the quality education spectrum.

Hybrid or "flipped" classrooms may bridge this gap in quality by incorporating MOOCs into the classroom. If professors are not already implementing this strategy, then students have the opportunity to do it themselves by supplementing their current studies with MOOC material in addition to the copious amount of OERs on the Internet—that is, if students even have the time to do so. Howard Horton, president of New England College of Business and Finance, wrote in the New England Journal of Higher Education that MOOCs might be the new "textbook" of modern day college courses:

> *As sourceware, MOOCs can be a major advancement over standard textbooks because they preserve the use of exceptional content ex-*

perts and expand the concept of the textbook by including internal assessment mechanisms and student-to-student interaction. Building on this concept, edX, the Harvard/MIT venture, is now saying its online courses will "improve" rather than "replace" campus-based education, and it has arrangements with Bunker Hill and other community colleges to teach courses around the MOOC content as one might similarly teach a class around a textbook. [31]

The step that edX is taking towards integration in traditional educational settings represents initial advancements among MOOC platforms to be included in the "flipped" classroom model. In efforts to make physically attending universities more attractive, according to an article by The Economist, edX is also selling its MOOC technology to universities like Stanford, to augment existing teaching. [32] If higher education is to respond to the MOOC phenomenon with its integration into "flipped" classrooms, then more work needs to be done on how MOOCs can augment or potentially improve education, along with how to best utilize class time. [33] For now, undergraduates can take advantage of this resource independently to aid or expand their knowledge base that will be intrinsically or extrinsically meaningful to them. As most testimonials on the value of online learning come from motivated students, MOOCs may benefit undergraduates with clear goals and confidence in their abilities, even after graduation, to build upon what they have learned in traditional educational settings. [34] For prospective undergraduates, however, in addition to worries of college debt, MOOCs will inevitably impact their educational choices in hopes of getting a job or going to graduate school.

In terms of getting a job, future college graduates may have to enhance their resume even further and adapt to the MOOC phenomenon. In a job climate that demands knowledgeable employees with many traditional experiences, such as formal postsecondary education, internships, summer jobs, and life experiences, many existing MOOC-subscribers appear to be potential job seekers, who use MOOCs as a resource to gain technical knowledge, while bypassing college credits and fees. [35] In fact, according to an article published by The Economist, Udacity, a MOOC platform, is working with companies to train future employees having established partnerships with several firms, including Google, AT&T, and Georgia Tech. [36] This could compensate for employers' common observation that many graduates lack the proper pool of knowledge to contribute immediately, if employed, compared to existing personnel. [37] Almost half of the employers surveyed in 2011 by the Accrediting Council for Independent Colleges and Schools complained about the skills gap and argued that specific workplace training rather than broad-based education should be emphasized. [38] Furthermore, employers' hiring behaviors indicate that knowledge takes precedence over educational expertise. [39] In the end, people, who already have traditional college degrees, may be equally qualified or less qualified job candidates compared to non-degree-seeking people who have completed targeted MOOCs . [40] Unless professional or graduate school is the student's goal after undergraduate studies, it seems that they will immediately face a more competitive job market that looks for well-suited, credentialed candidates. Indeed, the market of online learning through for-profit and non-profit ventures has reaffirmed the thought that any college degree is the ticket to prosperity. [41]

This competitive scenario between degree-holding and non-degree job-seekers will likely play out, as long as MOOCs remain accessible and massive, but may not be an issue just yet for professional school applicants. For instance, MOOCs could prepare undergraduates for medical or nursing school, but will not impact professional education overall, as face-to-face, hands-on components are essential. [42, 43] To date, no pre-medical program is offering academic credit for taking a course through a MOOC. [44] However, the American Council on Education has certified required and recommended pre-medical courses offered by Coursera and Udacity. These include "Introduction to Physics," "Introduction to Statistics," "Introduction to Genetics and Evolution," and "Calculus: Single Variable" to be taken for credit upon successful completion of a Credit Final Exam. [48] This encourages universities to grant credit to undergraduate students who complete these courses. Nonetheless, for these professions and other related fields such as law, degrees are still required in order to matriculate into professional school. However, the trend of pursuing knowledge over a degree presents critical questions in regards to professional organizations and the consumers of their services. The focus on knowledge, rather than a degree may ultimately undermine the "insured," "bonded," or "legal" process of professional work, and lead to complacency with the creation of a new role: the legal "laymen." [45] The concept of earning a MOOC education is still in its early stages and society will have to adapt quickly as we still predominantly rely on credentials as a hallmark of professionalism and expertise in a particular field.

Overall, MOOCs offer a cost-effective opportunity for undergraduates, as potential MOOC subscribers, to further their knowledge, enhance their resume, and, perhaps, provide a competitive edge against non-degree seekers under the higher education, credential-seeking paradigm in hopes of prosperity. Failure to realize that MOOCs offer career-related training may leave future college graduates inadequate in the eyes of employers compared to qualified job applicants, who completed targeted MOOCs. It is worth mentioning that this may apply to certain technical fields and not professional fields such as Medicine or Law. Undergraduates must be aware of what it means to achieve a higher education, in regards to MOOCs and their career goals. These implications are according to the current state of MOOC offerings, and will undoubtedly change as MOOCs continue to develop in the market of higher education. After all, major MOOC platforms have been around for less than a decade. Therefore, the points I have made so far beg validation through research findings, which are currently insufficient. [46, 47] Ultimately, current MOOCs have the potential to supplement or augment learning in the classroom whether independently on the part of the student or through classrooms flipped on the part of professors.

Conclusion

Like many undergraduate students, I held the predominant view that obtaining a degree is synonymous with being on a path to prosperity, or at least financial stability. However, MOOCs are now in the market of higher education and encourage a greater emphasis on knowledge seeking than degree seeking. I have suggested that career-oriented rationales may be the main basis for utilizing MOOCs as more than simply an OER. In general, MOOCs are in their early stages and society will have to quickly adapt to their implications for higher education. Nonetheless, as a cost-effective opportunity for undergraduates, MOOCs are beneficial tools to further knowledge, enhance resumes, and, perhaps, provide a competitive edge against non-degree seekers. The quantity of published literature pertaining to MOOCs will surely expand as time progresses, as the experimentation between MOOC platforms, colleges, and universities unfolds under the current pressures of soaring tuition and increasing enrollments at institutions across the US. An area of interest to investigate further includes an assessment of whether learning is really happening across MOOC platforms and whether MOOCs can successfully facilitate different types of learning.

Notes

[1] Bencini, R. (2013). Educating the Future: The End of Mediocrity. *Futurist*, 47(2), 40–44.

[2] http://www.ted.com/talks/daphne_koller_what_we_re_learning_from_online_education.html.

[3] Bencini (2013).

[4] Liyanagunawardena, T. R., Adams, A. A., & Williams, S. A. (2013). MOOCs: A Systematic Study of the Published Literature 2008-2012. *International Review of Research in Open & Distance Learning*, 14(3), 202–227.

[5] Liyanagunawardena et al. (2013)

[6] Delbanco, A. (2013). MOOCs OF HAZARD. New Republic, 244(5), 28–33.

[7] Cooper, S., & Sahami, M. (2013). Reflections on Stanford's MOOCs. Communications of the ACM, 56(2), 28. doi:10.1145/2408776.2408787

[8] Bates, T. (2012, August 5). What's right and what's wrong about Coursera-style MOOCs. Online Learning and Distance Education Resources. Retrieved from: http://www.tonybates.ca/2012/08/05/whats-right-and-whats-wrong-about-coursera-style-moocs/

[9] Delbanco (2012)

[10] Cooper & Sahami (2013)

[11] Liyanagunawardena et al. (2013)

[12] Pritchard, S. M. (2013). MOOCs: An Opportunity for Innovation and Research. Portal: Libraries and the Academy, 13(2), 127–129. doi:10.1353/pla.2013.0015

[13] For the first systematic review of published literature related to MOOCs, see Liyanagunawardena et al. (2013).

[14] Liyanagunawardena et al. (2013)

[15] Cooper and Sahami (2013)

[16] Adams, S. (2013, December 11). Are MOOCs Really A Failure? *Forbes*. Retrieved from: http://www.forbes.com/sites/susanadams/2013/12/11/are-moocs-really-a-failure/

[17] Grossman, R. J. (2013). Are Massive Open Online Courses in Your Future? *HR Magazine*, 58(8), 30.

[18] Adams (2013).

[19] Liyanagunawardena et al. (2013).

[20] Pritchard (2013).

[21] Adams (2013).

[22] Adams (2013).

[23] Grossman (2013).

[24] Grossman (2013).

[25] NDG Staff Writer. (2013). Next-generation MOOCs tackle budget-cuts at state universities. *North Dallas Gazette*. Retrieved from: http://northdallasgazette.com/2013/12/13/next-generation-moocs-tackle-budget-cuts-at-state-universities/.

[26] Shennan, A. (2013). Can MOOCs Work with Liberal Arts? : New England Board of Higher Education. *New England Board of Higher Education*. Retrieved from: http://www.nebhe.org/thejournal/can-moocs-work-with-liberal-arts/.

[27] Bates (2012).

[28] Grossman (2013).

[29] Crawford, T. H. (2013). Rediscovering the Material World. *Chronicle of Higher Education*, 59(34), B22–B23.

[30] Horton (2013).

[31] Horton, H. E. (2013). COOCs Over MOOCs. *New England Journal of Higher Education*, 1–1.

[32] The attack of the MOOCs; Higher education. (2013, July 20). *The Economist*, 408(8845), 55(US).

[33] Cooper & Sahami (2013).

[34] Delbanco (2013).

[35] Bencini (2013).

[36] The Economist (2013).

[37] Bencini (2013).

[38] Grossman (2013).

[39] Bencini (2013).

[40] Grossman (2013).

[41] Bencini (2013).

[42] Bellack, J. P. (Ed.). (2013). MOOCs: The Future Is Here. *Journal of Nursing Education*, 52(1), 3–4. doi:10.3928/01484834-20121227-10

[43] Harder, B. (2013). BMJ Careers – Are MOOCs the future of medical education? *BMJ Careers*. Retrieved November 29, 2013, from: http://careers.bmj.com/careers/advice/view-article.html?id=20012502

[44] Harder (2013).

[45] Bencini (2013).

[46] Liyanagunawardena et al. (2013).

[47] Pritchard (2013).

[48] http://www2.acenet.edu/credit/?fuseaction=browse.getOrganizationDetail&FICE=1008160; http://www2.acenet.edu/credit/?fuseaction=browse.getOrganizationDetail&FICE=1007444

Getting Educated: Liberal Arts v.s. MOOCs

by Justin Redona
Student Fellow, The Berglund Center for Internet Studies

Creativity expert Sir Ken Robinson presented a TEDTalk [1] on how the current education culture in America is working against the three principles with which the human mind flourishes. These principles are as follows: (1) human beings are naturally different and diverse, (2) curiosity drives human progress, and (3) human life is inherently creative. In other words, in order for meaningful learning to occur in our students, conditions that uphold these three principles will favor their success and perhaps the success of education in America. Massive Open Online Courses (MOOCs) add another dimension to our education culture as an iteration of distance learning. However, learning through MOOCs has its limitations, and whether or not learning is significantly happening is difficult to assess. Under the pedagogy of which MOOCs operate, I believe that the MOOC phenomenon perpetuates our current education culture since certification of obtaining knowledge from MOOCs is measured by how well students perform on tests and conform to a set of standards. A close proximity between the teacher and student is crucial to learning, and we shouldn't be furthering the distance between them—even at the higher educational level. MOOCs, although seemingly novel, will not provide us with the valuable knowledge and wisdom that a traditional liberal arts education may bring. We should be careful to avoid focusing too much on replacing traditional brick-and-mortar institutions with MOOCs if people are to become well-rounded, successful learners. On the other hand, MOOCs possess great potential for acquiring technical knowledge, as most courses are offered in mathematics and the sciences. Therefore, despite the rising cost of college tuition, people should not completely give in to MOOCs as an alternative, because pursuing a degree at a traditional brick-and-mortar institution still has its worth.

My previous article, "Pay Attention, MOOCs on the Loose!", [2] presented a brief overview of what MOOCs are and the implications they have for undergraduate students. I will discuss general implications for professors and colleges and universities in detail later. Courses that are normally reserved for enrolled undergraduates at elite institutions, such as Harvard and the Massachusetts Institute of Technology (MIT), are now freely available to anyone with

Internet access. MOOCs are worth discussing because "well-branded institutions have helped legitimize MOOCs and sparked interest—and apprehension—of many less-renowned colleges and universities." [3] Although course instructors may suggest that potential MOOC-learners possess prerequisite knowledge, a lack of such background does not prevent people from taking a course. The bottom line is that anyone with Internet access can participate.

This virtually free model of education essentially questions how valuable obtaining a higher education may be to young minds that are in the midst of pursuing a degree. If more people latch onto this MOOC approach, then what will it mean to be qualified among the professions across the many disciplines? The experts of tomorrow that take a variety of targeted MOOCs may be the equivalent of today's experts, who hold PhD or Master's degrees. Northeastern University President John Aoun goes as far as to suggest that "MOOCs could result in the emergence of a two-tiered educational system with one tier consisting of a campus-based education for those who can afford it, and the other consisting of low and no-cost MOOCs." [4] Although this is a possibility of things to come, I agree with the common notion that some people in higher education support: MOOCs cannot fully replace the value of a college education in brick-and-mortar institutions.

Indeed, the college campus with its many resources and expert faculty is an effective learning environment that has been the norm for years. But can a MOOC produce an equivalently effective one? According to Kop et al., "The structure of the learning environment, the place and presence of learners and educators within institutional boundaries, and the nature of knowing and learning are all challenged by the fast pace of technological change." [5] Information can be transferred, stored, disseminated, shared, and retrieved within a MOOC. This dynamic information flow allows MOOC-subscribers to respond, engage in dialogue, and interact through MOOC platform websites, Facebook groups, or other subject-relevant websites with forum functionalities. As long as students are engaged, it appears that learning should take place.

However, the very fact that MOOCs remain "massive" implies an inability to foster individualization. While it is true that MOOCs can bring together a diverse population of students from all over the world, MOOCs cannot cater to each and every student. Indeed, one of the challenges involved with teaching a MOOC is how to best serve and engage a great number of registered students. For instance, a professor from Harvard Divinity School who recently led an EdX MOOC allowed students to comment on reading material through an EdX website, a Facebook group, and another supplementary website with a forum format. [6] Although this does allow a sense of collaboration and interaction with the course material and fellow MOOC-subscribers, there still remains a large "distance" between the teacher and the student. Therefore, the "massive" nature of MOOCs seems to be non-conducive to Robinson's first principle for human flourishing. MOOCs bring a flashy, tech-savvy product along other traditional approaches to higher education, but professors and students in the same room seems like the best option in the context of learning among a group of diverse individuals.

In addition to Robinson's three principles of human flourishing, Robert Scott, President of Adelphi University, proposes three aspects of learning in the context of what he calls the current "imagination age": history, imagination, and compassion. [7] Furthermore, Scott supports the idea that a "truly liberating undergraduate education," one that is broad and diverse, "requires a faculty member and a student engaged in learning together." [8] For instance, traditional brick-and-mortar schools that have lecture classes allow opportunities for students to actively engage in learning, whether it be in the form of visiting office hours, asking questions in the classroom, or going to an on-campus tutoring center. It may be true that one can learn history and become imaginative as a result of going through MOOC content. However, this can only occur to an extent, because MOOC platforms control what type of MOOC content surrounds. Perhaps the material is not relevant enough to the MOOC learner, resulting in no strong connection to the material and therefore nonexistent engagement.

This brings us to the lack of compassion during the learning process. One cannot fully become engaged in learning without being compassionate. This is an apparent concept best illustrated by data released by Harvard and MIT during the month of January 2014 after performing a study on their MOOC offerings. According to their study, among the "841,000 registrants for the MOOCs that were offered by these two schools through the EdX platform in 2012 and 2013…only 5 percent of this population actually earned completion certificates." [9] Getting more registrants engaged in MOOC participation is clearly a challenge, and everyone may not be a compassionate learner.

Education that is broad and diverse more aptly lends itself to creating an environment that facilitates engagement amongst compassionate learners. A liberating education achieved through internships, service learning opportunities, and study-abroad experiences contributes to the development of good character, encourages engaged citizenship in ultimately preparing individuals for careers and commerce. [10] Likewise, Barry Schwartz, a professor at Swarthmore College, conveys the value of a higher education when students are prepared to answer four critical questions: (1) What is worth knowing? (2) What is worth doing? (3) What makes for a good human life? And (4) What are my responsibilities to other people? [11] Both Scott and Schwartz view the greater importance of a liberal arts education through brick-and-mortar institutions over MOOC alternatives. MOOCs, in this sense, are only finite, information-dispensing online resources for educating individuals at large.

Given the right conditions, it is possible that MOOCs may provide a suitable learning environment. Robinson's second principle for human flourishing is based on curiosity and the third principle is based on creativity. Rather than focusing on the information-dispensing model, sparking curiosity and creativity among MOOC learners may be the best route than simply relying on purely lecture-based formats. Although, close learning (i.e., proximity between the teacher and the learner) is a huge obstacle among MOOCs, incorporating social media and local study group meetings may compensate for this deficit.

However, despite the possible compensations, this downfall might just be the "Achilles' heel" for MOOCs. Robinson noted in his TEDTalk that "high-performing systems in the world...individualize teaching and learning." [12] Close learning requires the individualization of teaching and learning. It is through close learning that teachers are able to engage students, spark their curiosity, individuality, and creativity. According to Scott Newstok, a professor at Rhodes College, "at no stage of education does technology, no matter how novel, ever replace human attention. Close learning can't be automated or scaled up." [13] Even if MOOCs can improve the effectiveness at which MOOC-subscribers learn online, they probably will not be as successful as the traditional liberal arts education model.

The ideal form of pedagogy for MOOCs would need to be dependent on the subject being taught, as not all subject areas are best taught in the same manner. Ideally, in connection with educational psychology, MOOCs seem to best suit the needs of the cognitive and affective domain. The fact that MOOCs are offered on the Internet presents challenges for addressing the psychomotor domain. Therefore, the ideal MOOC would need to address all these areas, through innovative modalities far beyond lecture videos, multiple-choice assessments, and writing assignments. In addition, the subject area itself would have to be enticing enough to draw in a broader student population that would be engaged in learning and commit full participation. Incentives, in addition to statements or certificates of accomplishments, should be built into the MOOC approach to facilitate such engagement. These are all points that I think would improve what MOOCs are today. As it remains, however, MOOCs pose great implications for professors and educational institutions.

General Implications for Professors

Professors are essential components of a college education. Therefore, it is important to consider the relevant issues that the MOOC phenomenon presents in higher education. Viewpoints of professors vary from philosophical disinclination to scholastic stardom. As mentioned before, some professors who oppose MOOC-pedagogy insist that learning by doing is more effective. [14] Some professors also oppose MOOCs because it might "perpetuate the 'information dispensing' model of teaching." [15]

Nonetheless, beyond the scale of brick-and-mortar institutions, the advent of MOOCs has created a new stage to showcase top-notch professors. Experts, who facilitate MOOCs, may become celebrities among thousands of MOOC-subscribers, sparking inspiration among the masses, and influencing them with their intellectual work. Daniel McFarland, a Stanford University professor, observes, "I want to do anything I can to get my material out there," and goes on to say that "the more people who have access to it in any form, the better." [16] However, rather than considering access and quantity as being more important than quality, I argue that MOOCs ultimately hinder individuation when it comes to quality learning. Professors who get involved in MOOCs reach online masses at the cost of providing individual, responsive attention to their students.

Professors may actually end up being more impactful on a micro-level, influencing a finite amount of students, because teaching to the masses on a scale of thousands sacrifices opportunities for individuation. Another downside includes all the popularity among "a few charismatic professors with star quality and platform skills" that may complicate the hierarchy of professorship, possibly rendering mediocrity inadequate. [17] Collectively, this marks a reduction in educational quality, where MOOC-subscribers can be shunned due to the massive amount of course participants, too large for one professor to handle—even with the aid of a few graduate teaching assistants. Unfortunately, any further details on how MOOCs affect the work of professors in the field of higher education is not within the scope of this discussion and will have to be explored elsewhere.

General Implications for Colleges and Universities

It seems that participating universities have taken the stance that everyone ought to be educated. As long these courses are being offered for free with no ties to credit or a degree, elite universities allow themselves to be viewed as offering a philanthropic form of continuing education through MOOC platforms. [18] MOOCs are new services on the market that provide another educational option for current undergraduates. Indeed, MOOCs may be competing for the same market as colleges and universities.

At the same time, they could also be used as a supplemental service in higher education. And as college tuition rises and enrollment increases, MOOCs are bound to gain popularity as long as they operate on a "freemium" model. [19] The current challenge involves infusing MOOCs with a transformative learning experience to protect major losses in revenue, and any disruptions that MOOCs cause will depend on the willingness of institutions to grant credit for which students do not pay tuition. [20, 21]

In the long run, professors may just become the brand of education rather than the institution itself, and college administrators are worried about this notion. [22] Since MOOC-instructors have the potential to educationally impact the masses, higher education may centralize around professors rather than administrators, placing teachers at the forefront at educational institutions. MOOCs may give professors a greater voice that extends beyond the walls of a university, whereby people view the institutions based on which ones MOOC-instructors are affiliated with. As long as MOOCs continue to offer education as a free commodity, college and university leaders will be scrambling to find innovative solutions as revenues are shrinking. [23]

Education, in terms of a commodity within academia, is a valuable process of learning that culminates in acquiring a tangible credential, thereby certifying mastery of a specific knowledge base. Students and their families have financially invested in this commodity, traditionally. MOOCs alter this long-established view of education as, rather, something that virtually anyone can take advantage of without substantial financial investments.

Conclusion

While MOOCs offer a pedagogical modality that seems attractive in acquiring academic credentials, students should prioritize learning something meaningful over something that will make them employable. [24] Currently, MOOCs are practical for obtaining technical knowledge, primarily, surrounding mathematics and the sciences, as most MOOC offerings are relevant to these fields. However, there is potential for MOOCs to improve the effectiveness at which teaching and learning happens. Everyone including employers, professors, administrators, and students at large will need to be aware of the pros and cons of a liberal arts education compared to MOOC alternatives in order to tackle critical questions surrounding the qualifications and credentials of future "educated" citizens.

Notes

[1] http://www.ted.com/talks/ken_robinson_how_to_escape_education_s_death_valley.html.

[2] http://bcis.pacificu.edu/interface/?p=5236.

[3] Carver, L., & Harrison M., L. (2013). MOOCs and Democratic Education. Liberal Education, 99 (4). Retrieved from: http://www.aacu.org/liberaleducation/le-fa13/carver_harrison.cfm.

[4] Carlson, S., & Blumenstyk, G. (2012, December 17). For Whom Is College Being Reinvented? *The Chronicle of Higher Education*. Retrieved March 2, 2014, from: http://chronicle.com/article/The-False-Promise-of-the/136305.

[5] Kop, R., Fournier, H., & Mak, J. S. F. (2011). A Pedagogy of Abundance or a Pedagogy to Support Human Beings? Participant Support on Massive Open Online Courses. *International Review of Research in Open & Distance Learning*, 12 (7), 74–93.

[6] Clark, P. (2014). The Next Problem for MOOCs Starts With a Rap Genius Intern. *Bloomberg Businessweek*. Retrieved March 1, 2014, from: http://www.businessweek.com/articles/2014-02-26/the-next-problem-for-moocs-starts-with-a-rap-genius-intern.

[7] Scott, R. (2013). Thoughts on a "Liberating" Education. *Liberal Education*, 99 (4). Retrieved from: http://www.aacu.org/liberaleducation/le-fa13/scott.cfm.

[8] Scott (2013).

[9] Clark (2014).

[10] Scott (2013).

[11] Schwartz, B. (2013). What Higher Education Should Be For. *Linkedin*. Retrieved from: http://www.linkedin.com/today/post/article/20130905123357-91343717-what-higher-education-should-be-for?trk=corpblog_0913_chipcutter_influencers.

[12] http://www.ted.com/talks/ken_robinson_how_to_escape_education_s_death_valley.html.

[13] Newstok, S. (2013). A Plea for "Close Learning." *Liberal Education*, 99 (4). Retrieved from: http://www.aacu.org/liberaleducation/le-fa13/newstok.cfm.

[14] Crawford, T. H. (2013). Rediscovering the Material World. *Chronicle of Higher Education*, 59 (34), B22–B23.

[15] Kolowich, S. (2013). Why Some Colleges Are Saying No to MOOC Deals, at Least for Now. *Chronicle of Higher Education*, 59 (34), A8–A8.

[16] Grossman, R. J. (2013). Are Massive Open Online Courses in Your Future? HR Magazine, 58 (8), 30.

[17] Grossman (2013).

[18] Bates, T. (2012). What's right and what's wrong about Coursera-style MOOCs. *Online Learning and Distance Education Resources*. Retrieved from: http://www.tonybates.ca/2012/08/05/whats-right-and-whats-wrong-about-coursera-style-moocs/.

[19] Grossman (2013).

[20] Shennan, A. (2013, February 26). Can MOOCs Work with Liberal Arts? : New England Board of Higher Education. *New England Board of Higher Education*. Retrieved November 29, 2013, from: http://www.nebhe.org/thejournal/can-moocs-work-with-liberal-arts/.

[21] Kolowich (2013).

[22] Grossman (2013).

[23] Grossman (2013).

[24] Schwartz, B. (2013). What Higher Education Should Be For. Linkedin. Retrieved from: http://www.linkedin.com/today/post/article/20130905123357-91343717-what-higher-education-should-be-for?trk=corpblog_0913_chipcutter_influencers.

Is the Internet Changing Journalism Too Much?

by Jennifer Hofer
Student Fellow, The Berglund Center for Internet Studies

As society becomes more dependent on the Internet, the expectation on other forms of media is to adapt as best as possible in the name of advancements. This expectation is harshest on journalism as it simultaneously challenges the definition of journalism, changes the way journalism is read and written, alters the expectations of what a journalist needs to do, and forces educators to re-evaluate the entire teaching model in order to train journalists for a job that may not exist anymore. Journalism's adaptation to the internet is therefore changing every aspect of journalism, from the tasks to the education process.

A journalist used to be a person who worked for a newspaper or news channel, but as new news platforms have emerged, the definition of a "journalist" has needed to become more fluid because "in this age of blogs and WikiLeaks the definition of journalist has been challenged and changed... How can one say that a blog about topical news is any less valid?" [1] Without a stable definition right now, journalism is currently in a state of flux that Lia-Paschalia Spyridou et. al. explains, is affecting it "as a practice, a product, and a profession." [2] This shift stems from the uncertainty of whether journalism should be considered "a craft or a profession." [3] These are the two main contrasting forces in journalism. One side believes journalism to be an art form that takes time and dedication, and the other sees it as a business tool to make money. Even people within the field are arguing about how to label it. As is, the writers tend to view journalism as a craft, while anyone on the business side tries to emphasize journalism as a profession. Unfortunately, the industry doesn't have the luxury of being considered a craft right now, and instead emphasis needs to be on journalism as a profession and a business, to keep up with the changes being forced upon them. This isn't a matter of pride anymore, but a matter of survival. Companies are losing momentum, and will suffer drastically without the focus of staying financially afloat. Lawrence Pintak goes as far as saying that journalism needs to "continually re-tool, or die." This is because "20% more people now get their news from digital sources," [4] and that number is continually increasing. As the world becomes more dependent on digital files and documents, the use of paper lessens, and the expectation is that information will be available in other formats. Newspapers have become increasingly digital, making the news more accessible to the next generation of readers, but this change is to the dismay of the journalists who have been writing for print since the beginning of their career. A change to digital news doesn't just change the platform in which the news is read, it also changes how it must be written. An online report is shorter, and focuses on getting the details out as fast as possible, rather than expanding on the story and taking the time to create an in depth piece.

There is a sense of nostalgia from sitting in a deep Lay-Z Boy recliner on a Sunday morning, a mug of coffee to your side, and opening the first page of a large newspaper. The sound of the paper opening and the recognizable soft texture of the newspaper won't last forever, though. Mitchell Stephens admits that, "some of the discipline's most cherished practices will have to change." [5] The web is constantly expanding, technology is constantly becoming more advanced, and so journalism needs to be able to grow as well. The world isn't ever going to stop changing. The only way to sustain a form of media is to be flexible, and change as the world does, because "what's state-of-the-art technique may well be obsolete tomorrow." [6] The shift from print to digital is just one many that is occurring because of advancements in the internet, and it is the large amounts of recent changes that are making journalists upset. With the internet being a multi-media platform, there is pressure for sites to use these capabilities and incorporate other forms of media. "News is becoming platform-agnostic: print is just one of several delivery vehicles a 'newspaper' must utilize." [7] It's no longer enough for a news source to succeed with print alone. The incorporation of a website to distribute news is vital to reaching a large audience, and with the different platform comes a different structure for writing. A journalist can't just copy and paste the same article, because a website needs to follow the rules of the web, rather than that of the newspaper. The internet focuses on speed and brevity, as well as incorporating multiple different facets for sharing information. By not abiding by the expectations of the internet, news websites risk losing readers who can go to competing news sources for their information. Images or videos need to be incorporated, and articles should be briefer to hold the attention of the audience. These changes are what concern journalists. "Most of the journalists said they are willing to adapt, and most have done so, but their primary concern is sacrificing quality journalism for faster, softer, inaccurate piecemeal web nuggets." [8] It is the drastic changes that worries the journalists, as well as the negative impact this may have on their writing if they have to change their style, and focus on speed rather than quality of an article. Nicholas Lemann's defends their worries, observing "the quality of Internet Journalism is bound to improve over time, especially if more of the virtues of traditional journalism migrate to the internet." [9] Journalism is in a transition stage when it comes to entering into internet, and so people are still trying to understand the capabilities and the limitations. After there is an understanding of what can be done with the internet, journalists can utilize this information for their benefit. Until then, they are learning as they go to find what is successful in keeping the industry intact.

There is no way to reverse the influence the internet has had, and will continue to have, on journalism, so the only way to continue in the industry is to try and follow along as best as possible. For anyone within the profession, it is clear that the job is changing. There is a continuing decrease in available jobs, and the stress put on news companies is reflected in the continuing list of expectations for the industry. According to Scott Reinardy, "The State of the Media 2009 Annual Report said about 5,000 full-time journalism jobs disappeared in 2008… Between 2005-2007 newspaper stocks lost 42% of their value. In 2008 it grew much worse as newspapers dropped 83% of their remaining value." [10] The newspaper industry is in a decline right now, and while the whispered words of "journalism is dead" isn't a proven statement, it is well on its way unless drastic measures are taken. News organizations are being pressured to reconsider root values and practices by the technology that is being created in order to preserve some semblance of journalism, and not allow the entire medium to die out. In order to cut costs, jobs have been lost, or condensed. "News workers… are being asked to do more (writing, stories or shooting video for the web, compiling photo galleries, blogging, etc.) with less (layoffs, buyouts, hiring freezes, etc.)[sic]." [11] This forces the journalists to put in more hours and learn entirely new programs, as well as understand how to portray a news story best through those programs, or become another statistic in the count of journalists who have lost their jobs. Success in journalism now lies in understanding that "proficiency in computer technology and the internet has become central to the ability of journalists to do their jobs." [12] While there is leniency in teaching current employees the programs and skills necessary for an internet-based news story, there isn't any for new hires. An employee isn't likely to hire someone who is incapable of doing their job without constant instruction. With jobs scarce, new hires need to have these skills to keep up with the strong demands of the job, and to stand out against other applicants, when the employer is hyper-selective of whom they hire. According to Lawrence Pintak, "print and broadcast organizations alike that are hiring tell us they will not employ a graduate who does not have multi-platform skills." [13] This media knowledge is now a crucial skill that employees need to have to be able to keep up with the demands of the industry.

The way to combat these changes in the industry is to focus on how journalism is taught. If the education process can change, then these students will be better prepared to enter into a field of unknowns, and still succeed.

Barbara Kelley explains this by suggesting that, "as the mediascape morphs at breakneck speed... Journalists who succeed amidst change will be those whose education taught them to think critically." [14] The issue with the present education system is that the future jobs in this "media industry" may not exist right now. Essentially what needs to be studied more in-depth is what Jo Bardoel calls "Network Journalism." This is a form that focuses on the main features in journalism (interactivity, hypertextuality, multimediality and a-synchronicity) to educate on the concept of journalism more than the act. [15] If the focus of education is to teach students how to conceptualize the meaning of journalism, rather than to just churn out a pretty story, than the basis of journalism can be shared throughout the different platforms, and keep its integrity. This concept can then be molded however necessary to fit the specific needs of the news, because these students would be trained on how to work around the unknown. With technological changes happening so quickly, it is necessary for students to face the idea that the job they aimed for then they began school may be completely different when they enter the work field. By expecting changes in the industry, it gives students a better opportunity to succeed with the differences, and brace themselves for the unknown.

According to Mitchell Stephens, "the present education needs a heart transplant." [16] This education system is still training students for a job in journalism, but the training is old and outdated. The worry that journalism schools have with change is that a focus on multimedia will build a generation of technicians, rather than thinkers and journalists. The key is to find the balance in teaching the art of journalism, as well as the technical skills that will be necessary to be journalists. In this new phase of journalism it will not be the student who is the most grammatically correct, who dots there I's and crosses their T's, that is the most successful. The most successful student will be the one who can take the information given to them and adapt it to any given situation.

Journalism cannot turn back now. It is on a set, society-driven path, and, in order to survive, it must meet the demands of technological advancements. The best it can do is brace itself and try and get through the transition phase of becoming a multimedia vehicle for sharing information. If journalism can work with elasticity, being able to bend and weave as necessary while still keeping its core value, it will succeed. There is a danger in holding on too tight to old ideas, because they make it difficult to follow a successful business path. With print journalism on the decline, the only way for journalism to survive is to incorporate digital news as well. It is the integration of the multiple different methods of sharing information that will keep journalism alive throughout the current changes. It is possible for journalism to thrive with the internet, it just may be in a different format that how it was 20 years ago. Print is just a small aspect of an entire package labeled "media journalism," and journalism can be shared throughout each of the different mediums.

Notes

[1] Defreitas, Nick. (2011). How The Internet Has Changed The Definition Of "Journalist." *Gateway Journalism Review*, 41(323), 20-21. pp. 21.

[2] Spyridou, L.-P., M. Matsiola, A. Veglis, G. Kalliris, and C. Dimoulas. (2013). Journalism in a State of Flux: Journalists as Agents of Technology Innovation and Emerging News Practices. *International Communication Gazette*, 75(1), 76-98. Pp. 77.

[3] Mensing, Donica. (2010). Rethinking [Again] the Future of Journalism Education. *Journalism Studies*, 11(4), 511-23. pp. 514.

[4] Pintak, Lawrence. (2013). J-School Survival Tools. *Chronicle of Higher Education* 60(11), B4-B5.

[5] Stephens, Mitchell. (2000). A J-School Manifesto. *Columbia Journalism Review*, 39(3), 63.

[6] Kelley, Barbara. (2007). Teaching Journalism. *Communication Research Trends*, 26(2), 3-13. pp. 5.

[7] Pintak, Lawrence. (2013). J-School Survival Tools." *Chronicle of Higher Education* 60(11), B4-B5. pp. B4.

[8] Reinardy, Scott. (2010). Need For Speed onto Internet Clashes with Journalistic Values. *Newspaper Research Journal*, 31(1), 69-83. pp. 79.

[9] Lemann, Nicholas. Journalism without Journalists. *The New Yorker*. pp. 3.

[10] Reinardy (2010) pp. 70.

[11] Reinardy (2010). pp. 70.

[12] Spyridou, L.-P. et. al. (2013). pp. 83.

[13] Pintak (2013). pp. B4.

[14] Kelley (2007). pp. 5.

[15] Bardoel, J. (2002). The Internet, Journalism and Public Communication Policies. *International Communication Gazette*, 64(5), 501-11. pp. 504-505.

[16] Stephens, M. (2000). pp. 63.

Android app creation goes to elementary school

by Steve Rhine

In the dark ages of technology, about ten years ago, if you wanted to make a website you had to learn html. Does this look familiar to anyone?

```
<html> <head> <meta charset="UTF-8"> <!-- TemplateBeginEditable
name="doctitle" --> <title>Untitled Document</title> <!--
TemplateEndEditable --> <!-- TemplateBeginEditable name="head" --> <!--
TemplateEndEditable --> <style type="text/css"> <!–
body {    font: 100%/1.4 Verdana, Arial, Helvetica, sans-serif;
background: #42413C;     margin: 0;      padding: 0;     color: #000; }
```

Now, programs such as Web Studio, Dreamweaver, Sandvox, and iWeb all make website creation easier thanks to WYSIWYG (what you see is what you get) interfaces. All the code is written invisibly as you drag and drop text, images, and other media on the page. Web based site creation tools have proliferated on the Internet. As a result, the pace of website construction has skyrocketed incredibly. The University of California at Berkeley estimates that 7.3 million new web pages are added to the Internet every day. [1] Easy access to simple web site construction tools took the power from the realm of trained coders and gave it to everyday consumers. While people argue about the numbers, our ability to know what is happening on the global Internet, and whether we are counting pages versus websites, Reuters estimates that we have over a half trillion web pages today. This is 15,000 times as many as we had a decade ago. Content on the web exploded with a shift in capability.

Table 1. Number of web pages on the Internet. [2]

1993	130
1994	2,738
1995	18,957
1996	603,367
1997	1,681,868
1998	3,689,227
1999	9,560,866
2000	25,675,581
2001	36,276,252
2012	550,000,000,000

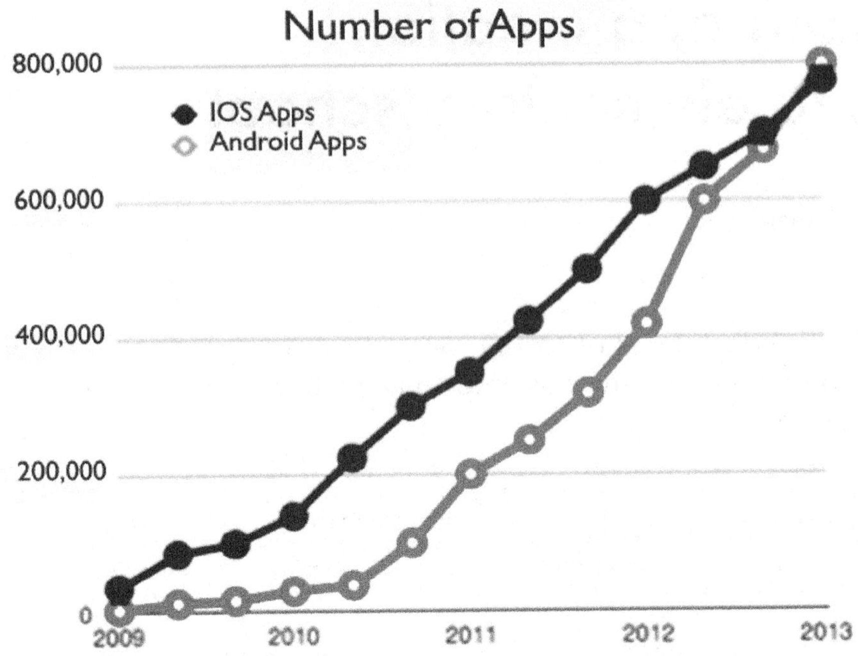

Figure 1. Number of apps created in iOS and Android.

That same evolution is potentially taking place in the world of apps for phones and tablets at a much more rapid pace. In six years, we have gone from not even knowing what an "app" is to about 800,000 iOS apps [3] and as many Android apps. [4] [5] Windows is trying to get in the game with about 30,000 apps currently. [6] While Apple had a big head start with the iPhone, the number of Android apps has closed the gap, and they are being created at a faster pace. These apps range from simple alarm clocks and calculators to apps that help doctors simulate surgeries for patients to understand. [7]

Meanwhile, one of the fastest growing occupations is software developers. The Bureau of Labor Statistics (BLS) estimates that the demand for developers will grow 30% over the next decade, much faster than the average occupation. [8] With a median wage of about $90,000, it is a profitable venture. However, there is a danger that outsourcing may limit that growth in the US, as programmers can be anywhere in the world. Nevertheless, opportunities for software developers are often surpassing the number of qualified people available.

While a great video on YouTube recently advocates for computer programmers, [9] [10] the growth area is actually for developers rather than programmers. The BLS estimates the demand for computer programmers growing at a rate of 14% over the next decade, slower than the average occupation. That said, knowing something about programming can help you design. Blogs are engaging in this conversation about how to meet the need for developers and defining what they should know. [11] [12]

In 2010, Google created a web based platform for app development that ultimately was taken over by MIT. The App Inventor program (http://appinventor.mit.edu/) is what Dreamweaver and iWeb were to website creation: the common person's access to WYSIWYG app creation. With drag and drop functionality students, as young as second grade, are writing their own apps. In fact, MIT runs a contest for programming using the App Inventor that includes K-8 students. [13] The first winner in that category was a seventh grade student in India whose parents were worried about school bus delays and whether he made the bus or not. His solution helps parents track their kids on bus rides home from school by using bar code scanning for students to check in and out from the bus while GPS tracks the bus location and automatically sends text messages to parents to keep them informed. His school is using the app this spring. Second place went to a third grade student in Wisconsin.

The App Inventor program has two parts to it. First, the design screen on which students can place objects such as pictures or buttons on the phone/tablet screen where they want them. This design side is the realm of software developers. What should it look like? What should it do? Students simply drag a button, sound, or capability (such as using the accelerometer) to the canvas. My fabulous app that lets you paint on any picture is shown in Figure 2. The tutorials are very easy to follow. While it took me an hour or so to get the idea, design of this app took about ten minutes.

Figure 2. Rhine's App.

The second part of the project is "programming" the code to make the app function. Without knowing any code, all you need to do is drag and drop.

The coding app is just a matter of which puzzle pieces to place on the canvas (see Figure 3). My Motorola Xoom tablet wirelessly connects to my computer and the App Inventor, so that I can see changes to my app as I make them. About 30 minutes later, I was painting the puppy (Figure 4)!

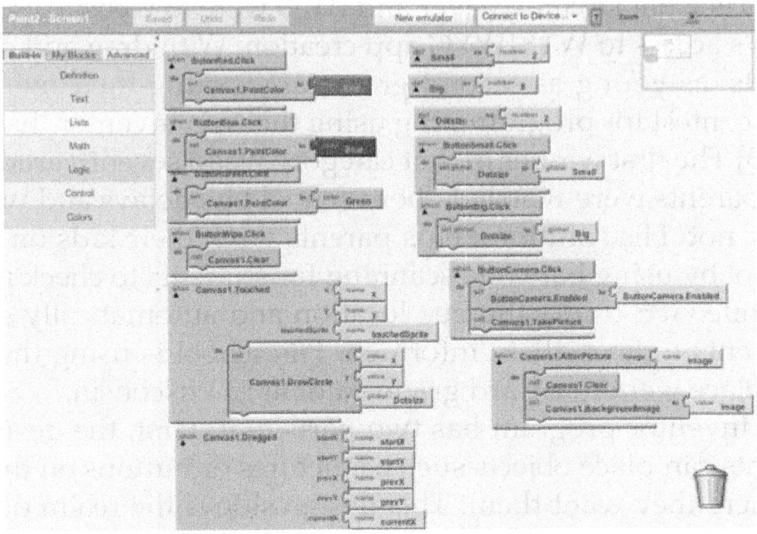

Figure 3. Coding Interface.

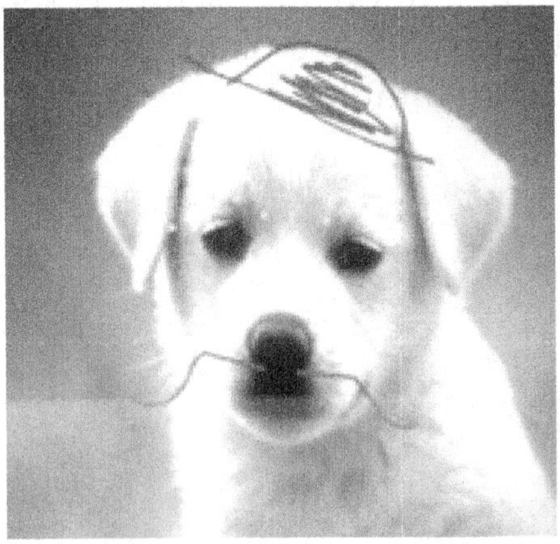

Figure 4. Painting the Puppy

Beyond the silliness is a path to success for students. Gaining the confidence to design their own apps and bring them to life can be a powerful motivator for the software developers of the future. Understanding how the code puzzle fits together will help developers in their design. Having instant access to the results, as ideas blossom in your head, can stimulate innovation. Time will tell if we are only using these tools to paint puppies or solve the problems of the world, like 7th grade student Arjun Kammar. But it seems to me, that bringing down the barrier of complex coding, as we have with html coding, opens the door to some cool possibilities.

Notes

[1] How Much Information? (2000). Retrieved from http://www2.sims.berkeley.edu/research/projects/how-much-info/internet.html

[2] Data was compliled from: BBC. (2002). Internet Starts to Shrink. *BBC*. Retrieved from http://news.bbc.co.uk/1/hi/sci/tech/1738496.stm; Zakon, R. (2014). Hobbes' Internet Timeline. *Zakon*. Retrieved from http://www.zakon.org/robert/internet/timeline/; halejrb-ga. (2003). Q: How many websites? [msg 1]. Message posted to http://answers.google.com/answers/threadview?id=172378

[3] Castello, S. (n.d.). How Many Apps Are in the iPhone App Store. *About.com*. Retrieved from http://ipod.about.com/od/iphonesoftwareterms/qt/apps-in-app-store.htm

[4] Castello, S. (n. d.)

[5] AppBrain (2013). Number of Android Apps. *AppBrain Stats*. Retrieved from http://www.appbrain.com/stats/number-of-android-apps; Google Play. (n.d.). In *Wikipedia*. Retrieved from http://en.wikipedia.org/wiki/Google_Play

[6] Microsoft claims to have over 100,000 apps for their phone, but there are less than 30,000 apps currently available in the Windows store. http://www.techrepublic.com/blog/window-on-windows/the-countdown-to-100000-windows-8-apps-falls-short/7199

[7] Husain, I., Aungst, T., & Lewis, T. (2012) The most innovative medical apps of 2012. *iMedical Apps*. Retrieved from http://www.imedicalapps.com/2012/12/innovative-medical-apps-2012/

[8] Bureau of Labor Statistics. Software Developers. In *Occupational Outlook Handbook, 2012-2013 edition*. Retrieved from http://www.bls.gov/ooh/Computer-and-Information-Technology/Software-developers.htm

[9] Code.org. (2013). What Most Schools Don't Teach [Web Video]. Retrieved from http://www.youtube.com/watch?v=nKIu9yen5nc

[10] Code.org. (2013).

[11] Code.org (2013); Dern, D. P. (2011).

[12] What today's software developers need to know. *Computer World UK*. http://www.computerworlduk.com/advice/applications/3304124/what-todays-software-developers-need-to-know/

[13] See: http://gallery.appinventor.mit.edu/#page%3DContest

Jambo Bwana Part 2: A Journey in Swahili as an Online Language

by Nicole Nowlin
Program cordinator, The Berglund Center for Internet Studies

Introduction

While the initial article relating to this experience (found here) was truly an experiential discussion on the endeavor, this second part is meant to examine the design of the program, as well as the various styles for teaching language virtually.

Cultural Explorations

In addition to the primary focus of language education built into the curriculum, the topics of each unit related directly to culture or life in West Africa, providing students with a broader understanding beyond language skills. Student projects, as they were not locked to the topic of the unit, could explore significant aspects of West African culture. While the amount of project freedom was difficult for some to handle, both because of a lack of known vocabulary and the challenge of choosing from so vast an array of topics, it did provide interesting opportunities for student research. This was conducted through interviews, search engines, media sites, and news outlets. The students used most technological resources at their disposal to complete their projects with plenty of relevant information.

Furthermore, students visited a leading fair trade wholesaler called Swahili Importers [1], located in Eugene, Oregon. The visit presented culture from a business perspective and also showed the impact of technology on trade. The Internet is a great example because it is a major part of the wholesaler's business. When the program is fully online, there may not be the opportunity for those same explorations outside of the regular classroom and coursework as there were in Eugene.

Technical Impressions [2]

The Swahili program and curriculum are unique in that they genuinely wish for extensive student feedback and criticism. Students are expected to be in charge of their learning. Deborah Cooke, head of the technology on the program, said very clearly to all students the first week of class, "You have power here. You have control over your learning journey. You have freedom. You have the creative options to explore your own learning path." [3] The Hermes [4] site was designed to be a guide for independent, self-directed learners. It provides clear instructions and expects a person to follow them; for the most part, the assignments are easily navigable. However, there are a few drawbacks with the design program used. Tables are difficult to code in the program, making it impossible to copy and paste tables from the assignment page into the program where they are to be posted because most of them are screenshots. Those tables that are not tend to have formatting issues and extend the unit chapter down quite far, especially when there are photos that are supposed to be matched with vocabulary words. The program also will not allow you to set links to open in a new window, which is very convenient for a student who needs to explore a link but doesn't want to have to find their way back to their course page. All links need to be opened with a right click to avoid this. The only other issues related to the learning management system were simple edits needed – misnumbered or mislabeled items, duplicate titles, etc. It is a very well crafted, detailed system.

The discussion board is generic and very easy to use. It does have a few issues with relation to duplicate titles from the same poster, so if a discussion board topic has the same title twice in a unit, there may be a problem posting it. Otherwise, posting and responding are extremely simple in the discussion board section. Also to be used for interaction was Blogger. [5] Assignments for Blogger disappeared about halfway through the curriculum in Swahili 1. While Blogger is more visually appealing—formatting-wise—than the discussion board, the interactions between students, conductors, and guides were just as easily completed on the discussion board. Blogger appears to be an extraneous item in the curriculum.

Wikispaces [6] was used for assignments that did not need student interaction, unlike the discussion board and Blogger. It also had assigned tasks throughout the course. Students complained they did not understand how to use Wikispaces and so did not do the assignments. However, I had never used the site myself and found it fairly simple to pick up in a matter of minutes. This could be my familiarity with technology, but most high school students today are as tech savvy, if not more so, than I have observed. Blogger received similar feedback. Unless a section is added to the site where each student could post assignments, or submit them to a shared folder Dropbox [7] style, or the conductor chooses to view all assignments on the discussion boards, Wikispaces needs to stay. It has purpose and functionality different than the Hermes site, so it is not a duplicate to the discussion board in the same way as Blogger.

Another new account for students to set up is a Google+ account. [8] For the hybrid pilot course, this was completely unused and rather useless, as students are not going to participate in a Hangout when they're living two doors apart. With full online course implementation, the Hangout feature on Google+, which is essentially free Skype for big groups, has the potential to be very useful in connecting families with conductors, guides, coaches, and other families.

I mentioned LinguaFolio [9] more than once. It is a fascinating program. LinguaFolio Students may add whatever languages they've studied and upload evidence to support their claims to various proficiency levels. Evaluators may confirm that the evidence is sufficient and the person meets that level. This program will not expire in the near future; students may continue to have access to it now that they have an account, and could potentially use it to show employers where their language proficiencies lie. This particular technological aspect introduced in the Swahili program – an online language portfolio – is fabulous and has a lot of potential. I would like to see it used at a university level. The only problem I saw with it was the actual uploading or creation of evidence. It is possible the condensed time made it more difficult for students to focus on selecting or creating evidence for specific Can Do statements. It remains to be seen if there are steadier updates during the regular online program.

Online coursework isn't for everyone, though, there are, as of this writing, no norms for evaluating a person's readiness for an online course. Some colleges are using controls to determine who would be successful in an online course, with the different workload and responsibilities that go with it. [10] A language-focused online course would be even more difficult. Such an evaluation of student success possibilities is likely in the hands of the contracting school, but would still be a recommended consideration for student success and retention. The goal of CASLS in this emerging activity of providing online language instruction is to make such instruction easier, so that anyone could potentially benefit from an online course, whether in language or in another subject area.

Curriculum Impressions

The subject matter of the curriculum was culturally relevant, while still remaining interesting and relatable to students. However, the format put the students into conversations with little understanding of how the language worked. The idea was for students to push themselves to learn and to be in charge of their own learning – they were the ones to make it work. However, all of the students, myself included, felt that we needed at least some structure. My general suggestion is to start the first unit with basic grammar and verbs, then end the first chapter of the unit with the dialogue using what was introduced, rather than beginning with it. I would add new verb tenses and perhaps noun classes through the other chapters in Unit 1, ending each chapter with a dialogue that expanded on what had been learned. By Unit 2, with some kind of a basis already established, I would go ahead and start the dialogue at the beginning and have students look up words they did not understand. From then on, students would have a basis from which to build, and would not feel lost and confused from the first conversation.

There were also strange gaps that, to me, seemed like basic information learned early on in most language programs. This could be my mind coming at it from a traditional language platform, but colors, animals, and foods, are usually learned early on in comparison to medicine, illnesses, and travel. I did discuss this with Director Falsgraf and commented on it earlier in this evaluation. I want to reiterate his point that "Whenever possible vocabulary should be learned for a purpose." [11] I do not disagree with this and even see its importance, but I also want to be able to have a general conversation. Knowing cat, dog, red, blue, and green can help in a very generic sense. The coursework followed two characters – Asante and Sarah – on their respective journeys in Tanzania and Kenya. Through them, we explored language and culture. While some students did not care for the story-based curriculum, I did not mind at all – I felt we could relate to the characters and build an image of the event through their activities.

I would still like to see some more common phrasing in the curriculum. I also feel the need to point out that we skipped sections in their entirety due to the time constraints of the hybrid intensive pilot course. Given more time, it is possible that during those sections we would have covered some of the items that felt strangely absent. When reviewing my ideas with Director Falsgraf, he commented that what I was pushing for was too comfortable a scenario. "Learning another language is not comfortable. Whether you are learning naturally in country or in a classroom, when confronting another culture and language you have to be uncomfortable. Giving lists of 'expected' vocab and testing students on exactly what they have been taught is comfortable, especially after 10+ years of being enculturated into this system." He did go on to clarify, though, that it doesn't work to frighten people too greatly with something different, and the unfamiliarity combined with a few of the other items discussed about the program may have contributed to some of the points discussed in this article. There is perhaps a middle ground to be found for what I see as an improvement still in keeping with the ideas of the program and its unique, challenging learning style. I did agree wholeheartedly with Dr. Falsgraf when he ended with, "We'll get better." [12]

The downside to the hybrid intensive that I feel may be corrected in the fully online course is a need for reinforcement. I mentioned it previously in the article, but it bears mentioning again. Immediately after the course, I could exchange polite conversation on a very basic level and perhaps throw in a few descriptions and sentences about familiar topics. Months later, I can still handle the greetings because we used them so often. I may remember several of the numbers, but we didn't count very high. I cannot tell time. For a year's worth of Swahili, my retention is very low with the effort everyone put in. This can be addressed for future intensives by repetition and reinforcement of material every day in the classroom, and also by adjusting the course schedule. I consider a year of high school language as equal to approximately one semester of lower division college language, which is four credits at Pacific. [13] Doing four university credits in three weeks is quite an undertaking. However, when doing 10 units of upper division university credit in eight weeks, I still had more free time than in the Swahili course and did not experience the same level of burnout. Students need more free time to absorb and unwind during the course.

In an online environment, it will be especially important for the Swahili families to support and reinforce each other, as there will be no instructor there in front of them. My other concern with the fully online course is Swahili conversation. Students will meet with the conductor, guides, and coaches to work on their conversation. The Fall 2012 course was designed to include several one-on-one appointments with coaches to work on conversation skills in an individualized fashion, and students were to be encouraged to utilize those abilities with other participants in the program. I do feel that observing the students as a group conversing with each other and the conductor would be beneficial as a way to see group dynamics and encourage comfort among family members with communication. [14] Focusing on the currently studied unit would be very helpful with both reinforcement and pronunciation improvement. Students may also retain more from the simple fact that most will be doing it on school computers in a semi-proctored environment, with less ability to distract themselves on other internet sites. The results of the fully online fall pilot will be presented by Director Falsgraf in a Berglund Center Roundtable in May 2013.

Online Language Learning Comparison

Over 152 million results appear when one searches Google for "online language learning." On the first page are familiar faces – Rosetta Stone, Live Mocha, etc. [15] It is curious that online education is so integrated into society, especially in an upper education echelon , when studies show the national average success rate is only about 50%. An online course is typically more difficult for students, not easier, as they require greater levels of self-discipline, not to mention strong academics and tech savvy. [16] Some researchers assert that "retention rates are 20% lower in online courses than in traditional face-to-face courses" [17] and that "retention may be improved by including face-to-face orientations or other face-to-face elements in online courses." [18]

I briefly touched on successful online learners, but wish to reiterate here that they are "motivated, independent, [and] self-directed." These students also "enjoy technology, have strong language skills, and are visual learners... They have positive attitudes and are willing to ask for help. Extroverted students are often more successful in socially interactive courses, while more introverted students tend to succeed in self-paced courses." The success of these students is also affected by the instructional method, such as frequent and timely instructor feedback,. Additionally, the use of various tools to support group activity, individual coaching, and speaking practice can make up for the lack of consistent instructor interaction inherent in an online course. "A combination of flexibility, independence, and experience with online tools has been associated with improved critical thinking, research, and computer skills." [19]

With this framework in mind of how a person is successful as an online language learner, let us consider a few comparisons to the new CASLS Swahili program.

Portal Zweite Chance (Portal Second Chance) [20]

This site is free and available in German only. Of special interest aside from the typical vocabulary and grammar exercises, it provides a self-evaluation and diagnostic testing to place students at different levels. It then automatically builds a learning plan based on level, curriculum, and the student's availability, which can be adjusted. Each week is evaluated and then the next is provided, individualized for the student. This provides quite a bit of independence and self-pacing as well as an automatic ability to advance when a level changes. [21] In comparison, the Swahili program does not provide a pre-evaluation as it is unnecessary for first year beginning students, but it does provide continual updating on progress through LinguaFolio. It also provides direct interaction through the conductor/guide/person-who-interacts setup. Currently, there are no grammar exercises particularly designed for the Swahili program, though it is heavy on the vocabulary.

Rosetta Stone [22]

You practice, you drill, and you listen quite a bit with Rosetta Stone. It is not structured in a particular context and you are not required to follow a set progression. There is no interaction with other people on this program in its usual form and it is best used in conjunction with other coursework or language practice, rather than by itself. It is generally easy to use and usage can be tracked by instructors. [23] It now offers an option called Totale, ringing in at approximately $1000, that includes RosettaCourse (basic Rosetta Stone), RosettaStudio (video chat with native speakers for interaction), and RosettaWorld (online language-related games community). [24] With Totale, Rosetta Stone upgrades from basic software that supports language but does not teach it to a fairly comprehensive program with a hefty price tag. CASLS provides a contextual story-based learning environment, guaranteed interaction with various individuals, language production and usage through projects, and peer interaction. Although it does not provide language-related gaming, the CASLS program does many of the same things with a more student focused approach.

Tell Me More [25]

A major competitor of Rosetta Stone, this program teaches words and phrases but also "includes a speech recognition component that analyzes pronunciation, presents a graph of speech, and suggests how to perfect it." There are also videos displaying how to physically make the sounds. [26] At $390 a year for six languages, it is a much better price point than Rosetta Stone, but it does not offer as much as Totale. The speech recognition is an interesting feature, but face to face with a native speaker, such as with the CASLS program, surpasses the computer based evaluation.

Livemocha [27]

New to Pacific University this year, Livemocha offers free basic lessons in any of its 30 languages with monthly or bi-annual subscriptions providing additional content and levels. For monthly users, eight recordings may be submitted for native speaker evaluation and recommendations, and for bi-annual users, two language examples per lesson may be submitted. All users have access to social networking groups and VoIP native speakers who in turn wish to learn English. [28] There is no set instructor for this program, as there is with CASLS.

Perhaps the most glaringly obvious issue with many online language learning tools is the lack of consistent contact with a native speaker (unless there is a high price to go with it). "The quality of feedback is important," according to Mike Levy, head of the School of Languages and Linguistics at Griffith University in Brisbane, Australia. "Sites with human contact work best," he said. "This shows the advantage of humans compared to computers. A computer is never as subtle or intelligent." [29]

Furthermore, in today's learning community, social networks and the theory of social constructivism are key to successful online learning communities, such as the families, clans, and tribes in the CASLS structure. Other programs have similar communities, but not to the structured, integrated level the Swahili program entails. Students create relationships and deal with real-world problems and projects, evidenced in the unit topics and the continuing stories of Asante and Sarah. "The ideal way to learn language in any situation or for any student has not been found. But one thing technology based language instruction must respect is the need for a cultural dimension to language learning....Any separation between language and the cultural context within which it functions is artificial. Language can't be separated from culture. Culture is language." [30]

But the question remains: how successful was the Swahili course in its pilot intensive phase? In order to be considered successful, the new system from CASLS needs to equal or exceed traditional language education results. Creating a solid basis of familiarity in East African culture was also a goal of the program. The success is mixed. While the students did learn much about East African culture in depth, including through numerous self-guided projects, they did not meet the proficiency goal of the program (Novice High) when examined by the CAP test.

Conclusion

If student interest is the key, then the program was successful; student surveys show 14 of 15 students feel motivated to continue studying Swahili, 14 plan to take Swahili 2, and 12 would take another Swahili summer course. 13 out of 15 felt the Hermes site was easy to use, as was the discussion board (10 out of 15), and the instructions for assignments were understandable (14 of 15). It is clear that students felt they did not have enough free time, as they disagreed with the statement "There was enough free time to prepare my project and explore campus" (13 of 15). 11 of 15 felt the class was too fast.

That being said, the more interesting results come from the Swahili exam taken by the students in Week Three. Scores 1-3 are novice levels, with 4 and up transitioning into the intermediate level. The test was multiple-choice reading comprehension, with the number and complexity of questions varying based on the students' scores as they progressed through the exam, followed by writing and speaking exercises to be graded by instructors. Due to time constraints, those portions of the exam were not graded, but the results of the multiple choice section are very interesting. Below is a raw data table on the overall scores. My own score is highlighted in yellow, showing me very much at Level 1 (beginning novice) with many of the other students. Highlighted in blue are some interestingly high results. To protect the identity of minors in the course, no identifying information such as year in school or Swahili in the home is included below.

Table-1. Report for College Readiness Academy, Class CRA-Swahili-2012.

Panel Name	Benchmark	Level	Test Time	Test Path [31]	Raw Score [32]
Swahili Reading	Beginning (C)	1	17 min.	RS,1E,2E	13.0
Swahili Reading	Beginning (C)	1	28 min.	RS,1E,2E	14.0
Swahili Reading	Beginning (C)	1	13 min.	RS,1E,2E	15.0
Swahili Reading	Beginning (C)	1	14 min.	RS,1E,2E	16.0
Swahili Reading	Beginning (C)	1	24 min.	RS,1E,2E	17.0
Swahili Reading	Beginning (C)	1	14 min.	RS,1E,2E	18.0
Swahili Reading	Beginning (C)	1	16 min.	RS,1E,2E	18.0
Swahili Reading	Beginning (C)	1	20 min.	RS,1E,2E	18.0
Swahili Reading	Beginning (C)	1	19 min.	RS,1E,2E	19.0
Swahili Reading	Beginning (C)	1	20 min.	RS,1E,2E	19.0
Swahili Reading	Beginning (C)	1	27 min.	RS,1E,2E	20.0
Swahili Reading	Beginning (C)	1	16 min.	RS,1E,2E	21.0
Swahili Reading	Beginning (A)	3	26 min.	RS,1E,2M,3M	30.0
Swahili Reading	Beginning (A)	3	34 min.	RS,1E,2M,3M	33.0
Swahili Reading	Transitioning (C)	4	72 min.	RS,1E,2M,3H,3M	39.0
Swahili Reading	Transitioning (C)	4	48 min.	RS,1E,2M,3H,3M	47.0

For a year's worth of Swahili, my expectation was to see students in the Beginning Intermediate to Beginning High range (2 or 3) but that was clearly not the result. Most of us did not retain the information and were frustrated by an inability to handle the proficiency exam. In no way were the instructors "teaching to the test." On the one hand, teaching to the test is an oft lamented style, but on the other hand, taking a test with no reference to the material is frustrating for the learner. 75% of us scored as true novices after the intensive, without consideration for writing and speaking exercises. I know my own writing and speaking exercises on the test were hardly high quality. Considering the two 3's and the two 4's, I conclude that those particular students either thrive in the style of learning environment around the course, utilized outside sources effectively as the program is designed to supplement their learning, or had prior knowledge of the language (i.e. heritage speakers). I am unable to confirm the impact of possible heritage speaking on the scores due to student privacy. Ultimately, I find myself disappointed with the scores after the course, but still hopeful that the program has the potential to bring more of those 3's and 4's to the other students with a little work.

Notes

[1] Swahili African Modern. (2012) Swahili Imports. Retrieved from http://www.swahili-imports.com/.

[2] Cooke, D. (2012a). Personal interview on 27 July 2012.

[3] Cooke, D. (2012b). Personal interview on 10 July 2012.

[4] Swahili. (2012). University of Oregon. Retrieved from http://hermes-fire.uoregon.edu/swahili/.

[5] See: http://www.blogger.com/.

[6] See: http://www.wikispaces.com/.

[7] See: http://www.dropbox.com/.

[8] See: https://plus.google.com/.

[9] See: https://linguafolio.uoregon.edu/.

[10] Jenkins, R. (2011). Why Are So Many Students Still Failing Online? Do Your Job Better. *The Chronicle of Higher Education*. Retrieved from http://chronicle.com/article/Why-Are-So-Many-Students-Still/127584/.

[11] Falsgraf, C. (2012a). Online interview on 25 Sept. 2012.

[12] Falsgraf, C. (2012b). Online interview on 10 Oct. 2012.
[13] See: http://www.pacificu.edu/.

[14] Falsgraf, C. (2012a).

[15] Online Language Learning Search Results. (n.d.) Google. Retrieved from http://www.google.com/.

[16] Jenkins, R. (2011).

[17] Ali, R & Leeds, E. M. (2009). The Impact of Face-to-Face Orientation on Online Retention: A Pilot Study. *Online Journal of Distance Learning Administration* 12(4). Retrieved from http://www.westga.edu/~distance/ojdla/winter124/ali124.html.

[18] Brau, M., Christian, S., Hill, B., McNair, D., Sandoz, S., & Taylor, C. (2010). Success and Retention in Online and Hybrid Courses. *Lane Community College*. Web. Retrieved from http://www.lanecc.edu/sites/default/files/assessment/hill-onlineteachinglearning2010.pdf.
[19] Kelly, M., Kennell, T., McBride, R., & Sturm, M. (2011). Fast Forward: An Analysis of Online and Distance Education Language Training. New Media Language Training, Inc. Citizenship and Immigration Canada. Retrieved from: http://atwork.settlement.org/downloads/atwork/CIC_Fast_Forward_Online_Language_Training.pdf.

[20] See: http://www.ich-will-lernen.de/.

[21] Kelly, M. et. al. (2011).

[22] See: http://www.rosettastone.com/.

[23] Kelly, M. et. al. (2011).

[24] Taub, E. A. (2010). The Web Way to Learn a Language. *The New York Times*. Retrieved from: http://www.nytimes.com/2010/01/28/technology/personaltech/28basics.html?_r=3.

[25] See: http://www.tellmemore.com/home.aspx.

[26] Taub, E. A. (2010).

[27] See: Livemocha.com

[28] Taub, E. A. (2010).

[29] Taub, E. A. (2010).

[30] Kelly, M. et. al. (2011).

[31] Test path consists of a series of bins. The first bin (RS) is the instructions, survey and sample item. The other bins each contain 15 items.

[32] Total items taken vary according to test path.

Directed Reading: A Strategy for Teaching Students to Read Mathematics

by Nancy Ann Neudauer, Ph.D.
Department of Mathematics & Computer Science, Pacific University

Abstract- Getting students to read the textbook is one of the major hurdles I face in teaching undergraduate mathematics. Students who do read the new material before hearing a lecture on it tell me that it is a tremendous help in understanding the lecture. Yet so few students do this.

Directed Reading offers students little choice but to read the book before coming to class. The students like it because it guides them through the reading and they follow the lecture more easily. Moreover, it saves precious class time on routine problems, and we can concentrate on subtleties and intricacies in the material.

1. Learning to Read

I have a problem getting my students to read their mathematics book. For years I would tell them to read the section before the lecture on that section. Occasionally a student would tell me that he or she had done this and that "it really helped." But for the most part the students admitted that they had not. I thought that maybe they did not wantto read the book, or maybe they did not like to read it. Many of them were struggling with mathematics. If reading the book really helped, why wouldn't they do it? Then it dawned on me—they didn't know how to read a mathematics book.

I thought back to how I had learned to read. Not back to sounding out the words and reading "See spot run. See Jane watch spot run," but rather to how I had learned to read for content. I remembered a long time ago—in second grade or fourth grade—reading a chapter in a social studies book and at the same time filling out a worksheet. The worksheet would have lines such as:

> _____________ is the capital of Spain.
> The major exports of Spain are _____________ and _____________.
> Most of the people of Spain speak _____________.

As I read, I would pick out pieces of information and fill in the blanks. At this point I was reading more than just words; I was expected to get some information out of what I was reading. The worksheet helped guide me, or direct me, in my reading.

2. Learning to read mathematics

Maybe I was right about the capital of Spain idea. But it seemed that 12 years after filling in Madrid we should be capable of a bit more than filling in blanks. And perhaps even more importantly, this was not exactly the type of content I wanted students to read for in a mathematics class. It wasn't that the students could not read, but that they could not read mathematics.

What exactly dowe want the students to glean from this reading? When they read a section before the lecture, whatwill help them to understand the lecture?

I was confronted with one more problem that helped me answer those questions: my lectures were each 65 minutes. I had been accustomed to teaching 50 minute lectures, and had even then thought the students' attention spans for new material were 35 or 40 minutes at best. Now with a 65 minute lecture I was worried I would be wasting too much of the time without the full attention of the class.

I could almost watch the students drift off. If at the board lecturing in calculus, for example, I would first introduce a new idea. The students would perk up a bit as I did some very simple examples. I would proceed to do some more complicated examples and would start to lose their attention. And just as I got to the subtleties—the really good stuff that maybe they really did need me for and could not just get from the book—they would drift off completely. I thought that if I could just get to that subtle stuff earlier—in the first 30 minutes—then maybe I could hold their attention long enough.

So this was my goal—to get to the more difficult, subtle problems in the first 30 minutes of lecture. I began to think about which material the students could learn from the book on their own. Students had complained from time to time that I didn't assign problems that were like the examples in the section. From precisely here came my idea: I would assign problems that were exactly like the examples, but I would assign them before I lectured on that material. That, I realized, was the sort of reading that the students could do, and in fact that they craved. Maybe at first they would not be reading all the words—but they would be absorbing some of the content. If I had lectured on section 2.3, an assignment might look like this:

Section 2.3 # 8, 10, 14, 15, 19, 22, 35, 36, 41

Section 2.4 # 1, 3, 4

where the Section 2.4 problems are mimics of the example problems in the text. I have had the opportunity to use Directed Reading in both upper- and lower-level courses, in courses for both mathematics majors and non-majors.

The following are a few examples of how I have used it.

3. Directed Reading in Calculus

Directed Reading in Calculus proved to be much more effective than I had anticipated. Where I had done several elementary examples in the past, I decided I would cut back to one, then move on to more complex ones. One day, for example, I was introducing integration by parts. I wrote ∫xcosx dx on the board. A student spoke up and said, "We've already done that." I pointed out that they had done , and he said, "It's the same thing." I then suggested that we try ∫tx-tdt. Another student pointed out that they had done ∫we-xdx. A third student said, "Can't we work on some harder ones, since that's what we'll have to do in the homework and on the test?"

As a result, I find that I can save 20 minutes of lecture time, the students have all at least attempted the more basic problems on their own and at their own pace, and they are able to follow the lecture better as we discuss the subtleties. And the students have what they want—homework problems that are exactly like the examples in the text. Occasionally, such as after an exam, I will not include a directed reading portion on the next assignment. The students will ask for it, arguing, "How can they be expected to follow the lecture if they haven't even looked at the material."

The types of problems that work well as directed reading problems are either a homework problem that closely mimics an example in the text or problems the students have done before but may need to review. With the former, the students carefully work through the example problem. With the latter, students are able to review at their own pace. For instance, in calculus I have found that students often do not remember very well absolute values, logarithms, solving systems of linear equations, and inequalities. Yet when I have spent a little time reviewing these in class, the students who remember them feel like I am wasting class time, while the students who do not remember think that I am going too fast. I find a pace that pleases no student. In working these problems before the lecture, the students are able to choose an appropriate speed until they feel comfortable with this review material.

Directed Reading serves another role here: In addition to saving lecture time, Directed Reading helps to bridge a gap between students of different abilities and with different backgrounds. Having students work problems before class, whether new problems or review problems, gets them all on the same page at the beginning of the lecture. Further, it allows the students to get there at their own pace.

4. Directed Reading in Abstract Algebra

Directed Reading in Abstract Algebra seemed to be a more challenging endeavor at first than it was in calculus. I was struck by the amount of material I needed to cover in this course, so I thought about what sorts of problems were more routine. Primarily I wanted to grade the students' proofs, but I also realized that to do the proofs the students would need to understand the structure as well. I found many straightforward and computational problems at the beginning of each section that required manipulating group elements, multiplying permutations, constructing group tables, etc.

I assigned these problems before lecturing on each section. Instead of collecting these computational problems, I would select some at the beginning of the lecture. Each student would write on a piece of paper which of those he or she could do. I would call on students to put their solution on the board. The students would receive one point for each problem they said they could do, but would lose 20 points if unable to do a problem when called on. The students received immediate feedback on their work instead of waiting for it to be graded, and they also had answers to their questions before the lecture had begun. I thought the negative points would keep the students honest and that the students would only claim to be able to do problems they actually could do, but students had different confidence in their answers, and some are risk takers. If I find this is not working well with a particular class, I change to giving points for students who volunteer to put a problem on the board. I teach abstract algebra differently from how I was taught it, and I have learned from Fraleigh's. article "Happy Abstract Algebra Classes." [4]

In comparison with previous times I had taught abstract algebra, there were noticeable differences. I used to work through many specific examples, covering every detail. Now I am able to cover deeper topics. Instead of presenting a lot of examples, I can mention them and the students will recall them as they have more familiarity with them due to working this all out on their own.

5. Implementation Difficulties

I have found the major stumbling block in the implementation of Directed Reading is the collection of the daily assignments and the quick turnaround necessary to incorporate the responses in that day's lecture. Turning in problems at the beginning of class does not allow me time to read them and modify the class to address questions raised or to skip material that is already clear to the students. Since the students are turning in a Directed Reading assignment on each class day, it becomes a paper-management and grading nightmare. Even if you can return the assignment at the next class, this rate of feedback may be inadequate for this method. We can circumvent the class preparation issue by having students e-mail the professor the day before; this allows time to modify the lecture to meet students' questions and understanding. This helps with lecture preparation but does not provide the quick feedback to the student that some of the newer online mathematics systems would. It also works better when the answers are in words rather than equations or mathematical notation. Some books have reading questions built in, like Beezer's First Course in Linear Algebra. [2] Others have computational problems that align well with examples in the section. A web forum can encourage online discussion of the topics before the class period, but this might not perfectly fit this model. With the huge number of new internet and online resources available, I believe that some combination of them will provide an appropriate forum to collect, assess, give feedback, and employ student understanding of new material. Ideally, the correct combination of these resources will help students to read better for content, thus not only providing the instructor and student feedback, but helping to develop their mathematical reading skills.

Many of the references on teaching students to read mathematics are targeted toward K-12 teachers [1] or pre-date internet current resources [3, 7], and are not widely employed. Recently, a nice overview called How to Read Mathematics appeared that will provide a great introduction to students (or faculty!) using Directed Reading in a course. [5]

Last year, to try to address some of the implementation and feedback issues with Directed Reading, I used WeBWorK for the Directed Reading questions. What is WeBWork? According to the Mathematical Association of America (MAA) website,

> *WeBWorK is a well-tested homework system for delivering individualized problems over the web. By providing students with immediate feedback as to the correctness of their answers, students can be encouraged to make multiple attempts until they succeed. With individualized problem sets, students can work together but will have to enter their own work to receive credit. The instructors are provided with real-time statistics, resulting in lesson plans that can be customized to better serve students. [6]*

We have a WeBWorK installation on our server, so students are given local accounts. WeBWorK gives them immediate feedback on their response, and instructors can choose to give them more than one chance to get a correct answer.

There were several advantages to WebWork. Students did receive immediate feedback to the Directed Reading questions and could then try again, potentially immediately correcting misconceptions. Students did not need to try to fit mathematical notation into an e-mail—some questions were multiple choice, but even for ones that were not, students commented that WeBWorK was easier for them than other online homework systems they had used. There were also some limitations. For example, problems from the existing library did not always align well to the book we were using. Instructors can write their own problems, but this can be a lot of work, and even modifying existing questions does not always go smoothly. Moeover, some of the existing questions had unexpected answers. Finally, I was not able to find suitable questions for each section or lecture.

I had planned to only use WeBWorK for Directed Reading questions, but quite unexpectedly I started using it for sets of review questions between exams and to check student understanding of routine computational exercises. Students liked these questions; if they had a good understanding of the material, it was an instant reward, and if they did not, they could practice and try again immediately. Also, these problems tended to be shorter and more straightforward than the text's homework problems. The increase of student understanding was measurable from this practice. However, there was still frustration and resistance. Glitches in the system and unexpected answers frustrated both students and myself. Some students felt like this was an additional requirement on top of their regular homework. When I implement this again, I will be sure to reduce the amount of other work commensurate with the time spent on WeBWorK assignments.

6. Other student reactions

Another obstacle in employing Directed Reading was a notion the students had that it was unfair to expect them to do a problem before I had "taught" them how to do it. Pointing out that they might have to read Romeo and Juliet before it was discussed in class, or to read a philosophy paper or a psychology chapter, did not shed any light. In fact, when I gave a talk about directed reading, I got the same reaction from some of the mathematics faculty in the audience. They asked how I could expect the students to do a problem that I had not yet discussed.

To combat this, the second semester I employed Directed Reading, I talked with the students about it in class, explaining what I thought the benefits were, and asking for their feedback. In subsequent semesters I have also put in the syllabus the following:

Read each section before I discuss it in class. Once we have gone over a section, reread it, and work through the examples. Sometimes it is difficult to read a mathematics book before coming to class. To guide you in this, each homework assignment will have a Directed Reading component. A few problems from the coming section with constitute this portion of the assignment. The problems will not be complex, but instead will mimic the examples in the text or will follow directly from the reading.

I have a Directed Reading component to each assignment. Now that the students expect it, their reactions are primarily positive, but it still remains a challenge in some classes. Students who like it feel that they are better prepared for the lecture, and often point out that the problems from the upcoming section are easy. And they are, in comparison with the challenging problems in the section I have lectured on, which are not just like the examples in the text.

There are benefits to using Directed Reading in both upper- and lower-level courses, in courses for both mathematics majors and non-majors. Non-majors benefit because they develop their mathematical reading skills, which they can bring to other technical reading they might have in future classes, and in their careers. The hope is that this will make them stronger independent learners, which is the transformation of students that we really hope to see in the undergraduate experience. Since we expect mathematics majors to read difficult and advanced mathematics independently for their capstone projects, developing these skills early and throughout their mathematics courses can better prepare them. Research mathematics presents unique difficulties for undergraduate students. It is unlike other sciences in that students cannot be put in a lab working on a hands-on experiment as part of a larger effort. It demands instead that they work conceptually with a high degree of independence on an abstract, unsolved problem. Even if a student simply wants to read some articles on new mathematics, finding an article an undergraduate can read is difficult. Once an appropriate article is found, having experience reading mathematics will be an asset. I hope that in learning to read mathematics in the earlier years of college, students will be more prepared to take on their own research projects in their later years.

Notes

[1] Barton, M. L., Heidema, C. (2002). *Teaching reading in mathematics: A supplement to Teaching Reading in the Content Areas: If Not Me, Then Who? 2nd Edition* (2nd ed.). Alexandria, VA: Association for Supervision and Curriculum Development.

[2] Beezer, R.A. (n.d.). A First Course in Linear Algebra. Retrieved from: http://linear.pugetsound.edu

[3] Borasi, R. & Siegel, M. (1990). Reading to learn mathematics: New connections, new questions, new challenges. *For the Learning of Mathematics*, 10, 9-16.

[4] Fraleigh, J.B. (2001). Happy Abstract Algebra Classes. *MAA Focus*, 21(8), p. 13.

[5] Gouvea, F. & Simonson, S. , (2011). How to Read Mathematics. In S. Simonson, *Rediscovering Mathematics* (pp. xvii-xxix). Mathematical Association of America.

[6] WeBWorK (n.d.). Mathematical Association of America. Retrieved from http://webwork.maa.org/wiki/

[7] Raphael, T. E. & Gavelek, J. R., (1988). Question-related activities and their relationship to reading comprehension: Some instructional implications. In G. Duffy & L. Roehler (Eds.), *Comprehension instruction: Perspectives and suggestions* (pp. 234-250). New York: Longman.

Forest Grove Conversations Contest 2013 "The Future Is Now: Citizens and Community in the Digital Age"

Introduction

The Tom McCall Center for Policy Innovations at Pacific University and the Friends of the Forest Grove Library co-sponsored the Forest Grove Conversations student contest this March. Students from the Forest Grove School District were challenged to submit their work for the chance to win cash prizes of 100 dollars for first place, 50 dollars for second place, and 25 dollars for honorable mention.

The theme for this year's contest was "The Future is Now: Citizens and Community in the Digital Age." Students had the choice of writing an essay, making a video, or submitting some other formatted project addressing one of the two prompts available. Option one was to interview someone who grew up before 1980 with the purpose of finding out how they interacted with those around them before modern technology and their views on modern technology and forms of communication. Prompt two asked students to imagine being archaeologists or historians in 2062 examining the Forest Grove Library and compare and contrast the state and function of the library between the future and the past.

Entries for the contest were submitted to the Forest Grove City Library by March 8. Essay submissions had to be between 250 and 500 words long and video or audio submissions had to be three to five minutes. There were three divisions for the contest: Elementary, Middle, and Senior Division.

The Elementary Division winners of Emmaus Christian School in order of first place, second place, and honorable mention are: Monique Ramberg, Lewis Beckett, and Sydney Webber. The Middle School Division winners in the same order are Stephanie Fachiol, Noah Drewrey, and Rachel Martins of Emmaus Christian School. Finally, the winner of the Senior Division is Joelle Bruckert-Frisk of Forest Grove High School.

The Interview

by Monique Ramberg
Elementary-First

In the twenty-first century, kids use technology to communicate. Talking to friends and family is easy because at the tap of a couple of buttons you're having a fun conversation. Today we use electronics to entertain ourselves. Texting is a quick and fun way to talk to someone. What people don't realize is that if you go back about fifty years, you will find a whole other world. In 1959, when my grandpa, Tom Hamilton, was ten years old, his life was different from mine in a lot of ways. Most things have changed: fashion, sports, prices, and especially technology. According to my grandpa, the only professional sport people watched was baseball. He said it was difficult to contact people when they were not at home because there were no cell phones. Back then, a burger at a fast food restaurant cost about fifteen cents, fries cost ten cents, and a normal snickers bar cost five cents. However he says some things are similar like school, houses, and food we eat. Today, most kids like me interact with friends and family, but not as much as we should. This is because there is always something else we are doing. My grandfather, a kind man who loves computers and remodeling things, said, "It amazes me how different the times are from then to now." He is right. As time goes on, life becomes much like a rollercoaster, with twists and turns as the new inventions just keep coming in. Everything changes. As I interviewed my grandfather, Tom Hamilton, at my house, he gave me examples of how his life was so different when he was a kid. To entertain himself, he listened to the news on the AM radio and watched baseball on a black and white TV. He was always outside playing sports and riding his bike or staying at his aunt and uncles farm in Iowa. He didn't have a microwave, a dishwasher, or a dryer.

My grandpa, Tom, had a fun childhood, and so do I, but they are far from alike. He was outside every second he could get, and that is one of the things that I appreciate most about him because he didn't have all the fancy gadgets we have now. I think it was cool to see that my own grandfather did all these things and wasn't focused on electronics. Because we have these things, it has affected the face to face communication between friends and family because when you are looking at a screen, you can't share moments or feel emotion with the people that you love. I think it is sad in some ways that people would rather type 'lol' on a screen than make physical contact with friends and family. As the time whizzes by in what seems like seconds, we should try to grasp the moment and appreciated all of the things we have.

The Forest Grove Library: Past and Present

by Lewis Beckett
Elementary-Second

What's the best way to spend an afternoon? Why of course it's to go to the Forest Grove Library! It has state-of-the-art gaming rooms. Thanks to the new technology, you can safely place a chip on your forehead, which allows you to play video games with your mind. If you want to read or research, you can check out books with the iPad 64. All you have to do to check out is scan your finger on the iPad dispensing machine screen. Then an iPad will pop out of the machine. There are the brand new, 2062 version of robot librarians here to answer your questions. You can grab a jetpack and explode like a rocket up 50 floors to have a snack at McDonalds. My favorite place in the library is the gaming room, so I went to play NBA 2k62. I decided to be the my favorite team, Portland Trail Blazers. I was playing against my least favorite team, the Miami Heat, in the finals. When I had reached the fourth quarter, I noticed some commotion outside of the window. I knew they were going to tear down the old library across the street, but most of the people did not look like construction workers. I paused my game to see what was going on. I took the teleporter over to the old library. It turned out that the construction crew found books, but with "paper," that is unusual! I put on my archaeologist badge to check out what else was there.

Right away, I found a 2013 issue of the "Forest Grove Times." I decided that 2013 was a great year to research. Apparently there were no video games that you could play with your mind. I read more and found that many of the books were written on paper. There were no restaurants in the old library and the librarians were actually people! There were no jetpacks either. One thing that is still the same is that there are still books, but the books are a lot different now then they were in 2013. I teleported back into the library wondering what it would be like one hundred years from now.

The Interview

by Sydney Weber
Elementary Honorable Mention

I picked up the phone to call my grandmother. I was excited to start writing my next paper but I needed to finish the interview first. What was your childhood like Nana? My grandmother, Janice, was born in a small suburb of Joliet, Illinois, on April 10, 1951. She had four brothers and one sister. She was the very youngest of the family. Her family settled down in a beautiful sunny California neighborhood when she was about 5 years old. The name of the little town was San Bernardino.

My Grandmother, or as I call her "nana" grew up going to public schools. The schools in the 50's where a kinder and safer place than they are today. Now, we worry about bullies and school safety daily. In class, they taught the same subjects such as, English, math, reading, history and science. The children did not have the tool of technology as we do today. Computers and laptops had not yet been invented. Primers and the Dewey decimal system at the library were used for all class subjects at school. She played outside and never had cellphones, I-Pads, or iPods! Her favorite sport was baseball. Nana's family was so big they were able to have two teams! Baseball and a delicious picnic were a favorite pastime for a lazy afternoon. She also enjoyed playing hide and seek and bicycling in her large neighborhood. Her five brothers and sisters were excellent playmates and lifetime friends. Her second oldest brother, Joe, is still protective of my Nana all these years later. Nana's family had an old fashioned TV. Her favorite show on television was Bonanza, a western cowboy show. Back then, their TV was black and white and had no remote. They had to always go to the movies to see films because they didn't have DVD'S . Her father, my great grandfather, always purchased Buicks over Fords. He felt they were the best family car. Over the years he owned brown, blue, red, and black Buicks. Now, you very rarely see a Buick on the road. Currently, people dress in tattered jeans and short shirts. My nana always wore dresses or skirts as a young girl. Pants came into fashion when she was in high school. She loved doing her hair in either a ponytail or braids.

Things have definitely changed between 1951 and now. My Nana had a wonderful childhood. Now, she lives near the Oregon Coast, and enjoys being a grandmother.

Archaeologist Prompt

by Stephanie Fachiol
Middle-First

Ivy's climbed up the side of the building by now, giving it an antique feel. It fits it, really, since it's one of the oldest buildings in Forest Grove now. Most buildings built before 2013 have been demolished and updated to fit the 2062 safety standards, but the city decided to leave the library up because the building reflects what's inside of it: knowledge. Old knowledge must be contained in an old building. I like to do my reports inside, sipping some clandestine hot chocolate when the librarian isn't looking. Practically everything in the building is the same as it was forty years ago, before I was born. The sections have remained unchanged; there's the study section, with only one or two college students cramming for that test they should have studied for earlier; the nonfiction section with the Dewey Decimal system that I have trouble with even now is still crammed with the musings of the centuries. The only difference there are the new additions about all the discoveries made since it opened; just past it, there's the fiction, packed with the imagination of long-dead writers and those still living, their voices collectively screaming in ink. The computers are nearby, the newest model. Somehow, last year, the library got a huge budget compared to that of the surrounding area, and the staff used it to update the computers. I like those computers. The touch-screen is easier to use than the clunky set I have at home, and the Internet's faster. Lastly, at the back, there's the database, the newest addition. That's where most people go nowadays, straight to the database. They just plug in their USB drive, download the information, and leave. What do they care about the rest of the library? It's retro. Besides, it's not updated to the safety standards. It isn't safe to hang around, so why bother? Why, indeed. Going to a database completely defeats the purpose of a library in the first place. Sure, it still has the same information and the same words, albeit on a screen, and it's even easier to get to. But doesn't this defeat the purpose? One must really dig through the mire of false writings and sift through opinions to gain true, actual knowledge, forming their own opinions and coming to their own conclusions. As an archaeologist, I can totally agree with the "digging" part. Imagine reading about the splendor of an ancient civilization and seeing a picture of the ruins. Now compare that to actually standing there, beneath towering arches that somehow have stood the test of time, and discovering that civilization's grandeur for yourself. It's the same with words and knowledge. It may be easier to get to with technology, but it's seeing it for yourself and finding it that's the important part, the key. Maybe that's why this whole building hasn't been completely replaced. There's a reason traditions are honored, and a reason that libraries are even now, in this digital age, still so irreplaceable.

2062-Forest Grove Library

by Noah Drewrey
Middle-Second

It is 2062 and the Forest Grove Library has been found. The real library was destroyed years ago, but with technology these days, we were able to create a virtual one. A holographic device that can capture fragments of time, normally used in crime investigations, was used to "resurrect" the library. Down to the last detail, this imaging device has created an exact replica of what used to be the Forest Grove Library.

Forest Grove is located in Oregon in the northeastern section of the United States of America. Oregon is a very green state that receives a lot of rainfall. The current population of Oregon is over 5,000,000 persons. Back in the year 2030 the library was burned down to be replaced with a DLB store, like every other library in the United States. DLB stores (DownLoadable Book) were created in the late 2020's and later became very popular in 2030. In the early second decade of the twenty-first century, buying books on tablets and phones became popular. Over the years, more and more people switched to the lighter and less expensive version of books. From Bibles to magazines, the screen books displayed everything, and didn't take up any room. With less and less people reading books, libraries weren't doing too well. In 2025, scientist created the DownLoadable Book, which is a pill containing a full book. When the pill was swallowed, the information made its way into your brain. With a simple thought you could access any book with you have downloaded. At first they were really expensive, and few were made, but over time more and more and been developed and made. With the value of the dollar going down and the number of U.S. currency going up, people were shocked to hear that a single DLB would only cost one dollar. At the time, in 2030, all libraries were demolished and DLB stores replaced them. Later they made more and more versions of the DLB. From DownLoadable Video Games to DLB and diet pills combined. DL pills became the next best thing, and sent many companies out of business. We have determined that many people used to study at this library. With a large amount of actual books, this place was great to prepare for something. There were many outdated computers used to locate books and research topics online. Time has done a lot to libraries. As successful as this one seemed to be, it is hard to imagine it would be completely demolished and replaced with a pill store. Comparing the Forest Grove Library to the DLB's we have today, I'm really appreciative to science for what it has done. I would hate to actually check out a book and bring it back later. It is just wasted energy.

Rachel Martins Interview: Communication Before the 1980s

by Rachel Martins,
Middle Honorable Mention

Rachel: Hi I'm Rachel and I'm here to interview my mom about how life was before the 1980s. So mom, how did you interact with your friends and your family before the 1980s?

Rachel's Mom: Before the 1980s we interacted by a phone, and the phone... was attached to a chord that was attached to... a phone base that in our home was on a wall. And that's how we would call our friends.... [M]aybe, if we were lucky, they'd have answering machines, but not usually.... So if we called, and nobody answered, we would just keep trying to call, until we reached them. We didn't have any computers, we didn't have any email, we didn't have any cellphones yet, or anything like that, so if I wanted to call one of my friends and get together to hangout.... I had to call them over and over, until I reached them. Then, we could make our plans and go from there.... [T]he other thing that we didn't have is—let's say I called my friend and they were already on the phone, then the phone line would be busy, until they hung-up—... we didn't have call waiting, where it would let us know that somebody else is trying to reach you, so we would just have to keep trying until they hung-up and would answer our call. The other thing we had back then was a party line,... when more than one house shared a phone line..., when that happened sometimes you would pick-up the phone to call somebody and... another house would be using the phone, and you would have to wait until they hung-up, so... you could use the phone and call the person, so we shared a line with two or three other households.

Rachel: Is life now way different than it was back then?

Rachel's mom: It's totally different, and what's changed it so much is computers, cellphones, texting,... voicemail, we just didn't have any of that... so it's totally different.

Rachel: So, what do you miss, from before the 1980s?
Rachel's Mom: ...[W]hat I miss from back then is that we didn't have all the

distractions of the computers and cellphones and Internet and email and all of that kind of thing.... [W]e didn't have cable either, so we would play games and we would go outside... and it just seems like we did... a lot of other activities that just didn't involve electronics at all, so it was totally different. I kind of miss writing on paper because nowadays everything's done, like you don't mail letters as much and things like that because of email, so I kind of miss writing letters and you know getting letters in the mail and things like that too.

Rachel: So what is your favorite electronic now?

Rachel's Mom: My favorite electronic now—I really like my iPhone, a lot. And one thing I like about it, is that I can use it for so many things, but if I am running around town, or shopping, or something like that, and there's some information I want to look-up quickly. Maybe, it's like if I'm shopping and I want to compare prices or if I'm out and about and I want to see what time a movies playing and things like that. I can just find out that information in just an instant. So I really like my iPhone.

Rachel: That's good. So, do you think it's much faster than back then?

Rachel's Mom: Things are way faster than back then... just people moving more quickly. You know, there's so much going on all the time and yeah, I think it's way faster now than back then.

Rachel: Do you think that texting instead of calling is better?

Rachel's Mom: Sometimes I think it's better. If you just... have a quick question or want to send somebody a quick message that maybe... doesn't even need a response. Like if I want to text you, my daughter, "hey Rachel I love you and I just want to let you know." I think texting can be really cool about that and if you have more time to talk or if you want to actually have a conversation, you can make a phone call.

Rachel: That's nice, thank you. Thank you for giving me this great opportunity, because I really enjoyed learning about all the electronics back then, and my mom had a great time too.

The Future is Now: Citizens and Community in the Digital Age

by Joelle Bruckert-Frisk
Senior-First

I scanned my eyes over the deteriorating heaps that previously existed as a library. The occasional breeze caused the unprotected rubble to tremble in response. The support beams bowed their backs in defeat. This would not be an easy demolition. The city requested the lot be excavated and then cleared for the building of another shopping center. The majority of the citizens were pleased to have the eyesore removed, but the few who could recall the library prospering in its golden years protested. I again scanned the piles of rubble, pondering where to begin. The whispering breeze suddenly amplified to a howl. It was an explosion of dust and rubble, paper and words. A screech escaped from the wind, but then it ceased. The dirt and decay that cloaked the remains was taken away with the torrent. All that remained were the books. Books, those ancient artifacts now foreign to us. Over the years, books fell from popularity. New technologies emerged daily, each time further eclipsing the written word. I grasped the nearest book and stretched its aching spine. It was a book of poems. The worn pages tumbled down a well-trodden path, revealing their secrets. The determined yet tired words stood stoically on the page. I looked up and down their graceful curves, the poem read: "Do not go gentle into that good night, old age should burn and rave at close of day; rage, rage against the dying of the light. Wild men who caught and sang the sun in flight, and learn, too late, they grieved it on its way, do not go gentle into that good night" (Dylan Thomas).

Suddenly, the wind thrust its icy searching fingers toward me, tearing the book from my hold. Paper thrashed in the air, beaten by the wind. No. Not just paper, words. Words, shaped and molded. Words that were not just words. Words that could be mine. Words that were mine. Words I would not destroy. The library was full of these words, and I would not destroy them. I, like the words, was determined. I would not demolish this library. I would resurrect this library. These piles and heaps that existed in the past as a library would remain a library. I strode, with purpose, off of the building foundation. I would be the voice for the words confined in this crumbling building. I would shout and scream and stand my ground until these words echoed from every wall.

The Future is Now: Citizens and Community in the Digital Age

HEALTH CARE

Volume 13

Use of Technology in Occupational Therapy Rehabilitation from an Elderly Perspective

by Julia Naumes
2013 Excellence in Internet Research Award Winner

Through advances in medical research, nutrition, hygiene, and technology, people are living longer today than in the past. Today, as the Baby Boomers begin to reach retirement age, it is expected that the elderly population in the United States will increase significantly in the near future. The use of rehabilitation therapy is an important intervention for elderly patients to maintain their quality of life and sense of self. Specifically, "Rehabilitation therapy comprises various treatments aimed to restore, improve, or increase functional independence, prevent further loss of function, and maintain or improve quality of life for individuals living with physical illnesses or conditions". [1] Occupational, physical, and speech therapies are examples of rehabilitative therapies (RT) that are utilized by many elderly patients.

Occupational Therapy (OT) in particular is a commonly used RT aimed at improving the quality of life of patients by enabling them to do things they highly value (e.g. occupations). Since patients have varying occupations, therapists need to use creative techniques to address a variety of needs. In recent years, technology has been used to help meet the needs of patients in a variety of ways, enabling them to stay socially active, maximizing independence, and assisting in mobility, driving, hearing, typing, and communication needs. [2] Many clinics and long-term elderly care centers are beginning to incorporate virtual rehabilitation (VR) into their therapeutic practices using programs and modules such as the Nintendo Wii and the OMNI Virtual Rehabilitation (VR). VR is defined as "the use of interactive simulations created with computer hardware and software to present users with opportunities to engage in environments that appear to be and feel similar to real world objects and events". [3] As the world of medicine becomes more technologically based, it is important to understand how the growing elderly population perceives technological

Literature Review

The Nintendo Wii is the most researched gaming console in therapeutic settings. Research by Deutsch, examined the feasibility of using the Wii gaming console for physical therapy rehabilitation. They chose the Wii for of a variety of reasons—including affordability, ability to let the client sit while participating, knowledge of performance and of results, allowance for multiple users, and ability to be analyzed biomechanically and for motor control requirements. [4] For example, the option of sitting is important for many elderly clients because some cannot stand for long, or at all. In many situations it is not safe for them to stand for long periods of time. Also, allowing clients to sit lessens the negative impact fatigue can have on therapy.

Compared to other Virtual Rehabilitation (VR) consoles, the Wii allows more patient access to quality care. Research shows that the Wii is preferable to other forms of VR because it is cost-effective, has good graphics, and is fun for clients, which encourages them to work harder and socialize with other people.[5] Accomplishing therapeutic goals while having fun offers strong motivation for patients to work hard. Further, being able to have fun while in a group therapy setting is a way for patients to feel socially connected.

Preliminary research shows that the use of the Wii gaming console in therapy settings has positive affects on patients' quality of life, primarily because it increases their group interactions and provides social support. [6] Although many elderly patients rarely engage in group interactions, research shows that social support and social interactions are critical for sustaining a sense of self and improving quality of life. [7] Connecting with one's former self also is a highly motivating factor for many people. As people age, they lose their ability to engage with life in the way they once did. This is due largely to physical changes in their bodies, disease, and injury. Sports that clients were once involved in, such as golf and/or bowling, can connect clients with their former selves and passions while doing similar but modified actions on the Wii. [8] Research demonstrates that staff members at rehabilitation clinics perceived many benefits for patients who used the Wii as a therapy modality. [9]

Higgins, Horton, Hodkinson, and Muggleton (2010) found that while using the Wii, clients were distracted from their physical pain, which enabled them to continue therapy sessions longer and thus reap better treatment outcomes. The positives noted included increases in general mobility and physical activity, greater persistence with therapeutic activity, social interactions and social skill building, heightened self esteem and confidence, connections with former self, and pacification of challenging behaviors. [10] Bell and colleagues also found that patients typically spent more time doing their therapeutic activities when playing the Wii when compared to conventional therapy techniques, (e.g., learning how to use aids for dressing and improving balance). [11] Such findings were also supported by Halton who discovered that clients often forgot about their physical limitations while using the Wii for rehabilitation purposes. [12] Conventional therapy can be repetitive and boring for patients; however, the variety in tasks that VR allows can be rewarding for patients. [13] This, along with the feedback given by the VR consoles and connection with former self, helps keep patients motivated and engaged.

Although there has been a great deal of research done on the use of gaming consoles, like the Nintendo Wii, as therapeutic devices, little research has been done on how the elderly population perceives the use of technology in therapy. The Wii is similar to the OMNI VR, a device also used in many rehabilitation settings. Little research has targeted other forms of VR, like the OMNI VR. This leaves a significant hole in the elderly experience of this particular program. Further technological advances indicate a need for research on how elderly people feel about using technology within rehabilitation settings. Typically the elderly population in the United States is less comfortable with technology than the rest of the society and few consider themselves digitally literate. [14] However, as digital literacy becomes essential to performing many daily tasks, it is important to understand the elderly experience. [15] By researching the technological needs of the elderly population, VR can be improved and hopefully cost-effective, enabling more patients to access the care. It is also important to see how VR can extend the rehabilitation process and improve the quality of life of senior citizens.

The current study focused on the experiences of patients at an elderly care facility in a small rural town in the Northwest United States. Patients use the OMNI Virtual Rehabilitation system during Occupational and Physical Therapy sessions to improve balance, endurance, and coordination. Hopefully, the information collected will be used to enhance the experiences of both current and future patients utilizing technology driven rehabilitation. Findings will be shared with staff and directors so that they can better meet their population's needs. This information could prove invaluable since gaming consoles are typically designed for young people, and so do not always work well with the physical and mental impairments that come with aging.

Methodology

Six semi-structured interviews were conducted with elderly rehabilitation patients, male and female. Initial contact was made via referrals from the rehabilitation team at the care facility. Once co-participants agreed to participate they were contacted in person to discuss the parameters of the study and to schedule interview times. After obtaining written informed consent, the principal investigator (PI) began the interview. Participants were interviewed using a semi-structured interview protocol about their experiences using technology, of the rehabilitation process, and of using technology within the rehabilitation process. The themes of the questions included, (1) experiences with technology prior to OT, (2) experiences of OT, (3) experiences with the OMNI Virtual Rehabilitation, and (4) adherence rates and motivation. Additional questions were asked to gain further clarification and/or provide additional details to previous comments. Interviews lasted from 10 minutes to 2 hours and were an average of 60 minutes, depending on the depth of co-participants' responses. All of the interviews were audiotaped and later transcribed verbatim. In addition to conducting the interview, the PI also took field notes to describe the physical location of the interview and any other behaviors of the co-participants not caught on tape. The final sample size was dictated by data saturation; the concept of saturation refers to the point at which no new information or themes are being obtained in the interviews. [16]

Data Analysis

The data was analyzed in a number of ways. After the interviews were transcribed from audio to text, co-participants were sent a copy of the written interview to verify their responses and ensure that the representations were correct. The PI began the initial stage of analysis by identifying codes, or important concepts, that emerged during the data collection process. The PI then invited members of her research group to question, challenge, and reinforce the interpretations in order to assure they were fully supported in the interview transcripts. [17] The use of a research group enhanced the rigor of the interpretative process as well as provided inter-rater reliability. [18] All members of the research group were required to sign a confidentiality agreement form. The PI also worked with the group in developing a thematic structure for the data. This process involved the identification of "meaning units," grouping the meaning units into sub-themes, and clustering sub-themes into major themes or categories.

Results & Discussion

Two main themes emerged from the data analysis—Psychosocial & Functionality (Figure 1). The psychosocial theme illustrated the value elderly rehabilitation patients placed on the psychological and sociological benefits of using technology within rehabilitation. The psychosocial subthemes included, Keeps Mind Engaged, Distraction from Pain, Limitations, & Disability, Connection with Former Self, Social Interaction, Fun, and Confidence & Digital Literacy. The majority of the Psychosocial subthemes were consistent with previous research cited in the Literature Review. However, Keeps Mind Engaged and Confidence & Digital Literacy were new concepts. The functionality theme indicates that to increase adherence rates and motivation, the patients must find the technology interesting, easily accessible, and rational. The subthemes here included Setup & Ease-of-use, Increased Strength & Endurance, Game-like, and Adaptability. The main barriers to using technology in rehabilitation settings were Confidence & Digital Literacy and Setup, the rest of the subthemes that emerged were positive.

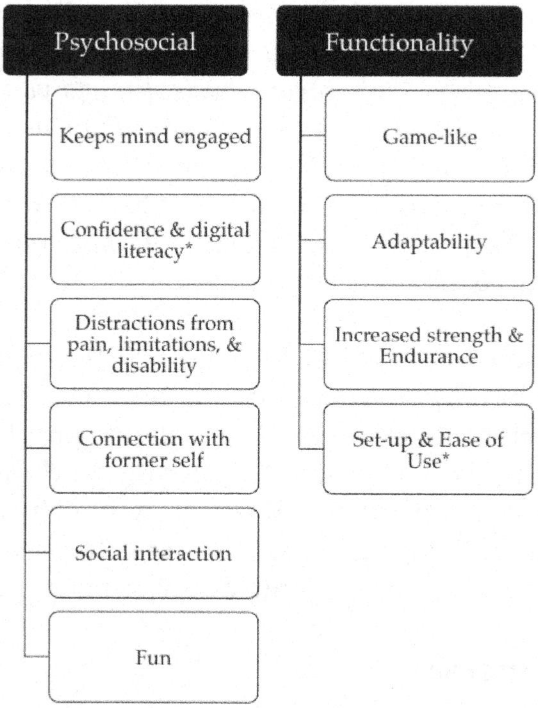

*Figure 1. A visual depiction of the themes and subthemes found in the research. Note. * Indicates a barrier to technology use.*

Keeps Mind Engaged

Participants stated that both the OMNI VR and the Nintendo Wii helped to keep their mind engaged and that cognitive awareness was one of the most beneficial aspects of using VR in the therapeutic setting. This is exemplified when Sam said:

There's lots of benefits. [The Wii] keeps you thinking. It keeps your mind working. If it weren't for that, what would I do? Sit in a chair all day long because I'm not physically able to work. But at least that keeps my mind thinking.

This demonstrates the importance Sam placed on being able to use the Wii in his day-to-day life and that it added to his quality of life. Similarly, a sufferer of Multiple Sclerosis (MS), Betty, felt the use of VR enabled her to focus mentally and physically on her surroundings for greater mobility.

I don't think I played all the games. They would do them at different speeds, but they really made you pay attention. Depending on the game you really had to be paying attention up here, you were using your brain, your eyes, and whatever physical parts you had to use. Whether it was standing or you just really had to focus on the objective of the game and then do your best at whatever you were supposed to be doing. Whether it was moving your feet to a certain spot on the screen or whatever, you really had to focus and that helped you physically and mentally (Betty).

For Betty, the use of the OMNI VR allowed her to exercise her mind and body, be more aware of her surroundings, and lessen the risk of falling. This is especially important for patients with balance problems since they are at a higher risk of falling. [19] The literature review did not reveal cognitive engagement as an important theme in VR research, which suggests that this is a new concept in this field. It would be beneficial for further research to specifically focus more on how VR affects cognitive awareness.

Confidence & Digital Literacy

Many co-participants felt their digital literacy was a barrier to their use of technology. For example, Whitfield said, "my wife runs the computer and she has troubles with it, so I don't even try." His lack of self-confidence affected his ability and motivation to operate a computer. Similarly, Sam said, "Well, it [technology] hasn't affected me much because I haven't used it. I don't know how to use it. I went through the tenth grade and then to farming. I never graduated." Sam's lack of education, knowledge, and experience prevented him from attempting to use technology.

These findings are supported by research conducted by Morris. Morris found that older people are missing out on the benefits of technology because of perceived barriers to e-literacy. Barriers include "lack of interest, feeling too old, fear of new technology, lack of access to IT, lack of IT skills and experience, cost, concerns about security, and problems with associated disability". [20] Similarly, Pietrass found that the elderly population utilizes technology for rational purposes, whereas youth use it playfully. The co-participants in this study stated that they would not use technology unless they saw the point in it, also known as functionality. Many participants used technology to pay bills, increase strength and endurance, and to communicate with loved ones, all of which they saw these as functional uses for it. [21]

Distraction from Pain, Limitations & Disability

Interestingly, The OMNI VR offered a distraction from pain, limitations, and disability. This was supported by previous research that found the Nintendo Wii, a form of VR, enabled patients to continue with therapy sessions for longer amounts of time. [22, 23, 24] For example, Doonie describes one of the first times she used the OMNI VR:

> *The OMNI VR, yes ... it tested my endurance. The first one was the bingo game and the first two times I played I wasn't too lucky with getting a bingo very quick. There was the one where you chase the bugs off the stepping-stones and another where you do a puzzle. I like puzzles. These things were entertaining. They weren't something that I would get tired of too easily. Other than the bingo. But, be that as it may, I got through that and it made the time go faster, by far. I didn't realize I'd been in there as long as I had when they finally says, "Okay you're gonna go back." I says, "thank you," cause I was exhausted. I mean more than I thought I could be. I couldn't sleep that night I was so exhausted.*

This quote also demonstrates the importance of therapists' awareness of each individual's limitations and to be mindful of not pushing the patient past their endurance level. This is especially important for elderly populations because they are more susceptible to injuries.

Connection with Former Self

As discussed in the literature review, VR allows patients to connect with their former selves by allowing them to participate in similar motions and sporting activities they once did. [19, 20] For example, Sam said that he and his wife regularly used the Wii because it enabled them to golf, which was an important activity in their lives when they had greater physical mobility. As Sam said:

Well I've always been a sportsman. I golf on it [the Wii] all the time. And once in a while we will change over and play something else, but mostly golf. It is a very good, very nice machine ... It's a good machine to golf with. Because I'm more or less held to a chair anymore. I don't get up and run around like I used to. I've had a good life though.

Although Sam can no longer physically golf, he is able to participate in a similar activity using the Nintendo Wii. This also tied into the theme of social interaction because he was able to connect with his wife and grandchildren by competing with them virtually.

Social Interaction

Social interaction is a subtheme that emerged both in the previous research and in this current study. In the following quote Doonie discusses the importance of social interaction in her life, along with the ease-of-use and adaptability of the OMNI VR.

The first time I saw [the OMNI VR], I was very impressed. I like the colors. I like the ease-of-use, that's a biggie! I like that there's different levels of everything. In fact I was thinking of asking them where I could pick one up! Haha. I wouldn't be against using one at home, for a couple of reasons. If the grandkids come in while I'm doing it, they could join me! They could manage it as well. And, they'd get bored with it, I'm sure, cause they're young. But you know, for me, it's the kind of thing that would probably help me get through the winter (Doonie).

Doonie valued the ability to connect with her grandchildren and husband and demonstrated that the OMNI VR could be used as a vessel to facilitate social interactions. She also stated that it would help her to continue exercising throughout the winter months, which were a struggle for her because she typically exercised outside when the weather was nice.

Fun

Similarly, patients value rehabilitation that is fun because it helps keep them interested and engaged in the process. Fun and game-like are two related subthemes that emerged. Whitfield explains how he values that VR can be more fun than traditional rehabilitation.

Well it was rehab, but it was things that are fun to do. And it makes a big difference if it isn't just straight rehab... The picnic one where you stomp out the ants and things like that. That was kind of fun! And then bouncing the Ping-Pong balls was kind of fun. And they do, try and make things so you have some interest in really doing what it is and it's a lot easier than just plain rehab.

Halton also found that when patients enjoy their rehabilitation experience they are able to work harder and longer. [24] Doonie covered such subthemes in the following quote.

Keeping it interesting. And I think even someone who doesn't like computers, who doesn't like dealing with them, I really think it's a way to keep them engaged, to keep them interested. And the graphics are beautiful on that program. To me, that's the biggie. Yeah, I think that, if nothing else, that's the main thing. And maybe the fact that it can be changed easily. Changed out. The program can be tweaked sometimes. And even the different levels. And you've got that all built in. I think that's fantastic. I think it's a really worthwhile program.

Doonie explains that the OMNI VR has many attributes that are valued by the elderly population, such as being appealing to the eye, easy to operate, fun, and useful. One of the most important topics in rehabilitation is adherence rates once the patients return home. Having a fun program that physically and cognitively benefits the individual is a great asset for improving quality of life and increasing adherence rates.

Adaptability

Rehabilitation programs need to be adaptable in their intensity level so that as the patient develops neural control and physical fitness levels they can continually be challenged. [25] The OMNI VR is adaptable in that you can perform from standing or sitting positions, can change the number of puzzle pieces, and a variety of difficulty levels in virtual rehabilitation. Doonie describes her experience of the adaptability of the OMNI VR:

It could be done from a standing position, that's the way I've done it. And then the puzzle game, there's a good selection of easy to hard pictures to choose. And, it's nice that they've got a choice of how many squares, for me I think they chose 25 squares per puzzle.

The adaptability allows the VR to be made developmentally appropriate as increases in skill-level and physical ability occur.

Increased Strength & Endurance

The primary goal of elderly rehabilitation is to increase strength and endurance so patients are able to safely return home. Therefore, this is a strongly valued attribute of the OMNI VR. It has been demonstrated that OMNI VR helps patients increase their strength and endurance levels. For instance, Fern said, "Well I don't know exactly when it happened, but it was great when I started getting stronger." Betty expands this when describing how she perceived the OMNI VR has helped her deal with her MS symptoms.

> *You had to really concentrate and test how you needed to react and where you needed to react. Whether it was your hands, or your feet, whether you were standing somewhere. Some of them involved sitting and then standing, then sitting, then standing repeatedly. Some of them were standing, then moving, or sitting then, using your feet to direct whatever was going on on the screen. So it was quite a wide variety and it helped to build strength. The therapy was some of the best things that happened here and really helped to build my strength. I got a lot of exercises to do that I did in therapy and then I could do them everyday. I am still doing them everyday so that I can retain what I gained during therapy before I go onto assisted living and don't lose any of that.*

To Betty it was very important to be able to retain the gains from rehabilitation in order to continue living a quality life.

Set-up & Ease-of-use

A deterrent to many elderly patients attempting to use technology is having a long or complicated set-up. Doonie discussed how she was not motivated to use the Nintendo Wii. "It's too much for me to set it up. You know after the grandkids have used it, I have to re-set it up for me. I guess I'm just not into it enough to care." She has utilized both the Nintendo Wii and the OMNI VR and compared both consoles on their ease-of-use.

> *Wii is hard for me because first you're supposed to fill in all this personal data. And then they do all the measuring. I suppose if I ever got into it, I might enjoy it, but I never got into it. By the time I got into it*

I'd wasted so much time, I felt like that I didn't want to bother with it. And so, truly I doubt if I've used the Wii more than 5 or 6 hours in the 7 years I've had it. Now with the OMNI VR, you know, I've only been here about 10 days and I haven't had that much use with it. But the first time they showed it to me, I liked the colors, I like the graphics, I like the way it was point and click and you were doing your exercise. You didn't have to fool with a lot of setup. You know, I've got scales, I can weigh myself. I don't need the machine to do that for me. I've got my own physical ability that tells me that I'm getting better. I did like the page that shows the goals that I've accomplished, or how many mistakes I've made, cause I go against myself now and then. But I think the ease of use is probably the biggest benefit to that. And I would think that would be true to also the therapists. You know, they don't want to spend all their time getting setup and everything. If they can go turn on a button and put you in position, and you can do it, that's a good program to me. Something that doesn't get overly complicated.

Conclusion

Virtual Rehabilitation is a great tool for the elderly population to utilize in maintaining physical and mental engagement, connection with former self, and maintaining or increasing physical fitness levels. The elderly population interviewed was receptive to the use of VR and perceived many positive attributes associated with it. Since this study has a small sample size, more research is required to extend the findings to a larger elderly population.

The co-participants who had the highest amount of social support also had better health and a more positive outlook on life. Future research should look into the relationship between outlook, social support, and health. Although this was not within the bounds of this study, it would be interesting to see how these three variables relate within the elderly population and to research how to increase social support in elderly rehabilitation centers so health and perspective on life may be improved.

Elderly rehabilitation centers could further support their patients by setting up a transition program to help interested patients continue to use VR; for example, staff members could create a document for patients to refer to when setting up the OMNI VR, Nintendo Wii, or Xbox Kinnect. They could also assist patients with technical difficulties so they adhere to the rehabilitation program while at home.

The facility where the research was conducted did not have a Nintendo Wii for the patients to utilize. Investing in one could be beneficial for patients to enable them to connect with their former selves, distract them from their ailments, and increase the social connections and support between patients and staff members. The addition of a fun, competitive, and therapeutic device could greatly increase perceptions of the clinic and rehabilitation experience by giving patients something to look forward to while they are not doing therapy or visiting with loved ones.

Notes

[1] Rehabilitation Therapy. (n.d.). In MD Guidelines. Retrieved from http://www.mdguidelines.com/rehabilitation-therapy/definition

[2] Halton, J. (2008). Virtual Rehabilitation with video games: A new frontier for occupational therapy. *Occupational Therapy Now*, 9(6), 12-14.

[3] Weiss, P. L., Rand, D., Katz, N., & Kizony, R. (2004). Video capture virtual reality as a flexible and effective rehabilitation tool. *Journal of Neuroengineering and Rehabilitation*, 1(1), 1-12.

[4] Deutsch, J. E., Borbely, M., Filler, J., Huhn, K., & Guarrera-Bowlby, P. (2008). Use of a low-cost, commercially available gaming console (Wii) for rehabilitation of an adolescent with cerebral palsy. *Journal of the American Physical Therapy Association*, 88(10), 1196-1207.

[5] Halton, J. (2008)

[6] Bell, C. S., Fain, E., Daub, J., Warren, S. H., Howell, S. H., Southard, K. S., Sellers, C., & Shadoin, H. (2011). Effects of Nintendo Wii on quality of life, social relationships, and confidence to prevent falls. *Physical & Occupational Therapy in Geriatrics*, 29(3), 213-221.

[7] Bell et. al. (2011)

[8] Halton, J. (2008)

[9] Higgins, H. C., Horton, J. K., Hodgkinson, B. C., & Muggleton, S. B. (2010). Lessons learned: Staff perceptions of the Nintendo Wii as a health promotion tool within an aged-care and disability service. *Health Promotion Journal of Australia*, 21(3), 189-195.

[10] Higgins et. al. (2010)

[11] Bell et. al. (2011)

[12] Halton, J. (2008)

[13] Burdea, G. C. (2003). Virtual rehabilitation – Benefits and challenges. *Methods of Information in Medicine*, 42, 519-523.

[14] Pietrass, M. (2007). Digital Literacy Research from an International and Comparative Point of View. *Research in Comparative and International Education*, 2(1), 1-12.

[15] Riman, C., Ghusn, H., & Monacelli, E. (2011). Differences in Computer Performance

Across Age Groups. *Physical & Occupational Therapy in Geriatrics*, 29(3), 169-180.

[16] Guest, G., Bunce, A., & Johnson, L. (2006). How many interviews are enough? An experiment with data saturation and variability. *Field methods*, 18(1), 59-82.

[17] Pollio, H. R., & Thompson, C. J. (1997). *The phenomenology of everyday life: Empirical inhvestigations of human experience*. Cambridge: Cambridge University Press.

[18] Thomas, S. P., & Pollio, H. R. (2002). *Listening to patients: A phenomenological approach to nursing research and practice*. New York: Springer Publishing Company.

[19] Finlayson, M. L., Peterson, E. W., & Cho, C. C. (2006). Risk factors for falling among people aged 45 to 90 years with multiple sclerosis. Archives of Physical and Medical Rehabilitation, 87(9), 1274-1279.

[20] Morris, A. (2007). E-literacy and the grey digital divide: a review with recommendations. Journal of Information Literacy, 1(3), 2

[21] Pietrass, M. (2007)

[22] Bell Et. Al. (2011)

[23] Higgins Et. Al. (2010)

[24] Halton, J. (2008)

[25] Weinberg, R. S., & Gould, D. (2010). Foundations of Sport and Exercise Psychology (5th ed.), Champaign, IL: Human Kinetics.

Building a web-based collaboration system for effective, engaging, and interactive teaching of undergraduate Speech Science curriculum: A REVIEW OF A BERGLUND CENTER FOR INTERNET STUDIES FELLOWSHIP

by Kerry Mandulak, PhD, CCC-SLP
School of Communication Sciences and Disorders, Pacific University

Introduction

The discipline of speech science is one of the foundational areas of communication sciences and disorders (CSD). Students often perceive the undergraduate requisite class of Speech Science as "difficult, irrelevant, and terrifying" [1]. In order to both increase interest in the specialized discipline of speech science and help bridge the gap between science and clinical practice, a solid, engaging, interactive class at the undergraduate level is needed.

With new advances in digital signal processing and freely downloadable acoustic analysis software, the speech science classroom could be changed dramatically. Instead of a class where students are mystified, intimidated, and anxious about the material, students could be instantly involved and interacting with easily accessible resources. Engaging students with laboratory activities and clinical applications of class content could bridge the gap between the science of speech production and its relationship to their future clinical practice. Introducing students to course content in ways that are viewed as accessible and relevant, rather than daunting or arduous, promotes a transformation of attitude toward speech science that could happen at the undergraduate level. As these same well-informed students progress into graduate programs to become clinical practitioners of speech-language pathology or audiology, a positive outlook and willingness to engage with and use technology will change how they approach future clinical practice.

Unfortunately, despite the importance of science to the foundation of clinical practice, interest in speech science has declined in our discipline. There is a current shortage of individuals receiving a Ph.D. in CSD, and, therefore, a shortage of doctoral level instructors at university programs. More importantly, of the 150,000 members of the American Speech-Language-Hearing Association (ASHA) [2] only a small percentage work in academia and an even smaller number identify themselves as speech scientists. [3] Speech scientists are essentially small fish in a big pond [4] and lack the benefit of experiencing a critical mass at any given community-building event, such as the ASHA annual convention, or within the context of an academic department or an area of clinical specialty.

The consequence of the doctoral shortage and small percentage of speech scientists within the field are twofold. New instructors are tasked with teaching the course with a lack of expertise in the subject area, in addition to the extensive time and effort for initial course preparation with few resources. Knowledgeable instructors have to actively seek collaboration and fresh teaching resources, expending time and effort that competes with their many other responsibilities, including research and service, in order to improve their current teaching. Speech Science is a required class for undergraduate curriculum in CSD programs throughout the country, yet there is no established central repository for course content materials that could support effective and efficient teaching by the inexperienced or seasoned instructor.

The purpose of this manuscript is to describe the challenges and successes of the process that was undertaken to build a web-based resource for teaching speech science curriculum, in addition to how selected resources were used and evaluated within the classroom environment. Preliminary data gained from weekly student questionnaires will be presented to illustrate how the end users of the course content responded to the introduction of various types of online media and interactive lecture techniques. Future directions and ideas will be presented regarding the continued work on this project.

Methods

The four main goals of this project were to do the following: 1) build a website that would function as a primary resource for any instructor teaching the required undergraduate speech science course in a CSD curriculum; 2) collect peer-reviewed and openly shared course content; 3) establish video demonstrations of specific instrumentation or previously available media resources; and 4) create a discussion forum that would allow community building and collaboration among speech scientists engaged in teaching and research.

Building the Website

As a starting point, current online and media resources that were available were collected. Finan & Tasko [5] [6] had begun this process with the creation of a website based in Google Sites that functioned as an introductory repository of video examples, pedagogical resources, physical models, and software resources. The current project was designed to expand and develop that current site. These resources were collected and categorized, along with other currently available resources that were found through a focused Internet search. A variety of options were found to be available including online courses, software downloads, video demonstrations, and textbook sites. These assorted findings covered a wide spectrum of topics as well, including: acoustics, phonation, phonetics, anatomy, and neuroanatomy. Relevant search terms representing specific aspects of curriculum, such as "source-filter theory," "vocal tract – larynx," and "spectrograms" were used, in addition to searching in fields other than communication sciences and disorders, such as linguistics or physics. The rationale for including any specific resource was that it made a classic concept typically taught in speech science curriculum both interesting and interactive. [7]

Wordpress (http://www.wordpress.com) was chosen as the platform on which to build and expand the website. Because of both the static and dynamic nature of a blogging platform, the ability to accommodate comments on blog posts, in addition to static pages that contain significant content, which were important features, in order to allow those who visit the site to interact with the material, ask questions, and pose discussions. The new website (http://speechsciencetoolbox.wordpress.com) [8] was designed to foster community, first and foremost, and by doing that, supporting both teaching and research interests focused on speech science of those that participate.

Content

There are sections for both the new and seasoned instructor of speech science curricula. Within the section for the new instructor, descriptions and informal reviews of textbooks, sample syllabi, and curriculum examples are posted. For the new instructor, the goal is to have a place to start building their course. Communication sciences and disorders programs will have various ways that speech science content will be delivered within their own curricular structure, whether it be a stand-alone class or within another course (such as anatomy and physiology of the speech mechanism), and so offering instructors examples from multiple university programs was deemed to be important. The contributors to the website will be offering material to be shared openly, whether it be a syllabus structure, lecture notes, or outlines of the content covered within a course. For the seasoned instructor, resources posted will include ideas for laboratory assignments, online resources, software ideas, and video demonstrations, in order for experienced teachers to enhance their course.

Because the addition of content to the website could become time consuming in terms of editing, vetting, and reviewing for any one (or a few) person(s), the creation of an editorial board will be established by the creators (Finan & Tasko) and other main contributor (Mandulak) to the website. At this point in the website creation process, the editorial board is not yet needed, but will be used in the future as the number of contributors and level of participation increases.

Discussion Forum

Because one of the goals of this website is to build and foster community among speech scientists, a central discussion forum is essential to build a critical mass of those involved in this specific area of practice and research within the larger speech – language pathology community. The discussion forum portion of the website will be updated weekly, and allow for subscription through email (via RSS feeds), so that end users of the website will be alerted to new posts and discussion threads on a regular basis. Topics could include teaching ideas, research interests, and special "ask the expert" type of postings in order to encourage online interaction and learning opportunities, from the undergraduate to post-doctoral level.

Enhancing a Course Using Speech Science Toolbox: One Example

As part of my Berglund Center for Internet Studies (BCIS) Fellowship, I used resources available on http://speechsciencetoolbox.wordpress.com in my undergraduate speech science course taught in the spring semester of 2014 at Pacific University within the School of Communication Sciences and Disorders. There were 15 students registered for class. I planned to integrate the use of online resources and media into all three modules of the course. In-class, hands-on activities were planned [7] in addition to interactive lecture techniques, in order to augment the traditional, standard lecture format that I had previously used to deliver content. Another change to the course included initiating weekly assignments that incorporated both content questions, for students to review their own understanding of learning objectives, and a laboratory type experience related to course content. To support student learning through and participation in these, I created screencasts of assignment details or procedures and posted them to YouTube. Because many digital resources and acoustic analysis tools are highly accessible and no-cost, requiring students to complete these type of assignments independently, outside of class was a new endeavor for me as an instructor. I was particularly interested in how students would respond to these types of learning experiences, both in their achievement of learning objectives for class and their interaction with course content material.

As the first assignment for class, I required the students to complete a Learning Styles Inventory to self-identify and understand their own personal learning style. [9] The students gave me a copy voluntarily and kept a copy for themselves. I collected this data, in order to compare their responses on their learning styles questionnaire to their preferences for learning within the class environment.

Q'aire: COMPLEX SOUNDS

1

Please respond to the following questions about the content focused on COMPLEX SOUNDS (1 = strongly agree, 2 = agree, 3 = neutral, 4 = disagree, 5 = strongly disagree).

	1	2	3	4	5
I understand the difference between a pure tone and a complex sound wave.					
I understand the relationship between fundamental frequency and harmonics (and vice versa).					
I could explain the differences between a periodic and aperiodic complex sound wave.					
I could independently and accurately draw a line spectrum of a complex periodic sound wave.					
I could independently and accurately draw a continuous spectrum of a complex aperiodic sound wave.					
The You Tube video explaining the web animation for Fourier Analysis / Complex Periodic Sounds was helpful to complete the assignment.					
I am confident that I have solid answers to the questions posted for the WEEK 2 Reading Assignment.					
I felt comfortable with the pace of delivery of new information within class.					

2

Which of the following was the MOST helpful for your learning with regard to this specific content?

- Reading before / after class (pages 25 - 29)
- Lecture (Complex Sounds)
- In - class activities (drawings, working with the waveforms within lecture together as a class)
- Online animations / media (Fourier Analysis)
- None were helpful

3

Which of the following was LEAST helpful for your learning with regard to this specific content?

- Reading before / after class (pages 25 - 29)
- Lecture (Complex Sounds)
- In - class activities (drawings, working with the waveforms within lecture together as a class)
- Online animations / media (Fourier Analysis)
- All were helpful in some way

4

The following concepts / ideas are still confusing to me and could use some additional explanation:

Figure 1: One of the weekly questionnaires administered as part of the study.

I used the Questionnaire activity on the Moodle Learning Management System to collect weekly feedback on the students' perception of their own learning of course objectives and their beliefs about what helped them learn best (or least) over the past week.

The options for the choices of most or least helpful activities for learning stayed the same across questionnaires, but the specifics of each were changed for each week. Because the class is still being taught and data collection is in process, a preliminary data analysis will be provided with some general trends and themes from the student feedback. IRB approval was obtained through Pacific University, and the use of student feedback data was approved for exempt review with a waiver of consent.

Results

Preliminary data analysis from the first module of class (Basic Acoustics) revealed consistent trends. Of the three modules of class (Basic Acoustics; The Source: Respiratory and Phonatory Physiology; and The Filter: Articulation and Resonance), the first unit (Basic Acoustics) is classically the most challenging in terms of learning concepts and applying them to the clinical aspect of speech – language pathology. For many students, the concepts, which focused on the physics of sound, introduce terminology and mathematical equations that are unfamiliar, abstract, and, possibly, difficult to understand.

There were four questionnaires administered during the first module in class: 1) Simple Harmonic Motion (SHM)/Waveforms; 2) Complex Sounds; 3) Frequency/Pitch/Intensity; and 4) Resonance/Source & Filter. The following table details the responses specific to their experiences with the in-class activities and online media/resources, rated as most or least helpful, for their learning in the first module, Basic Acoustics. Of the 15 students, the survey response rate varied from 10 to 13 responses per week. Students were not required to complete the surveys as part of class requirements.

In-class activities ranged from hands-on endeavors (tying a hex nut to a string to create a swing and represent simple harmonic motion that they could manipulate during class; using Play-Doh to illustrate the Source-Filter theory) to activities that I did alongside the students (working through logarithmic equations relating to intensity and pressure, after having them work in pairs or small groups, reviewing homework activities in class to ensure and reinforce understanding). Online media and animations referred to content on external websites that was shown in class, used in homework assignments for independent learning, and supported through the use of screencasts I designed to assist in completing homework assignments.

It should be noted that the consistent weekly response to "least helpful" by the overwhelming majority of students was the textbook reading for the course. Engaging students through the use of the textbook in class continues to be a challenge for me as an instructor, but the focus on in-class, interactive activities, in addition to the inclusion of online media and animations, was the main improvement in course content that was planned for the current semester.

Table 1: Preliminary student responses specific to their experiences with the in-class activities and online media / resources, rated as most or least helpful for their learning in the first module, Basic Acoustics.

Title of Questionnaire (Content Area)	Student report of "most helpful" for learning	Student report of "least helpful" for learning
Simple Harmonic Motion / Waveforms	In – class activities (over half of class)	Online media / animations (less than 20% of class)
Complex Sounds	In – class activities (over half of class)	Online media / animations (approximately one-quarter of class)
Frequency / Pitch / Intensity	In – class activities (over half of class); online media / resources (about 10%)	"All were helpful" (approximately one-quarter of class)*
Resonance / Source and Filter	In – class activities (over half of class)	"All were helpful" (approximately half of class)*

** the option "all were helpful" was added for the third questionnaire (Frequency / Pitch / Intensity) and remained on all questionnaires that followed.*

Discussion

The data from the student questionnaires provided a preliminary and exploratory look at the effect of including interactive lecture methods and online media resources into the speech science classroom environment. The pattern of students finding in-class activities the most engaging was intriguing. Although the majority of class time was still spent in traditional lecture format, for efficiency of delivery of course content, the incorporation of these activities reflected increased engagement and interaction from the student perspective. These activities were discovered through existing resources available on the original Speech Science Toolbox Google Site, in addition to the presentation at the American Speech – Language – Hearing Annual Convention that I participated in with Finan, Tasko, Dromey and Neel. [7]

The finding that the data for the first two questionnaires (Simple Harmonic Motion / Waveforms; Complex Sounds) indicated that students found the online media / resources "least helpful" was also thought provoking. Several differing perspectives could be considered. First, I may not have presented them in a way that facilitated their own learning or connection to the content. Second, the resource may not have been as relevant as I perceived in relation to the content or the student's level of understanding. Third, the students may have been getting used to the format of class, the type of materials being used, and the type of content being presented at this early stage of the semester. I believe it takes several weeks of "buy-in" for students to begin to see how the foundational concepts of Speech Science connect to the bigger picture of the subject matter and its relevance to clinical practice. Finally, the presentation of the resource in class could have been done differently. Regardless of the reason, having only used these resources for the first time in class this semester, the feedback from the students will be helpful in reconsidering their use or presenting them in an alternate way in class. Continued use of the resources and other teaching techniques will drive the process of continued improvement in the instructional methods used in the classroom.

A more complete analysis of the current data set will be carried out in the future. Relationships between what worked best for the students learning (as perceived by themselves) and the type of learning style with which the students' identify (collected at the start of class), will be another way to explore the questionnaire data. I hope to disseminate these and other findings from this study and project at future national meetings of the American Speech – Language – Hearing Association and through relevant publications.

Conclusions

The Speech Science Toolbox website will continue to evolve and change. Establishing this site as a resource for instructors and repository for teaching resources was the first step. As more instructors, speech scientists, and students of speech science become more involved, the hope is that this small community will grow and provide opportunities for all of us to learn from one another. In addition, it is anticipated that students from the undergraduate to post-doctorate level will continue to appreciate the contribution of speech science to our overall field of speech – language pathology. The class that no student looked forward to having to sit through will be a class that engenders curiosity, enthusiasm, and engagement, from both the student and the instructor.

Notes

[1] Berkowitz, S. S. (2012, April). Out of the lab...and onto the laptop. Paper presented at the Annual Meeting of the Council of Academic Programs in Communication Sciences and Disorders, Newport Beach, CA.

[2] Brook, G. (2012, May 15). ASHA Members: 150,000 Strong and Growing. *The ASHA Leader*, 1, 10 – 13.

[3] Finan, D. & Tasko, S. M. (2012a). Toward a Speech Sciences community. *Perspectives on*

Speech Science and Orofacial Disorders, 22 (1), 14 – 20.

[4] Finan, D. & Tasko, S. M. (2012b, November). The argument for building a speech sciences community. Paper presented at the Annual Convention of the American Speech-Language-Hearing Association, Atlanta, GA.
[5] Finan, D. & Tasko, S.M. (2012c). Speech science toolbox. Retrieved from https://sites.google.com/site/speechsciencetools/
[6] Tasko, S. M., & Finan, D. (2011, November). What's a formant: Toward a speech science toolbox. Paper presented at the Annual Convention of the American Speech-Language-Hearing Association, San Diego, CA.

[7] Finan, D., Tasko, S.M., Dromey, C., Mandulak, K.M., Neel, A. (2013, November). Speech Science: Does anybody know how to teach this stuff? Paper presented at the Annual Convention of the American Speech-Language-Hearing Association, Chicago, IL.

[8] Finan, D., Tasko, S.M., Mandulak, K.M. (2014). Speech science toolbox. Retrieved from http://speechsciencetoolbox.wordpress.com/

[9] Felder, R.M. & Soloman, B. A. (n.d.a.) Index of Learning Styles (ILS). Retrieved from http://www4.ncsu.edu/unity/lockers/users/f/felder/public/ILSpage.html

Continuing Mobile Medical Education: The College of Optometry Web CE Mobile App Project

By James Kundart, OD, MEd, FAAO FCOVD-A
College of Optometry, Pacific University.

Introduction

Evidence-based medicine has been defined as "the conscientious, explicit, and judicious use of current best evidence in making decisions about the care of individual patients." [1] Before the Information Age, evidence-based medicine was much more difficult to practice. Without fast, random access to real-time information, it is no wonder that it's opposite—eminence-based medicine—was the standard of care for so long.

Eminence-based medicine might be defined as decision-making in consultation with senior medical staff. [2] Somewhat surprisingly, eminence-based medicine is the still the standard in many places. It is understandable in situations that lack access to information technology, but that is not the only reason. It is often the case that the busy clinical setting also limits real-time access to evidence. Put simply, it's often faster just to ask those around you when faced with a treatment dilemma.

Mobile technology changes this equation. The portability of the smartphone and quick-access time of mobile apps makes evidence-based medicine more readily available to all but the busiest and remotest health care providers. Also, as the standard of care changes, mobile apps hold great promise for use in continuing medical care education, as long as health care providers trust the evidence. High-level patient care has created a need for rapid access to emerging evidence.

Continuing Mobile Medical Education (CMME) has evolved to address this need. CMME can be evaluated by traditional criteria used for promotion in health care academia. These criteria include clinical services, research and scholarly work, education, and public service.

This article aims to explore some ways in which mobile apps are effectively used in health care, and specific applications to continuing education for optometry on the web. These ways include:

1. Improved clinical diagnosis of visually-distinct conditions.
2. Improved clinical treatment for complicated conditions.
3. Improved availability of evidence for research and scholarly work.
4. Pyscho-social applications for patients and allied health personnel.
5. Home monitoring of patient conditions and home training of physicians.

Each of these is discussed in detail, below.

1. Improved Diagnosis for Visually-Distinct Conditions

CMME can be used to help in diagnosis, particularly for conditions that are photographable. In eye care, one of these is diabetic retinopathy. While this condition can lead to leakage of capillaries in the retina and elsewhere, there are subtle changes that even seasoned eye doctors can miss if they are not trained in diagnosis of diabetic retinopathy (DR). See Figure 1 for an obvious case of diabetic retinopathy.

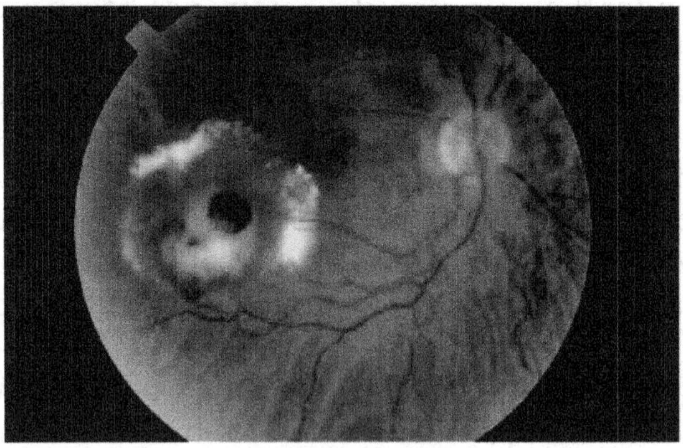

Figure 1: Proliferative Diabetic Retinopathy. [23]

A study by Sundling et. al. [3] in Norway looked at the ability of optometrists to identify this condition from photographs send by e-mail. With a sensitivity of 67% and a specificity of 84% for any DR, and a paltry 54% for subtle non-proliferative DR, only 4 out of 74 optometrists were able to meet the required standard of 80% sensitivity and 95% specificity for diabetic eye disease. This is a significant finding, because there are likely over 100,000 Norwegians with diabetes in this small country, about one-fifth of whom have DR.

In an unrelated Norwegian study, Jemec and colleagues [4] investigated whether a web-based course with electronic support from a dermatologist would change behavior with regard to atopic dermatitis. Specifically, the student investigated topical steroid treatment duration and the referral rate to dermatology between the web course participants and a control group of doctors. The course used was complemented by color audio-video footage. While the treatment interventions by primary care doctors did not change, the referral rate decreased from 30% to 11% with the web-based course on this acute disease.

2. Improved Treatment for Complicated Conditions

CMME has been proposed for increasing early detection of common disease, as well as for the training of healthcare workers dealing with potentially fatal diseases like HIV/AIDS.

Vision screenings have been shown to be effective, low-cost interventions to detect amblyopia (lazy eye) and strabismus (eye turns) in school-aged children. Unfortunately, pediatricians have less than a 20% vision screening rate for children, and, thus, often fail to detect lazy or turned eyes. [5] As a result of low screening rates and imperfect screenings, only about one in three children with strabismus or amblyopia are detected in primary care settings. Online education was not entirely successful in remediating this deficit in these busy doctors, particularly with regard of the fact that more than one-third of lazy eyes are undetectable by pediatricians.

In a 2009 study, which is nearly venerable by modern technology standards, CMME has also been used to train HIV/AIDS healthcare workers in Peru. At the time of the study, routers to provide wireless connections and portable solar chargers were necessary to keep the smartphones working, due to lack of infrastructure and healthcare providers. The authors write that "Peru does not have an adequate healthcare workforce to meet the population's demand for services." [6] The use of pre-tests, clinical cases, Skype-based discussion, review, and assessment were designed to effectively teach these overworked healthcare providers. See Figure 2).

Two things were discovered in this study. First, a combination of synchronous and asynchronous learning, using Skype and forum participation, was vital to training these workers with 90% compliance. Secondly, even "One of the best smartphones in history on any platform" [7] was not as robust as the contemporary iPhone accessing Skype and social media at the time. Technology rapidly changes, but it may remain true that not all platforms are created equally when it comes to CMME.

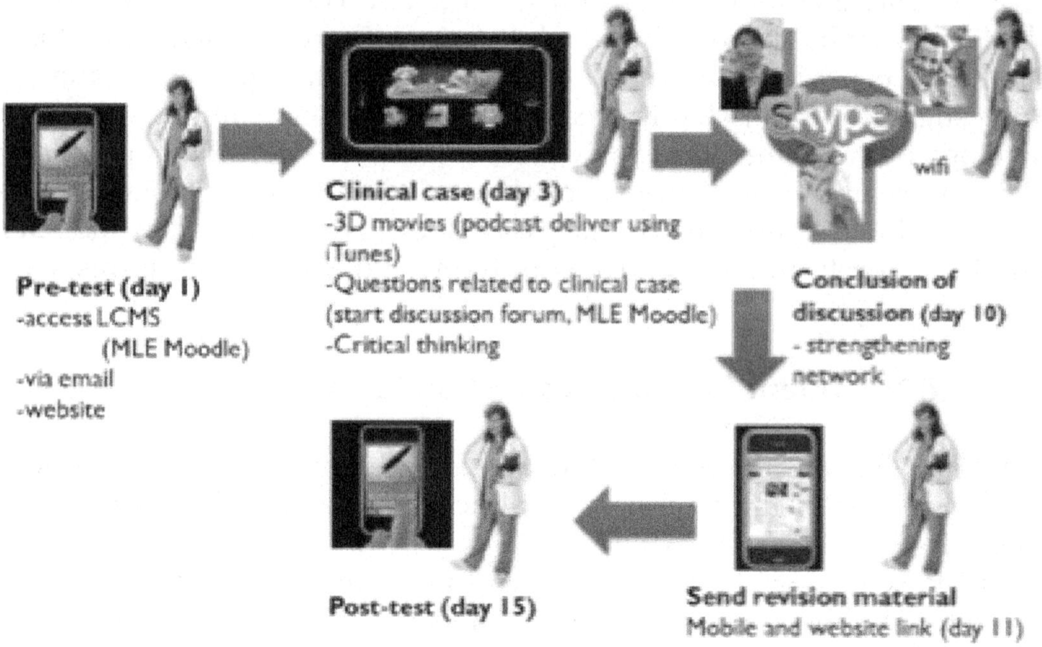

Figure 2: Flow of five clinical modules for HIV/AIDS training in Peru. [6]

3. Improved Availability of Evidence in Clinical Settings

Another approach to CMME is to make textbooks widely available to doctors in training. A landmark study by Hardyman et. al. [8] from 2013 discussed a medical textbook-smartphone interface called "iDoc". After surveying hundreds of doctors, who used iDoc and submitted case reports, there were several important and specific results of this study. First, to answer clinical questions, trainee doctors still relied on senior staff 80% of the time and ancillary medical personnel just over 50% of the time, with negligible changes from baseline. What did change is reliance on peers, which reduced from 70% to 58% after iDoc was introduced. Use of the iDoc library was significantly higher for first-year and male trainees and for medical skills queries, especially, when senior staff was not available. The patient problem they needed to solve determined their preferred information source. For instance, hard-copy texts were still preferred for speed of access for information-based queries, while senior staff members were relied on for complex queries that were harder to search. Clearly, electronically-searchable textbooks are still a niche resource.

A much smaller study took place with a half-dozen doctors in Botswana. [9] With 40 physicians for every 100,000 citizens and where almost 25% of the population under age 50 is HIV positive, Botswana has some overwhelming health challenges. Even in the cities like the capitol

Figure 3: Universtiy of Botswana Home Screen showing ePocrates and uCentral mobile apps. [9]

Gaborone, Internet connectivity is limited and functioning desktop computer access even more so. On the upside, since 2009, three-quarters of the world's mobile devices are in use in developing countries and this trend is only expected to continue. Mobile apps like ePocrates, 5-Minute Clinical Consult, and especially uCentral were most popular. Most of the doctors used the smartphone access for supplementary reading outside the hospital and requested increased access to medical journals. See Figure 3 (above).

4. Psycho-Social Applications for Mobile Apps in Healthcare

A novel application for mobile devices in mental health is to gather confidential intake and history forms from young clients. Whitehouse et. al. [10] note that this patient population are at higher probability for "engaging in risky behavior." There is a standard review of these risk factors, called "Home Education, Eating, Activities, Drugs, Depression, Sex, Safety (HEEADDSS)," but the authors note that "time constraints and patient/provider discomfort reduce implementation," at least when administered on paper. By making this survey electronic for the 12-18-year-old digital natives whom they serve, the study cites a 99% uptake and completion rate of the 90-question survey in ten minutes or less. The app-based survey is called TickiT, and the process banner (showing tablet use, secure uploading, and upward-trending results) is shown in Figure 4.

Figure 4: TickiT process banner for high-risk behavior history survey [10]

Medical residents were most positive with this survey, while the (presumably older) surgeons were the least positive. The authors also document their trial-and-error experience with icons and color schemes appropriate for their pediatric and young adult audience. This demographic does not include most doctors, unfortunately.

One neglected aspect of CMME is reflection. Renner and colleagues explored app-based reflection, individually and collaboratively, and its effect on hospital staff job satisfaction. [11] The authors defined reflection as "a process "in which people recapture their experience, think about it, mull it over and evaluate it." While reflection increases job satisfaction, it does not occur by itself and needs support. This author might add the additional value of reflection is to determine the muddy points of a lesson, web-based or otherwise.

5. Transportability of Health Professional Skills and Training

Usually, as technology evolves, it becomes smaller. This was not the case with handheld devices. Many will recall that the smaller personal data assistant and smartphones preceded the larger tablet among mobile devices. For many physicians, CMME requires these smaller, pocket-sized devices.

A comprehensive review of the literature as of late 2012 was written by Ozdalga et. al. [12] In the year prior, the authors discovered over 2300 medical apps for smartphones. Just 60 of these were identified as involving patient care, medical reference, or continuing education. An example of CMME using specialty challenges is shown in Figure 5.

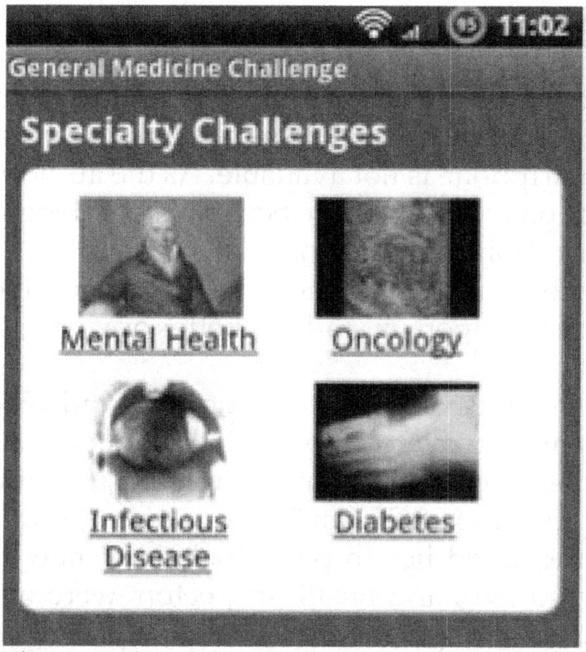

Figure 5: Specialty challenges used for CMME [12]

Several examples are given, including:

- iWander, an app that allows for the location monitoring of dementia patients with GPS tracking.
- A Bluetooth electrocardiogram (ECG) that allows a patient to monitor heart function while exercising or during sleep apnea.
- Automatic gait and balance monitoring in post-stroke patients using an accelerometer placed in their shoes.
- Monitoring of diabetic control and malaria treatment with proper data entry and review by the health care team.
- Patient apps for alcohol abuse, exercise, relaxation, smoking cessation, and weight loss.
- iTriage, providing location and waiting times for local emergency rooms.
- Epic, which allows doctors to access electronic health records from their smartphones.

While the smartphone alone is not a medical panacea, it is clear that it has the potential to improve independent living for those with health challenges. However, without the monitoring of health care personnel or the FDA, the authors "did not find evidence that apps led wellness." The article also takes on the unsubstantiated claim that ePocrates helps reduce medical errors and saves 20 minutes of doctor time per day.

The authors warn of smartphone apps weakening interprofessional relationships among healthcare personnel and engendering self-diagnosis among patients. Most ominously, they warn of disastrous results when there is over-reliance on medical apps and a smartphone is not available. As the authors put it, "as we become more dependent on technology, we become more dependent on it working flawlessly, with catastrophic implications when it fails." It seems worrisome that the day is near when a dead phone battery renders doctors impotent. However, the wave is clearly upon us, and, for better or worse, these objections are unlikely to stop it.

Since medical apps can also be used by doctors at a time and place of their choosing, they have the potential to overcome CMME bottlenecks. Many places have taken advantage of this fact already. For example, Rajasekaran et. al. [13] report that in India, up to 50 hours of CE can be taken online, but it has traditionally been used for training allied health personnel about new pharmaceuticals. In this case, doctors, nurses, and health inspectors were offered a training program on immunization. The goal was 50% eligible participation, equal test scores to in-person training, and to "obtain a 20% completion rate in lesser time." The training was offered through lectures delivered to mobile devices and a custom social networking page. The authors claim good success by using peer-to-peer learning.

This brings us to the College of Optometry's mobile app project, and the feasibility of creating and persuading optometric physicians to use a mobile app with podcasts, instead of text courses for continuing education.

Web-Based Continuing Education in Optometry

Like most state-regulated healthcare professions, optometrists require annual continuing education (CE) to maintain their professional licensure. In Oregon, that requirement is 18 hours per year. While at least half these hours need to be completed in person, at live lectures, quality web-based continuing education can make better patient care available to doctors in remote locations, who cannot easily afford to take much time away from their practices to attend regional or national meetings. In states like Oregon, up to 50% of these credits can be obtained by distance education, usually meaning online. Yet, there are limited venues for quality online CE in optometry.

The College of Optometry at Pacific was one of the first in the nation to offer web-based continuing education courses. These courses have traditionally been text-based, with illustrations. In text-based courses, every 3000 words would be counted as a credit, pending passage of a ten-question multiple-choice test at the end. Resembling a journal article, these courses have been praised for their quality and are popular in over a dozen states, and accepted for credit in all of them. They have been taken internationally as well. Because of this, at its peak of popularity, the Web CE site generated significant revenue for the College each year.

Continuing Education Challenges

However, the audience for these online CE courses is changing. There is increasing competition for text-based courses. Many are industry-sponsored and free. In recent years, webinars and similar multimedia courses have become popular. All of these changes have resulted in the slow attrition of the Pacific Web CE revenue. Our recent addition of PayPal has been a huge improvement, but by itself is not sufficient.

To continue to ensure Web CE success, a better interface is needed. While text-based courses with heavy, color illustrations lend themselves well to smart phones and tablets, the young, busy OD would often prefer a high-quality podcast format.

Podcast courses have been offered since the University adopted iTunesU several years ago, but to be most effective, an application (or "app") is necessary.

This proposal details how to make the Pacific Optometry Web CE finically viable for the foreseeable future.

II. Method and procedures

Current Web CE offerings [24]

While constantly changing, at this writing, the Pacific Web CE site currently offers 20 courses and 27 credits, all approved by the Council of Optometric Practitioner Education (COPE). Additionally, there are many archived courses for which the COPE approval has expired, and there has not been an application for renewal. This makes it by far the largest program of its kind in the county (see Appendix A).

To access the written courses, the practitioner can simply click through to the illustrated text, which has always been available free to read or print in PDF format for those who prefer hard copy. Doctors pay for their continuing education certificate only if they take the COPE-approved exam.

However, as of this printing, the large portion of these courses (10 courses and 11 credits) are in podcast format, with most new courses expected in this format. Instead of prose text, these courses have a written outline at most, and a podcast with synched audio available – if the doctor can access it. A written transcript in mobile-friendly format, along with a mobile app, would be very useful moving forward. Part of the reason is the podcasts are not very user-friendly.

iTunesU Accessibility

Audit reports indicate that while they are the minority of courses currently offered for Pacific Web CE, the written courses are still our most popular. The reasons for this discrepancy are not always clear. Sometimes, the podcast audio quality may be to blame. Other times, it may be the doctor's ability to access the podcast that makes these courses sell more slowly than expected.

The University has made these courses possible by offering a public channel on the Apple website, iTunesU. [25] However, it costs the University to make these freely-accessible podcasts searchable from iTunes.com. Instead, doctors must login to the above website as a guest, and then download the podcast onto their hard drive. This requires the downloading and installation of free iTunes software, and the ability to navigate it.

The Proposed Solution

Since podcast course are meant to be accessed to mobile devices, downloading them to a laptop or desktop, and then synching with a mobile device, is rather cumbersome. Apps are the solution to this problem. iTunesU has a free app available, but apparently doesn't allow easy access to our website. Therefore, a custom app for all major smartphone and tablet platforms is the ultimate solution to our transition to a combination of traditional text-based and the new podcasted Web CE courses. This would also be a recruitment tool to help find new, young authors for our courses.

Writing an app is normally a $10K proposal if a subcontractor is hired. The new Berglund grants, which funded 500 hours of work-study assistance, allowed us to direct the creation of one an app and mobile-friendly course transcripts for our existing and new web CE courses. The latter required more than typing and medical transcription experience, as the text files needed to be converted to illustrated PDF format for the Seattle Clouds template.

With regard to app programming, we used a template from Seattle Clouds, which allowed us to construct five app platforms (iPhone, iPad, Android, Kindle and web-based) for $600, including tech support. Although Seattle Clouds continued to own the code, the apps belong to the College of Optometry, and cost about $900 each to build from the template. Maintenance costs are separate and will likely average at least $200 a month as new courses are added and old ones are archived.

There was little hardware or software needed for this project that we did not already own. A PowerMac laptop was obtained on loan from University Information Services. Along with Seattle Clouds template, we used funds from a Faculty Development Grant (for 2013-2014) to get a tablet device (iPad), Kindle Fire, and iPhone 4 to Beta test the app on those platforms. Of course, the Android platform needed to be tested as well. A personal phone was used for this purpose. Lastly, for $15, a copy of iMovie was purchased to allow splitting of the podcasts into 25 MB chunks.

Future Directions and Conclusions

While the release of our mobile app to the iTunes App Store has been delayed until the new Pacific University mobile-friendly wireframe website is completed in the summer of 2014, we have learned several lessons for moving forward.

Based on the evidence, the evaluation of the mobile app for optometry could include the following testable hypotheses:

1. Testing for each course based on visual inspection of photographs of ocular tissues, like cornea, iris, and retina, as was done in the Norwegian diabetes study. [3]

2. Rates of referral to specialists can be decreased with proper audio-visuals such as video, as in podcast courses on visually noteworthy conditions like atopic dermatitis. [4]

3. Many busy physicians will not necessarily improve their ability to perform screenings for referrals outside their specialty by using an app alone. [5]

4. Recognize that not all platforms are equally fast and easy to use, thus, even the best app for CMME will be prone to platform limitations.6

5. Medical textbooks available in mobile format may be most useful for medical skills inquiries in absence of senior staff [8] and in places that do not have reliable desktop Internet connection. [9]

6. Digital natives respond better to mobile technology, including patient intake and history forms, [10] but mobile app reflection on what is learned can be useful to health care providers [11] and teachers alike.

This may be especially true for the solo practitioner.

7. Mobile partnerships such as patient personal data entry for monitoring diseases like diabetes work best when monitored by health care personnel. [12]

8. CMME on new pharmaceuticals and immunizations works best when combined with social networking and peer-to-peer training. [13]

Appendix A: Bibliography of Web Continuing Education for Optometry

There are currently 21 schools and colleges of optometry in the United States. [14] Not all of these have online continuing education. The following is a summary of those that were easy to access, as of 05/23/2014:

1. Indiana University (Bloomington) School of Optometry: 14 courses (23 credits). [15]

2. Northeastern State University (Oklahoma) College of Optometry: 2 courses (20 credits). [16]

3. Pacific University College of Optometry: 20 courses (27 credits). [17]

4. Rosenburg School of Optometry, University of the Incarnate Word: 1 course. [18]

5. Southern College of Optometry (Memphis): 8 courses (9 credits). [19]

6. State University of New York (SUNY): 1 course. [20]

7. University of Houston College of Optometry: 10 courses (13 credits). [21]

8. Western University College of Optometry (Pomona, CA): 16 courses (46 credits). [22]

Notes

[1] Evidence-Based Medicine. (2014) In *Wikipedia*. Retrieved from http://en.wikipedia.org/wiki/Evidence-Based_Medicine

[2] Cassels A. (2012). Eminence vs. evidence. *The Cochrane Collaboration*, Retrieved from http://www.cochrane.org/news/blog/eminence-vs-evidence .

[3] Sundling V, Gulbrandsen P, Straand J. (2013). Sensitivity and specificity of Norwegian optometrists' evaluation of diabetic retinopathy in single-field retinal images - a cross-sectional experimental study. *BMC Health Services Research*, 13(17). 1-8. doi: 10.1186/1472-6963-13-17.

[4] Schopf T, Flytkjaer V. (2012). Impact of interactive web-based education with mobile and email-based support of general practitioners on treatment and referral patterns of patients with atopic dermatitis: randomized controlled trial. *Journal of Medical Internet Research*, 14(6). doi: 10.2196/jmir.2359.

[5] Marsh-Tootle WL, McGwin G, Kohler CL, Kristofco RE, Datla RV, Wall TC. (2011). Efficacy of a web-based intervention to improve and sustain knowledge and screening for amblyopia in primary care settings. *Investigative Ophthalmology & Visual Sciences*, 52(10), 7160-7. doi: 10.1167/iovs.10-6566.

[6] Zolfo M, Iglesias D, Kiyan C, Echevarria J, Fucay L, Llacsahuanga E, de Waard I, Suàrez V, Llaque WC, Lynen L. (2010). Mobile learning for HIV/AIDS healthcare worker training in resource-limited settings. *AIDS Research and Therapy*, 7(35), 1-8. doi: 10.1186/1742-6405-7-35.

[7] Segan S. (2013). The 10 Best Symbian Phones Ever. PC Magazine. Retrieved from http://www.pcmag.com/slideshow/story/307321/the-10-best-symbian-phones-ever/1

[8] Hardyman W, Bullock A, Brown A, Carter-Ingram S, Stacey M. (2013). Mobile technology supporting trainee doctors' workplace learning and patient care: an evaluation. BMC Medical Education, 13(6), 1-10. doi: 10.1186/1472-6920-13-6.

[9] Chang AY, Ghose S, Littman-Quinn R, Anolik RB, Kyer A, Mazhani L, Seymour AK, Kovarik CL. (2012). Use of mobile learning by resident physicians in Botswana. *Telemedicine and e-Health*, 18(1), 11-13. doi: 10.1089/tmj.2011.0050.

[10] Whitehouse SR, Lam PY, Balka E, McLellan S, Deevska M, Penn D, Issenman R, Paone M. (2013). Co-Creation With TickiT: Designing and Evaluating a Clinical eHealth Platform for Youth. *JMIR Research Protocol*, 2(2), e42. doi: 10.2196/resprot.2865.

[11] Renner B, Kimmerle J, Cavael D, Ziegler V, Reinmann L, Cress U. (2014). Web-based apps for reflection: a longitudinal study with hospital staff. *Journal of Medical Internet Research*, 16(3), e85. doi: 10.2196/jmir.3040.

[12] Ozdalga, E, Ozdalga, A, Ahuja, N. (2012). The Smartphone in Medicine: A Review of Current and Potential Use Among Physicians and Students. *Journal of Medical Internet Research*, 14(5), e128. doi: 10.2196/jmir.1994

[13] Rajasekaran R and Iyengar NCSN. (2013). Peer-to-Peer JXTA Architecture for Continuing Mobile Medical Education Incorporated in Rural Public Health Centers. *Osong Public*

Health Research Perspectives. 4(2): 99–106. doi: 10.1016/j.phrp.2013.03.004.

[14] See: http://www.opted.org/i4a/pages/index.cfm?pageid=3336

[15] See: http://www.opt.indiana.edu/ce/OnLine.htm

[16] See: http://optometry.nsuok.edu/ContinuingEducation/CMEOnline.aspx

[17] See: http://www.pacificu.edu/optometry/ce/online_ce.cfm

[18] See: http://optometry.uiw.edu/continuing/index.html

[19] See: http://www.sco.edu/onlinecontinuingeducation

[20] See: http://www.sunyopt.edu/education/academics/continuing_professional_education/online_nys_infection_control_course

[21] See: http://ce.opt.uh.edu/online-ce/courses/

[22] See: http://www.westernu.edu/optometry-continuing-education

[23] *The Pacific University Ocular Disease Digital Collection*. Retrieved from http://cdm15925.contentdm.oclc.org/cdm/singleitem/collection/p15925coll4/id/422/rec/2

[24] See: http://www.pacificu.edu/optometry/ce/online_ce.cfm

[25] See: http://www.pacificu.edu/itunesu/

Provider and Recipient Perceptions and Utilization of Email in Healthcare

by Susan Glinka, M.A.
PhD Candidate at Pacific University

Abstract-This study examines patient-provider email communication. Digital communication has changed the way people communicate but there is slow implementation of electronic communication in healthcare. A sample of 110 individuals was surveyed regarding their perceptions and utilization of electronic communication in healthcare. The current study found that 5.6% of healthcare providers contact recipients via email. The results show that 76% recipient participants feel positively toward email communication in healthcare; but only 44% of the healthcare providers feel positively toward provider-patient email communication. Finally the primary concerns surrounding electronic communication in healthcare are legal and privacy issues.

Introduction

The impact of technology on our everyday lives is staggering. According to Internet World Statistics, as of 2012 there are over 2.4 billion people using the Internet. [1] Given the widespread use of the Internet and the proliferation of email accounts, it is evident that electronic communication has revolutionized the way that people interact on a daily basis in business, personal, and commercial communication.

Even though digital communication through email has changed the way people communicate with each other, there is slow implementation of electronic communication in healthcare systems. Specifically, there has been limited implementation of electronic communication between providers and their patients. Although researchers have examined the use of email communication in healthcare settings, their results have been largely inconsistent and the current utilization of patient-provider email communication remains unclear. The present study seeks to examine the prevalence of electronic communication between patients and their providers, as well as explore patient and provider attitudes regarding the use and benefits of such communication.

Literature Review

Email Prevalence in Healthcare Settings

Despite email prevalence in personal and business communications, it has not had the same impact in the medical and health fields. Moyer, Stern, Katz and Fredrick explored the potential of implementing electronic communication in healthcare. The authors noted that increasing the accessibility of managed care could improve patient outcomes, intensify disease management strategies, and increase patient involvement with and understanding of their health care. This untapped resource for doctor-patient communication could aid in the development of the relationship between doctors and their patients. However, electronic communications are often met with concerns over equitable access, confidentiality, and privacy. [2]

Healthcare systems housed within university settings are quicker to integrate new technology into their existing systems. Neill, Mainous, Clark, and Hagen conducted a survey regarding electronic mail as a medium of communication at a university-based family medicine clinic. The results of this exploratory survey indicated that patients believed that email use could increase the speed, convenience, and access to medical care for refilling prescriptions, communicating laboratory results, and making appointments. However, the study results indicated that the handling of urgent matters would not be successful via email communication and should be left to the traditional communication methods such as office visits and personal phone calls. [3]

Fridsma, Ford, and Altman compared email use to other mediums of communication. They surveyed 444 internal medicine patients. Although half of the patients reported that they used email on a regular basis, patients reported that they used email less than the postal service, telephone, or fax for communicating with the clinic. [4] Similarly, Moyer, Stern, Dobias, Cox, and Kats examined email use patterns and attitudes among patients and primary care physicians. More than half (52.1%) of patients disclosed email usage for personal use, however, only 10.5% of the respondents reported having communicated with their doctor via email. The authors reported that patient-provider email is diffusing slowly because of patient concerns about efficiency and effectiveness. [5] To resolve this issue, managed care providers wanting to implement electronic communication systems should work to educate providers and recipients about the strengths and weaknesses that are involved with electronic communication.

Guidelines for Electronic Mail with Patients

Overall, electronic communication does not appear to be widely implemented in the healthcare setting. When electronic communication is utilized, the guidelines for patient privacy can be ambiguous. To best expand the use of electronic communications in healthcare, concerns about access, confidentiality, and privacy needed to be addressed. The American Medical Informatics Association (AMIA) Internet Working Group, Task Force on Guidelines for the Use of Clinic-Patient Electronic Mail [6] was developed to address the issues concerning effective communication between clinicians and patients. The communication guidelines are as follows: establish a turnaround for messages and do not use email for urgent matters; inform patients about privacy issues; establish types of transaction and sensitivity of subject matter permitted over email; instruct patients to address the reason for the message in the subject line of the email; request patients to put their name and identification number in the body of the email; configure automatic reply messages to confirm receipt; print all messages, replies, and confirmations for the patient's chart; send new messages to inform patient that requests have been processed; ask patients to acknowledge reading providers messages; maintain an email distribution list of patients, but do not send group mailings where recipients are visible to each other; and avoid using anger, sarcasm, harsh criticism, and libelous references to third party messages.

The second portion of the Guidelines for Use of Clinic-Patient Electronic Mail [7] covers how medical staff should treat patient information when utilizing electronic communication. The medico-legal and administrative guidelines included are as follows: consider obtaining patient's informed consent for use of email; use password-protected screen savers for all desktop work-stations in the office, hospital, and home; never forward patient-identifiable information to a third party without expressed permission; do not share professional email with family members; use encryption for all messages; do not use unencrypted wireless connections with patient-identifiable information; perform at least weekly backups of email onto long-term storage; and commit policy decisions to writing and electronic form. Following these suggested guidelines would keep patient information confidential and in concordance with the Health Insurance Portability and Accountability Act (1996).

These guidelines were established to standardize the use of electronic communication in healthcare. In the following sections, email trends in healthcare, adaptation of The American Medical Informatics Association (AMIA) Internet Working Group, Task Force on Guidelines for the Use of Clinic-Patient Electronic Mail [8] guidelines, and attitudes of healthcare providers and recipients toward electronic communication are reviewed.

Email Communication Trends in Healthcare

The prevalence of Internet use in healthcare settings and its impact on health care utilization are unclear. [9] Available estimates of Internet use and impact vary widely, making it difficult to focus policy discussions or design appropriate policy activities. Baker et al. sent surveys to over 60,000 US households. Analyzed responses included 4,764 individuals aged 21 years and older who were self-reported Internet users. The results indicated the following: 40% of the respondents with Internet access reported using the Internet to find information about health care; 6% reported using email to contact a physician or other healthcare professional; 33% of those using the Internet for health-related matters reported that the information found impacted their medical decision, although few reported that the information impacted health care utilization; 94% said that Internet use had no effect on the number of physician visits; 93% said Internet use had no effect on the number of telephone contacts with their provider; and less than 5% reported use of the Internet to obtain a prescription or purchase pharmaceutical products.

Given the general increase in Internet use and email communication, the opportunity to connect with healthcare providers through email would facilitate and enhance patient-provider communication. Despite the massive growth of Internet and email usage, provider adoption of this medium has been minimal. Brooks and Menachemi observed that only 16.6% of physicians surveyed have utilized electronic communication and only 2.9% use it frequently to communicate with their patients. The primary concerns they reported involved fiscal and legal vulnerabilities. The authors also found a difference in the type of physician adopting email communication, with community physicians being less likely than those who work at university or county hospitals to use email communication with their patients. Further, education of providers and recipients, in addition to improvement in the security and protocols surrounding electronic communication, is needed for the implementation and widespread use of email communication between patients and providers in healthcare settings. [10]

Menachemi, Prickeet, and Brooks reported that the number of attempts made by physicians using email to communicate with their patients increased from 2005 to 2008; however, the number of physicians who regularly use email to communicate did not increase significantly during this time. [11] Unfortunately, the authors reported a lack of adherence to best practices outlined by the AMIA Internet Working Group, Task Force on Guidelines for the Use of Clinic-Patient Electronic Mail. [12] This reported lack of adherence to best practices for electronic communication is unsettling because of the sensitive and confidential nature of health concerns. Although some healthcare providers have implemented email communication, there is a lack of oversight regarding patient privacy.

Healthcare Recipient Perspectives

Investigating the attitudes of healthcare recipients is an important part in determining whether or not there is a demand for electronic communication in the healthcare setting. Sittig, King, and Hazlehurst investigated how subjects who use the Internet and email view the potential of contacting their healthcare provider via email. A total of 954 users of WebMD (webmd.com), an open access database for medical information available online, were surveyed. The results indicated that 6% of those surveyed had used email to communicate with their healthcare providers. The main concerns with emailing healthcare providers that were identified were lack of access, limited privacy, and the potential of the email message to be read or intercepted by someone other than their healthcare provider. [13]

Couchman, Forjuoh and Rascoe surveyed 950 patients from nine family practice clinics to investigate how many of the patients were email users, as well as patients' willingness to utilize email to contact their healthcare providers and their expectations regarding email response time and content. They found that 54.3% of the patients were email users. Additionally, patients endorsed that they would use email for refilling prescriptions, non-urgent consultations, and to obtain laboratory results. [14]

Caretakers and parents often contact providers on behalf of someone else or their children. Kleiner, Akers, Burke, and Werner examined the email readiness of families who utilized the services of general pediatricians and specialty pediatricians from an integrated healthcare system. The researchers also surveyed the families' knowledge base and attitudes of the potential liabilities involved in using electronic communication with their healthcare providers. The results of this survey showed that parents who were 31-40 years of age were significantly more likely to use email. Parents at the general pediatric clinics were more concerned about privacy than those who were associated with specialty pediatric clinics. However, 74% of all parents surveyed were interested in contacting their pediatrician through email for getting test results, scheduling, and discussing symptoms. [15]

Houston, Sands, Jenckes, and Ford surveyed the experience of patients and providers who were early users of patient-provider email communication. The authors found that those who used email were more likely to have a college education, were younger, and did belong to a minority group. The most common topics discussed through email with physicians were laboratory results and prescription renewals. The benefits of email communication identified by the participants were the ability to save the email messages, efficiency, and the ability to ask more questions. [16]

Anand, Feldman, Geller, Bisbee, and Baucher conducted a content analysis of emails between providers and parents of patients in pediatric primary care. They also examined parents' attitudes about email communication with their providers. A total of 54 parents of patients, surveyed from two primary care pediatric clinics, participated in the study. The results indicated that 98% of parents were satisfied with email communications with their pediatrician. Additionally, 80% of parents felt that all pediatricians should use electronic communication, 65% stated that they would be more likely to choose a pediatrician based on their email use, and 63% were unwilling to pay for this service. [17]

In a follow-up study to the Couchman, Forjuoh, and Rascoe investigation, [18] Couchman et al. explored patients' expectations and willingness regarding the use of email communication with their healthcare providers. The researchers surveyed 2,314 patients from 19 clinics and found that 58.3% of patients had email access but only 5.8% of them had used email to communicate directly with their providers. Patients stated that they were more willing to use email for non-urgent matters such as refilling prescriptions (83%), minor consultations (82%), asking for a follow-up for direct communication previously made with their physicians (82%), and obtaining test or laboratory results (82%). Patients, in general, had high expectations for a rapid response time. The results of this study also showed a large difference in willingness and expectations by age group, education level, and income. Participants that were younger, more educated, and had higher level of income were more willing to use patient-provider electronic communication than the participants that were older, less educated, and had lower level of income. [19]

Kagen, Clarke, and Happ explored patients' and family members' interest and use of email with their health care providers after head and neck cancer operations. This study included 74 patients and 35 family members that were attending clinic visits after their procedures. The results indicated that 9.5% of patients reported using email to contact their surgeon or nurse and about 30% of those who did not use email to contact their healthcare providers were planning on doing so in the future. Symptom management and prescription refills were the most common items addressed in the emails from patients to providers. [20]

Katzen, Solan, and Dicker found that patients also favored email for increased efficiency, convenience, and timeliness of communication with their healthcare providers about general health problems. Additionally, the authors reported that 80% of patients surveyed favored posing a health related question to their physicians over email. Only 51% of the respondents were concerned about confidentiality or concerned that their email would not go directly to their physician. [21]

In a study investigating whether email communication enhanced patient care as well as examining some of the common barriers for implementing an email communication system, Leong, Gengrich, Lewis, Mauger, and George, surveyed 100 patients (67 patients using email and 33 patients not using email). The authors found that those in the email group reported higher levels of satisfaction with convenience of communication and the amount of time spent communicating with their healthcare providers. [22]

To explore electronic communication within the family medicine domain, Virji et al. surveyed 390 patients at a family medicine clinic to determine how many patients utilized email, how many patients were receptive to communicating with their physician via email, and the feasibility of providing medical education through email. The results indicate that 80% of the patients who used email were interested in emailing their healthcare provider and 42% were willing to pay out of pocket for the ability to email the clinic. [23]

Rosen and Kwoh conducted a survey to assess the pattern of email communication between patients and providers, measure the average amount of time providers spend on email communication with patients, and examine the satisfaction of families who had communicated electronically with their child's rheumatologist. Of the respondents, 86% endorsed that email increased access to their child's physician and 84% endorsed that more doctors should offer email systems. [24]

Regarding access to electronic communication in healthcare, older patient populations experience disparities such as lack of access to healthcare services and information. Electronic communication combined with face-to-face communication could improve quality of health care for older patients. The researchers polled a sample of 4,059 patients over 65 years of age. Although only 52 (1.3%) participants had used email to contact their physicians, almost half (49.3%) expressed interest in the possibility of using email to communicate with their doctor. [25]

Overall, healthcare recipients are excited about the possibility of communicating with their doctors through email. Some healthcare recipients are even willing to pay for this service. [26] [27] Despite the interest of patients to communicate with providers through email, only 5.8 to 10.5% of patients currently use email to communicate with their providers. [28] [29]

Healthcare Provider Perspectives

In addition to healthcare recipient attitudes regarding email in healthcare, it is also important to explore the thoughts of healthcare providers. The implementation of email into their daily practice may have both positive and negative impacts. Kleiner, Akers, Burke, and Werner examined provider and patient access to and knowledge about email communication. A total of 37 physicians participated in their study. The results indicated that 74% of the general pediatric physicians and 100% of the subspecialty pediatric physicians had general access to email. However, 79% of these doctors did not want to use email to communicate with their patients, reporting concerns regarding confidentiality and time demands. [30]

Investigating outpatient clinics, Moyer et al. examined email utilization patterns and attitudes toward email use among primary care physicians. They found that 61% of physicians thought email was a good way for their patients to handle administrative concerns. Those who used email more frequently were more comfortable with the idea of using email in their clinic. Contrary to previous studies, Moyer et al. found that the physicians and front desk personnel were more optimistic than were patients about using email to improve the patient-provider relationship. [31]

In a survey of physicians associated with large academic medical center outpatient clinics, Gaster et al. found that nearly 72% of physicians surveyed used email to communicate with their patients. Those who utilized email in this study were highly satisfied with its use. The main concern identified by the physicians, however, was confidentiality. [32]

Anand et al. (discussed in more detail above) examined email communication between parents of patients and providers. The researchers asked the doctors to estimate how much time they spent answering emails. On average, the doctors reported spending 30 min per day emailing patients. [33]

Regarding best practices for email communication in healthcare settings as well as physicians' adoption of email communication in their practices, Brooks and Menachemi examined factors associated with physician-patient email and reported on the adherence of the physicians to the guidelines of patient communication developed by AMIA Internet Working Group, Task Force on Guidelines for the Use of Clinic-Patient Electronic Mail. Of those physicians surveyed, 16.6% reported using email to communicate with patients, with only 2.9% reporting they used email frequently. Factors that were likely to increase the usage of email were physicians' age (decreased use with advancing age), race (less frequent for Asian physicians), medical training (more frequent in family practice and surgery), practice size (increased use in larger groups), and geographic location (increased use in urban populations). Only 6.7% of the physicians surveyed complied with at least half of the guidelines for electronic communication with patients. [34] [35]

Houston, Sands, Nash, and Ford examined the qualitative experiences of physicians who used email frequently with their patients. A total of 204 physicians reported using email on a daily basis to communicate with patients participated in the study. Commonly reported topics for email communication were discussions of new but non-urgent symptoms and questions about lab results. According to the results, 75% of the physicians were satisfied with email communication because of efficiency and perceived delivery of better care. Some aspects with which physicians were not satisfied were concerns about excessive time demand, medico-legal risks, and patients' ability to use email appropriately. [36]

In conclusion, electronic communication is not widespread within the healthcare environment. Even though attempts have been made by The American Medical Informatics Association (AMIA) Internet Working Group, Task Force on Guidelines for the Use of Clinic-Patient Electronic Mail [37] to set standards for electronic communication, they are not often enforced. [38] Healthcare recipients are often in favor of electronic communication in healthcare; however, healthcare providers express privacy and legal concerns.

Present Study

The present study is an investigation of the current prevalence of email communication between patient and healthcare provider. The existing literature indicates that email is only prevalent in 5.8 to 10.5% of patient populations [39] [40] even though both providers and patients often report being satisfied with the use of email communication. [41] [42] [43] An exploratory analysis will be conducted to determine if email use has increased in healthcare settings from the time of the aforementioned studies. It is hypothesized that there will be an increase in electronic communication in healthcare from the previously reported 5.8 to 10.5% of patient populations. [44]

Additional questions, including assessment of attitudes regarding email communication in healthcare settings as well as determination if providers and patients think email could enhance the patient-provider relationship will also be explored. It is hypothesized that both healthcare providers and recipients will respond positively to the idea of electronic communication in healthcare. Finally, it is hypothesized that concerns regarding electronic communication in healthcare will be predominantly related to privacy concerns over legal concerns as was found in previous investigations.

Method

Participants

One hundred and ten participants were recruited using a convenience sampling method (18 were healthcare providers (e.g., doctor, nurse, psychologist, etc.) and were 92 recipients). All participants were recruited either via email message or through a social networking site (e.g. Facebook). Requirements for participation were being over the age of 18 and having access to a computer.

Participants ranged in age from 18 to 69 years (M=26.8; SD=10.9). Of the 110 participants, 40 (36.4%) were male, 69 (62.7%) were female and one who self-identified as other (.9%). Self-identified racial ethnicity within the sample was as follows: 101 (92.7%) Caucasian, 4 (3.7%) Asian/Pacific Islander, 1 (.9%) Black, 3 (2.8%) Hispanic, and 5 (4.6%) other.

Materials and Procedures

Participants were asked to partake in a survey regarding the frequency, purpose, and location of patient-provider email communication; whether or not they have engaged in such communication; and their attitudes regarding email communication and health care. Providers and recipients completed a similar survey with minor differences in wording.

Upon entering the study website, participants were presented with and asked to read the document of informed consent. After agreeing to the conditions presented in the statement of informed consent, each participant was presented with a demographics questionnaire. Based on participant indication that they are either a healthcare provider or a recipient of healthcare services, individuals were directed to two additional survey measures, one regarding their attitudes and a measure of email and healthcare communication. All participants were presented with these two measures; however, the language differed slightly depending upon the participant indication of status (i.e., patient or provider). Once the participant completed these measures, they were thanked for their time and participation. The total participation time was approximately 20 minutes. The Pacific University Institutional Review board approved the study protocol and all participants were free to discontinue their participation at any time without penalty.

Table 1.Demographics of Sample (n = 110)

	Recipients n (%)	Providers n (%)
Total:	92 (83.6)	18 (16.4)
Gender		
Male	36 (39.1)	4 (22.2)
Female	55 (59.8)	14 (77.8)
Other	1 (.9)	-
Education		
High school	9 (9.8)	1 (5.6)
Some college/trade	31 (33.7)	1 (5.6)
2-year degree	6 (6.5)	2 (11.1)
Bachelors	32 (34.8)	8 (44.4)
Masters	8 (8.7)	5 (27.8
Doctorate	6 (6.5)	1 (5.6)
Ethnicity		
Caucasian	80 (87.0)	18 (100)
Black/African American	1 (1.1)	-
Hispanic	1 (1.1)	-
Asian/Pacific Islander	3 (3.3)	-
Middle Eastern	2 (2.2)	-
Bi-racial	4 (4.3)	-
Other	1 (1.1)	-

Table 2. Email usage (n=110)

	Recipients n (%)	Providers n (%)
Email Use (yes)	92 (100)	18 (100)
How often do you check email?		
Once a week or less	1 (1.1)	1 (5.6)
A few times a week	9 (9.8)	1 (5.6)
Every day	8 (8.7)	3 (16.7)
More than once a day	74 (80.4)	13 (72.2)
What do you use email for most?		
Work	35 (38)	9 (50)
School	8 (8.7)	1 (5.6)
Personal	49 (53.3)	8 (44.4)

Table 3.Details of Email Usage (n = 110)

	Recipients n (%)	Providers n (%)
Where do you use email?		
Work	69 (75)	15 (83.3)
Home	90 (97.8)	18 (100)
Other	26 (28.3)	3 (16.7)
Who do you email?		
Coworkers	58 (63)	13 (72.2)
Boss	56 (60.9)	13 (72.2)
Friends	70 (76.1)	14 (77.8)
Family	74 (80.4)	12 (66.7)
Companies	36 (39.1)	3 (16.7)
Professionals	35 (38)	9 (50)
Other	9 (9.8)	18 (100)

Results

Demographic Information

Participant demographic information, including gender, education, and ethnicity, are presented in Table 1.

All participants in the study reported that they use email. Information about frequency of email use and for what purpose email is utilized the most is presented in Table 2.

Table 3 contains information pertaining details of email usage within the sample. Participants were asked to "check all that apply" to obtain this data. The percentages that are presented in the table are those who positively endorsed the use of email in that modality.

Table 4.Health Information Online (n = 110)

	Recipients n (%)	Providers n (%)
Education regarding health concerns:		
Very educated	15 (16.3)	6 (33.3)
Somewhat educated	60 (65.2)	12 (66.7)
Neither educated or not	14 (15.2)	-
Not really educated	3 (3.3)	-
Uninformed	-	-
Research symptoms online?*		
Yes	83 (90.2)	4 (22.2)
No	9 (9.8)	14 (77.8)
Reliability of online information:		
Very accurate	4 (4.3)	-
Accurate	45 (48.9)	9 (50)
Neither accurate or inaccurate	35 (38)	8 (44.4)
Inaccurate	7 (7.6)	1 (5.6)
Very inaccurate	-	-

**Recipients were asked if they research their symptoms online; providers were asked if they encourage patients researching symptoms online.*

Email and Healthcare

Participants were asked a series of questions regarding how educated they perceived themselves to be concerning medical information presented online, whether or not they researched their health concerns or symptoms online (or in the case of physicians, whether they encouraged their patients to research health concerns online), and the accuracy of the information presented online. This information is presented in Table 4.

Table 5 presents the interest of recipients and providers in provider-patient email communication; if they have used email for such communication; and if so, what was the content of the email communication. The content portion of this question was restricted to common themes that were found to be popular for email communication between healthcare providers and recipients in the literature review.

Table 5.Use of Email with Healthcare Providers and Patients (n = 110)

	Recipients n (%)	Providers n (%)
Interested in emailing doctor/patient:		
Yes	79 (85.9)	3 (16.7)
No	13 (14.1)	15 (83.3)
Frequency of communication with health care provider via email:		
Never	54 (58.7)	17 (94.4)
Once	7 (7.6)	-
2-3 times	18 (19.6)	-
4-5 times	2 (2.2)	-
5 or more times	11 (12)	1 (5.6)
Reason for email:		
Scheduling	36 (39.1)	2 (11.1)
Billing	12 (13)	-
Health concerns	19 (20.7)	-
Question regarding symptoms	18 (19.6)	-
Refill prescriptions	23 (25)	1 (5.6)
Other	10 (10.9)	6 (33.33)

Table 6.Perceptions of Email Utilization in Healthcare (n = 110)

	Recipients n (%)	Providers n (%)
Feeling toward email in healthcare:		
Extremely positive	33 (35.9)	2 (11.1)
Positive	38 (41.3)	6 (33.33)
Ambivalent	18 (19.6)	8 (44.4)
Negative	3 (3.3)	2 (11.1)
Extremely Negative	-	-
Email good way to contact healthcare provider?		
Yes	55 (59.8)	3 (16.7)
Yes, but for administrative only	20 (21.7)	9 (50)
Yes, for admin and health concerns	12 (13)	-
No	5 (5.4)	6 (33.33)
Reasons you currently do not email healthcare professionals?*		
Lack of access	45 (48.9)	8 (44.4)
Response time is slow	13 (14.1)	4 (22.2)
Fear of being lost in the system	18 (19.6)	4 (22.2)
Other (Privacy)	-	15 (83.3)
Other (Legal)	-	12 (66.7)
Other	33 (35.9)	5 (27.8)
Could email improve patient-provider communication?		
Yes	88 (90.2)	13 (72.2)
No	4 (4.3)	5 (27.8)
Could email improve patient understanding of health and concerns?		
Yes	83 (90.2)	10 (55.6)
No	9 (9.8)	8 (44.4)

**Check all that apply*

Attitudes About Email in Healthcare

The perceptions of email use in healthcare settings, and whether or not such communication would enhance understanding between healthcare providers and recipients, are presented in Table 6. The reasoning behind current barriers to email use was a "Check all that apply" question, accounting for the larger reported percentages.

Discussion

The results of the current study are consistent what was previously found in the literature. The first hypothesis was that there would be a reported increase in adoption of email utilization in healthcare settings. According to prior research, email communication was only prevalent in 5.8 to 10.5% of patient populations. [45] [46] In the current study, the percentage of healthcare providers using electronic communication with recipients was 5.6%. In the sample surveyed, there was not an increase in electronic communication in healthcare.

Despite a lack of utilization, there are many examples within the literature of healthcare providers and patients being satisfied with the implementation of email communication. [47] [48] [49] The second hypothesis in the present study was that healthcare providers and recipients would respond positively to electronic communication. The results from the current study are that 76% of healthcare recipients surveyed feel positively toward email communication in healthcare; but only 44% of the healthcare providers sampled feel positively toward provider-patient email communication. All healthcare providers in this study endorsed email use for their personal lives. However, only half of the providers (n = 9; 50%) endorsed email use with healthcare recipients. Further, 85.9% of recipients of healthcare are interested in such communication, but only 16.7% of providers are interested. This disparity in interest could partially be responsible for the lack of integration of electronic communication in healthcare practice. Although healthcare recipients view email as a convenience, a majority of healthcare providers reported privacy and legal concerns (as detailed below).

The final hypothesis was that legal and privacy issues would be the primary concerns regarding the implementation of electronic communication in healthcare settings. While this was true for healthcare providers, the results of the present study show that the primary concerns of healthcare recipients are lack of access or opportunity fear of being lost in a complex system, and privacy. Prior research indicated the reasoning behind the lack of email communication in healthcare settings were lack of access, slow response time, legal, and privacy barriers. [50]

Included in this study were questions regarding provider and patient opinions on email potentially enhancing the patient-provider relationship and communication. Although providers did not endorse being interested in communicating with patients via email, 72% endorsed that email would be a good way to improve patient-provider communication. This is consistent with the findings of Kleiner et. al. and Houston et. al.. [51] [52] Further research should investigate the barriers between the desires to improve patient-provider communication and relationships their relations to concerns regarding lack of access, legal and privacy.

In regard to the use of the Internet to search for information regarding symptoms online, the majority of healthcare recipients reported that they do search their symptoms online, while the majority of healthcare providers do not encourage their patients to do so. The information that is available on the Internet regarding health concerns is vast and often not regulated. [53] Researching types of medical information available online is a difficult subject. Improved communication between the healthcare provider and patient surrounding online health information can have a positive impact on healthcare understanding and treatment adherence.

Limitations

There are a few limitations of the present study. This study utilized a small sample (n = 110) collected via a convenience sampling method through social networking sites (i.e., Facebook). The sample was homogenous in regards with racial ethnicity, with the great majority of the sample identifying as Caucasian and socioeconomic factors were not collected.

Further, the authors of the present study did not differentiate between healthcare provider settings. Higher rates of email communication have reported in urban areas and hospitals that are affiliated with universities. [54] Further examination of such geographic differences in the adoption of provider-patient electronic communication is called for. Also, exploring current models of electronic communication success in healthcare settings should be investigated. This could be used to create electronic communication systems between providers and recipients that better address common concerns.

Conclusions

Digital communication has changed the way people communicate in their personal, professional, and social lives. However, there is slow implementation of electronic communication in healthcare. The current study found a small margin of healthcare providers contact recipients via email, despite the results indicating most recipient participants feel positively toward email communication in healthcare. Further research should be conducted into the barriers between the adaptation of patient-provider email communication to enhance access and quality of healthcare services.

Notes

[1] internetworldstats.com/stats.htm

[2] Moyer, C. A., Stern, D. T., Katz, S. J., & Fendrick, A. M. (1999). "We got mail": Electronic communication between physicians and patients. *The American Journal of Managed Care*, 5(12), 1513-1522.

[3] Neill, R. A., Mainous, A. G., Clark, J. R., & Hagen, M. D. (1994). The utility of electronic mail as a medium for patient-physician communication. *Archives of Family Medicine*, 3, 268-271.

[4] Fridsma, D. B., Ford, P., & Altman R. (1994). A survey of patient access to electronic mail: Attitudes, barriers, and opportunities. *Annual Symposium of Computers Application in Medical Care*, 15-19.

[5] Moyer, C. A., Stern, D. T., Dobias, K. S., Cox, D. T., & Katz, S. J. (2002). Bridging the electronic divide: Patient and provider perspectives on e-mail communication in primary care. *Technology Assessment*, 8(5), 427-433.

[6] Kane, B., & Sands, D. Z. (1998). Guidelines for clinical use of electronic mail with patients. *Journal of American Medical Informatics Association*, 5, 104-111.

[7] Kane & Sands (1998)

[8] Kane & Sands (1998)

[9] Baker, L., Wagner, T. H., Singer, S., & Bundorf, M. K. (2003). Use of the Internet and e-mail for health care information: Results from a national survey. *Journal of the American Medical Association*, 289(18), 2400-2406.

[10] Brooks, R. G., & Menachemi, N. (2006). Physicians' use of email with patients: Factors influencing electronic communication and adherence to best practices. *Journal of Medical Internet Research*, 8(1), E2. doi: 10.2196/jmir.8.1.e2

[11] Menachemi, N, Prickett, C. T., & Brooks, R. G. (2011). The use of physician-patient email: A follow up examination of adoption and best-practice adherence 2005-2008. *Journal of Medical Internet Research* 13(1), E23.

[12] Kane & Sands (1998)

[13] Sittig, D. F., King, S., & Hazlehurst, B. L. (2001). A survey of patient-provider e-mail communication: What do patients think. *International Journal of Medical Informatics*, 61, 71-80.

[14] Couchman, G. R., Forjuoh, S. N., & Rascoe, T.G. (2001). E-mail communications in family practice: What do patients expect? *Journal of Family Practice*, 50, 414-418.

[15] Kleiner, K. D., Akers, R., Burke, B. L., & Werner, E. J. (2002). Parent and physician attitudes regarding electronic communication in pediatric practices. *Pediatrics* (109), 740-744.

[16] Houston, T. K., Sands, D. Z., Jenckes, M. W., & Ford, D. E. (2004). Experiences of patients who were early adopters of electronic communication with their physician: Satisfaction, benefits, and concerns. *American Journal of Managed Care*, 10, 601-608.

[17] Anand, S. G., Feldman, M. J., Geller, D. S., Bisbee, A., & Bauchner, H. A. (2005). Content analysis of e-mail communication between primary care providers and parents. *Pediatrics*, 18, 1283-1288.

[18] Couchman et. al. (2001)

[19] Couchman, G. R., Forjuoh, S. N., Rascoe, T.G., Reis, M. D., Koehler, B., & Walsum, K. L. (2005). E-mail communications in primary care: What patients' expectations for specific test results? *International Journal of Medical Informatics*, 74, 21-30.

[20] Kagen, S. H., Clarke, S. P., & Happ, M. B. (2005). Head and neck cancer patient and family member interest in and use of e-mail to communicate with clinicians. *Head & Neck*, 27, 976-981.

[21] Katzen, C., Solan, M. J., & Dicker, A. P. (2005). E-mail and oncology: A survey of radiation oncology patients and their attitudes to a new generation of health communication. *Prostate Cancer and Prostatic Diseases*, 8, 189-193.

[22] Leong, S. L., Gingrich, D., Lewis, P. R., Mauger, D. T., & George, J. H. (2005). Enhancing doctor-patient communication using email: A pilot study. *The Journal of the American Board of Family Medicine*, 18(3), 180-188.

[23] Virji, A., Yarnall, K. S., Krause, K. M., Pollak, K. I., Scannell, M. A., & Gradison, M. (2006). Use of email in family practice setting: Opportunities and challenges in patient- and physician-initiated communication. *British Medical Journal Medical Humanities*, 4, 18.

[24] Rosen, P., & Kwoh, C.K. (2007). Patient-physician e-mail: An opportunity to transform pediatric health care delivery. *Pediatrics*, 120, 701-706.

[25] Singh, H., Fox, S. A., Petersen, N. J., Shethia, A., & Street Jr., R. L. (2009). Older patients' enthusiasm to use electronic mail to communicate with their physicians: Cross-sectional survey. *Journal of Medical Internet Research*, 11(2), E18. doi: 10.2196/jmir.1143

[26] Anand, S. G., Feldman, M. J., Geller, D. S., Bisbee, A., & Bauchner, H. A. (2005). Content analysis of e-mail communication between primary care providers and parents. *Pediatrics*, 18, 1283-1288.

[27] Virji, A., Yarnall, K. S., Krause, K. M., Pollak, K. I., Scannell, M. A., & Gradison, M. (2006). Use of email in family practice setting: Opportunities and challenges in patient- and physician-initiated communication. *British Medical Journal Medical Humanities*, 4, 18.

[28] Couchman et. al. (2005)

[29] Moyer et. al. (2002)

[30] Kleiner, K. D., Akers, R., Burke, B. L., & Werner, E. J. (2002). Parent and physician attitudes regarding electronic communication in pediatric practices. *Pediatrics,* (109), 740-744.

[31] Moyer et. al. (2002)

[32] Gaster, B., Knight, C. L., Dewitt, D. E., Sheffield, J. V., Assefi, N. P., & Buckwald, D. (2003). Physicians' use of and attitudes toward electronic mail for patient communication. *Journal of General Internal Medicine,* 18, 385-389.

[33] Anand et. al. (2005)

[34] Brooks & Menachemi (2006)

[35] Kane & Sands (1998)

[36] Houston, T. K., Sands, D. Z., Nash, B. R., & Ford, D. E. (2003). Experiences of physicians who frequently use e-mail with patients. *Health Communications,* 15(4), 515-525.

[37] Kane & Sands (1998)

[38] Brooks & Menachemi (2006)

[39] Couchman et. al. (2005)

[40] Moyer et. al. (2002)

[41] Houston et. al. (2004)

[42] Houston et. al. (2003)

[43] Katzen et. al. (2005)

[44] As reported by Couchman et. al. (2005) and Moyer et. al. (2002)

[45] Couchman et. al. (2005)

[46] Moyer et. al. (2002)

[47] Houston et. al. (2004)

[48] Houston et. al. (2003)

[49] Katzen et. al. (2005)

[50] Brooks & Menachemi (2006)

[51] Kleiner et. al. (2002)

[52] Houston et. al. (2003)

[53] Delamothe, T., Purcell, G. P., & Wilson, P. (2002). The quality of health information on the Internet: As for any other medium it varies widely. *British Medical Journal*, 324, 557-558.

[54] Gaster et. al. (2003).

Digital Narrative Projects

Volume 13

Dotted Landscape: Berglund Center for Internet Studies Fellowship Review and Analysis Part 1

by Michael Geraci

A Digital Narrative Project

It's difficult to describe my Dotted Landscape project as anything other than a "web site about trash". In fact, when asked about this endeavor by friends and colleagues, there is a consistent, awkward pause, while I try to formulate a response that is worthy of everything that this Web site represents to me without overwhelming them with the entire back story and the thinking that rests below its surface. Before going into the myriad details about what this project really is, I will describe it in its simplest form in hopes that you will continue reading so that you will gain a certain appreciation for the degree to which this project plumbed the strata of my life since its inception.

The project website uses a display based on Google Maps as its primary interface. On this series of maps, I have plotted the location of actual garbage that I found along the roadsides of rural Washington County, Oregon — the county in which I have lived and worked since 1991. I set out to document the litter during the fall of 2011 over the course of ten bike rides, performed alone, that skirted the Western edges of the county. The rides covered 175 miles of public roadways. I snapped nearly 140 images of unique garbage lying in plain site and on public land with the aid of a GPS-enabled digital camera. By "unique" I mean that once a certain type of garbage, say a fast-food drink container, was documented, say a fast-food drink container, further encounters with that type were ignored.

The "unique" rule was not part of my original plan, but a mile or so into my first ride, around the cities of Banks and Roy, I came to the conclusion that documenting every piece of trash encountered during a 10-15 mile bike ride was going to be next to impossible. The amount of litter in our environment is simply overwhelming when you are aware of it. The alcohol containers alone, on the routes that I surveyed, would have numbered in the thousands, and, in my estimation, if spread out along the entire 175 miles travelled, would have punctuated every 300-400 feet of road. The pervasiveness of alcohol containers along roadways was a sobering realization that I was not prepared for. Assuming that they found their way to the roadside from the windows of vehicles, they tell a kind of story that has deeper implications for residents and travellers in rural areas.

With each of the ten bike rides comprising one page (or context) of the Dotted Landscape site, a Google map in "terrain" mode shows the general area of the ride. The garbage encountered on the ride is plotted on the map with custom designed map markers. Clicking one of the markers opens a modified version of the "info window" that users of Google's mapping service are familiar with. Styled with Google's default "word bubble" shape, the pop-up windows provide summary information and a photograph of the actual item as it was found. Eventually a link will be included to a page telling the item's "story." This "back story" concept is central to the idea behind the project. It's not just a site about garbage but a platform for the community to address their garbage and give it some life other than the one it has decomposing along the roadside. I want my fellow citizens to join me, in a virtual way, in making something slightly more interesting out of our detritus and this project is my attempt at enabling that conversation.

Figure 1. A screen shot of a map from http://www.dottedlandscape.org.

I located and implemented some open source tools for modifying the maps' info windows so that I could add a tabbed interface to them and style them in the overall aesthetic of the site, which eschews 'clean' lines and well-positioned elements in favor of the rough-edged and gritty nature of the subject matter I was featuring on the pages. That said, the graphic designer in me could not resist the need to select colors and set type in ways that enhance the experience and give it the slightest feeling of being intentionally crafted. Next to the map window on every page is a menu of all of the items plotted on the map in the order in which they were found during the ride. This is an interface element that affords users an alternate means of browsing the garbage found along that particular route. Clicking any of the listed items triggers the display of its info window in the map interface. This menu's generation and included functionality proved to be one of the project's first sizeable technical challenges for me. This will be addressed in section three of this document when I discuss the technical aspects of the project.

Figure 2. A screen shot of the info windows used on http://www.dottedlandscape.org.

About mid-way through the project's development, I convinced myself that a secondary interface — beyond the maps — would be useful in conveying the diversity in the body of trash documented, so for each route, I implemented a thumbnail gallery view where each item is seen in a tabular layout of small images that, when clicked, opens up a full-sized (800 x 600 pixel) view of the image in a typical "lightbox" effect, where the photo hovers over the dimmed page, thereby making it easier for the user to browse photos. The lightbox effect is a common experience on the Web and has been for a few years. Its use is well-founded in the psychological theory of "flow" made popular by Hungarian psychologist Mihaly Csikszentmihalyi who says that people are best served when they are allowed to fully immerse themselves in what they are doing. [1] It's not likely that Csikszentmihalyi envisioned people flipping through images of litter when he considered the notion of "flow", but as a Web designer, I am always trying to find ways to keep users engaged in the content and experiences featured in my sites.

If the Dotted Landscape project was really a Web site about trash, the above description would serve as an adequate summary of the project's more surface-level qualities, but it's really not as simple as that. In fact, it's actually quite complex and requires far more historical, psychological, and technical context to understand how this site about trash is really a reflection of a single person's experiences as a resident, cyclist, educator, and storyteller in Oregon's second most populous county. [2]

What Dotted Landscape is to me

Dotted Landscape is the confluence of three landscapes—three distinct realities flowing through my life, with their headwaters originating in 2007. As I consider them, these realities are somewhat amorphous and ill-defined in their forms as their offshoots tend to cross and intertwine along certain topics. For the sake of organizing the following segments of this document, I will categorize them as the "professional," "personal," and "technical'" streams of consciousness that came together in the planning and development of this project. The term "personal" here refers to aspects in my life that came into focus, or took on a certain clarity, as a natural result of internal and external changes I experienced in the time leading up to and throughout my work on Dotted Landscape. "Professional" refers to my full-time employment as an associate professor of media arts with specialization in digital media design and development — something I have done since 1999 and have enjoyed immensely despite the challenges inherent in teaching such transient and constantly evolving subject matter. Finally, the "technical" nature of my pursuits here might be seen as the bridge that connects the other two areas — the thread that connects my personal experiences to my professional undertakings. As Douglas Rushkoff wrote in his book of commandments for the digital age, Program or be Programmed, When human beings acquired language, we learned not just how to listen but how to speak. When we gained literacy, we learned not just how to read but how to write. And as we move into an increasingly digital reality, we must learn not just how to use programs but how to make them. [3]

This philosophy resonates in my life and in my teaching; for I believe that to become truly engaged as citizens in this digital world, an ongoing study and comprehension of digital technologies and their application to our lives is a fundamental skill. I appreciate and understand the importance of furthering my own fluency with modern web development tools that I see percolating throughout the Internet and using them in my personal life and in the curricula that I deliver to my undergraduate students in the media arts.

Conclusions: The road ahead

I envisioned Dotted Landscape as a platform for me to engage my local community in a discussion about our relationship to the place we live and its trash. At this point, that platform is poised and ready to start this conversation. My first step at working with the community came in May of 2012. At this time, I made contact with two different schools in Washington County, Fernhill Elementary in Cornelius and the Forest Grove Community School. In both cases, I was allowed to come meet with students to talk about my project and gather their thoughts about litter in their world.

At Fernhill, I visited the kindergarten class of Mrs. Craiglow-Cordes. There was a wonderful moment as I was telling the students about how much I loved the area where we all lived and so I did a project that reflected my feelings about Washington County. I asked them what they thought my project was about. One by one, students called out things like "the trees", "the mountains", and "the wildlife". I replied, "Those are great things to feature in a project. But I decided to do a project on… (pause) litter!" My statement was met by a unanimous "eeew" from the class. I proceeded to hand them printed photos of the garbage I had encountered on my rides and asked them to create stories about how that garbage came to be there. In their stories, I found a common theme: that garbage appears in our environment by mistake. It is as if these young minds can't quite fathom the idea that people toss things out on the road intentionally. Student after student told me about candy wrappers blown out of open car windows on blustery days, and children's toys falling out of their hands during a fall from their bike or scooter.

The experience was much the same with Ms. Reuter's first grade class at Forest Grove's Community School. I met with this class on a sunny day in the school's community garden on Main Street. Students at this school routinely hold class in this garden where they plant flowers and vegetables, and learn about environmental stewardship. I spent an hour here video recording students as they talked to me about why there's litter all around us and how it got there. These students were also reluctant to believe that people leave trash on the sidewalks and roads on purpose, but a few students hinted at the fact that there might be less litter if there were more garbage cans everywhere, therefore making it easier for people to dispose of their unwanted items. As we all left the garden that day, I was happy to witness numerous students stopping to pick up litter on their walk back to the school.

My third step in talking to the community was an interview with Dr. Alyson Burns-Glover in Pacific University's psychology department. Unlike the students, Dr. Burns-Glover relayed to me the psychology behind why people litter, which is related to the idea that it is perceived to be a victimless crime with little or no consequences to the perpetrator. Dr. Burns-Glover went on to talk about how the rural areas of the county are commuter routes to a population that drives to and from urban areas for work and, as such, there is no ownership of the environment by those who pass through it rather than call it their home.

In the future, I hope to connect with members of the local art and science community to get their interpretations of what our garbage says about us and what it means to our environment. I will then create small vignettes of these experiences and interviews and begin the process of adding these community "stories" to the Dotted Landscape site. Once that is underway, I will share the site with as many people and groups as I can to encourage participation in this online experimental narrative.

Looking back on the whole process and all that has gone into it, I extract a lot of pride in what I have accomplished and look forward to the next steps in the project and those that will follow it. I am grateful for the opportunity to create something that has such a personal connection to my life and the place that I call home. I am especially thankful for the support given to me by Pacific University, the Berglund Center for Internet Studies, my student research assistant, Austin Prohl, and my incredible wife, Jennifer Hardacker.

Notes

[1] Czikszentmihalyi, M. (2004). Flow, the secret to happiness. *TED2004.* Lecture conducted in Monterey, CA. [Web Video]. Retrieved from: http://www.ted.com/talks/mihaly_csikszentmihalyi_on_flow.html

[2] List of Counties in Oregon. (n.d.). In *Wikipedia.* Retrieved from: http://en.wikipedia.org/wiki/List_of_counties_in_Oregon

[3] Rushkoff, Douglas (2010). *Program or be Programmed: Ten Commandments for a Digital Age*. New York, New York. OR Books.

Dotted Landscape: Berglund Center for Internet Studies Fellowship Review and Analysis Part 2

by Michael Geraci

Landscape 1: Middle Life on the Roads of Rural Oregon

Two things have been consistent throughout my life: cycling and technology. I received my first bike at the age of five. It was a purple, single-speed affair complete with a banana seat. It took me a year to grow comfortable enough to ride off, a young explorer along the residential streets of Northeast Portland. As years passed, I traded up bikes and eventually transported myself around the city within a 25-mile area of my home. Cycling was not just an expression of youthful freedom, but the gateway to employment and a social life. Even after learning to drive and gaining access to a car, I rode bikes. Typically accompanied by a small pack of friends, I rode as a means of recreation, exercise, and exploration in the city and its surrounding areas. It was commonplace to head out on a Saturday morning and ride 10-12 miles to fishing holes along the Columbia River, or to the peaks of Portland's Rocky Butte and Mount Tabor Park. Pedaling a bike wasn't just something I did, it was a part of me, both as I was then and as I am today.

I got my first computer at the age of 15. It was a Commodore 64, which I connected to a 13" black and white television. I began teaching myself the Basic programming language, mainly for the purpose of creating simple text-based adventure games. Working on the computer connected with some visceral part of my brain. Even within the limited confines of the Commodore's operating system and programming language, the simple logic structures and modularized functionality just made sense at a fundamental level. Never quite a stereotypical "computer geek," I relished the computer's ability to create new expressions of creativity and storytelling.

My affinity for technology grew in college where I learned to use the earliest models of the Macintosh computer, with its novel, graphical user interface and mouse. In the years following my undergraduate college experience, I launched a career creating educational multimedia titles using Apple's innovative HyperCard application. I was at the right place at the right time as computers became the center of media convergence. First I watched the widespread adoption of the CD-ROM for media storage and distribution and then the arrival of the Internet and World Wide Web as a platform for sharing information in an increasingly rich and engaging format. In 1995, I began creating websites with a text editor and the earliest versions of Photoshop, Adobe's flagship software.

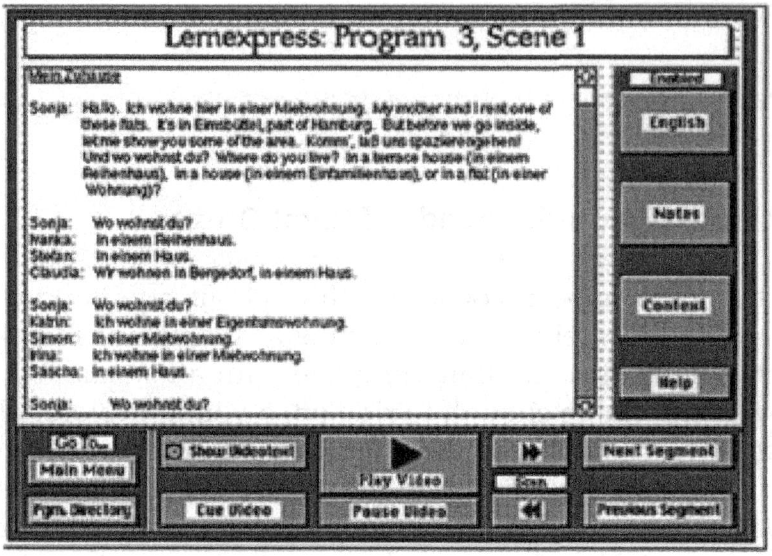

Figure 3. A screen shot from Lernexpress, an early project created by the author in HyperCard.

While my use of computers and technology continued to grow, I found myself living in Western Washington County, raising a family, and always cycling. As middle age approached, I took to my bike in the early morning hours as a form of exercise and meditation. Riding alone or with a friend, the sunrise ritual of pedaling along the roads of the county that bisected farms and logging communities, I began to understand, and appreciate, how much this place meant to me. While I never really sought the opportunity to leave the Pacific Northwest, it became very clear to me as I pedaled over the years that I probably could not bear to ever leave this truly amazing part of the country.

Juxtaposed with my growing acknowledgement of place as a fundamental part of who I am, was the omnipresent garbage. The roadways that were becoming the passages of my life were dotted with the refuse of others, cast out of car windows and left to decompose, however slowly, in the natural environment. I remember asking myself over and over during my rides "how do we live in such a beautiful place yet treat it so poorly?" Thus a seed was planted. I had found a subject for some future endeavor that would allow me to craft my own response and reconciliation for the conflict I witnessed along those miles of pavement.

In 2009, a budding relationship with an accomplished experimental filmmaker opened my eyes to experimental film as a new genre in art and expression. It was a new way to see the world and build a narrative around it with the layered complexity of poetry, image, sound, and personal reflection. I gained an appreciation and affection for the many non-traditional ways we have to share our experiences and bring to life the things that occupy our minds and souls. I didn't want to explore a new form of filmmaking, I wanted to see how the Web, now just a teenager, could become more than a platform for news and information. I wanted to delve into the ways that the Web could become the next platform for experimental storytelling and the conveyance of all aspects of our collective experiences as humans in an interconnected world.

My early inquiries in this realm turned up an interesting site hosted by Penguin Books in the United Kingdom. The We Tell Stories project sought to re-envision and re-tell the stories of six classic texts in a format that leveraged modern day technologies as more than just a vessel to hold the story but as a way to tell the story. The six stories on the site are told in ways that are unique to our digital lives. For example, the Charles Dickens classic, *Hard Times* [1] is told through infographics, a type of data visualization that has been around for hundreds of years, but has experienced a renaissance on the Web since 2008. Then, there is *Slice* [2] an adaptation of M. R. James' *The Haunted Dolls' House* told through a series of blog posts and tweets posted to the Web in 2008 by the story's characters. The one story that captured my attention and contributed to this germinating idea of mine was *The 21 Steps*, an adaptation of John Buchan's *The 39 Steps*, by Charles Cummings. [3] This story about an innocent bystander being swallowed up in an international mystery is told as a connected series of renderings and animations played out on a live Google Map of the United Kingdom and surrounding environs. With each segment of the story the viewer watches as the map changes position, zooms in and out of locations and plots the movement of the protagonist as his adventure unfolds (Note: recent changes to Google's mapping technology has rendered some or all of this story unusable. Such is the impact of change on the Web — a reality I am all too familiar with). All this was made possible through the growing availability of open source technologies on the Internet such as Google's powerhouse mapping platform. The 21 Steps represented how place — the setting for our stories — can be represented online and used as the digital text in today's modern form of storytelling.

Experiencing The 21 Steps was just the start of my Dotted Landscape project. It was not until I saw The Wilderness Downtown [4], a Web-based music video experience based on the Arcade Fire song We Used to Wait and a vision for how the modern Web could be transformed into a truly dynamic and personal storytelling platform. In The Wilderness Downtown, the user is asked to enter the address of his or her childhood home. What happens after that is a mesmerizing combination of filmmaking, animation, and programming played out in a geographical context that makes our own personal history the location of this compelling and inspirational story. I am not being hyperbolic when I say that this site changed my life and my understanding of what the Web represented as a platform for all of humanity to share its stories. It was the dawn of a new era in my personal life.

Landscape 2: A media educator shifts gears

In 1999, I started my career as an educator, teaching undergraduate courses in multimedia design, website development, and digital media production. This was still early on in the development of Internet technologies, so much of the curriculum I taught centered upon the creation of static Web-based presentations of content connected via traditional hyperlinked navigational systems. It was not until Macromedia (now Adobe) Flash started to find its way into mainstream websites that I was awakened to the idea that this platform was just getting started. I had not yet begun to appreciate what was possible with the technology I was teaching to students while feverishly attempting to stay current in my own knowledge and abilities.

Flash is a commercial application that quickly grew into a one-stop shop for interactivity, animation, and rich media experiences on the Web. I found myself pouring over books and online tutorials for hours before going into classes where I was educating students in the use of Flash. The curriculum focused on the creation and implementation of digital assets in Flash's timeline based user interface and ActionScript programming language. The Shockwave-Flash browser plug-in gave all Web surfers the capability to explore the rich environments that could be built in this format. In fact, the Shockwave-Flash plug-in found its way into the vast majority of all Web browsers and Internet connected devices and continues to be a viable technology for rich Internet applications (RIAs). [5] Flash provided a much-needed platform of development in many of my classes. I used it to teach animation, programming and website development for the first ten years of my career as a multimedia educator.

By 2009, Flash began to slowly fall out of favor as THE platform for rich media development. Technical advances on the Web and in modern browsers like Google Chrome and Mozilla Firefox combined with a growing lack of support for Flash content by major players like Apple and Google pointed to a new future of Web development. It would be based upon freely available technologies like the now mature and robust JavaScript programming language and its myriad code libraries that enhance functionality such as jQuery [6] and Prototype [7]. In 2010, Steve Jobs himself released an open letter on Apple's website saying it was time to move beyond Flash. [8] My world as an educator was changing before my eyes. My students were keenly aware that learning

Flash was not the best use of their time, and they were right.

Figure 4. A photo of some of the many books on Flash that are no longer relevant.

With nowhere to go but forward, in 2011 I shelved my dozens of Flash texts and started exploring the depths of a new toolset that would find its way into most of my classes. My gradual command of technologies, from HyperCard and HTML in the 1990's on through Flash in the 2000's, always came through the creation of my own projects. The act of imagining an end product and actualizing it via trial and error with a set of tools and techniques is by far the best way for me to learn the finer points of media design and development.

In the spring of 2011 I made the decision to create the project that would use the new technologies I had started learning to make my personal reflections about life in Washington County and all of its litter the centerpiece of a scholarly investigation of the Web as a storytelling platform. This was the true genesis of Dotted Landscape and the start of a new chapter in my life as a media creator and educator.

The Berglund Center for Internet Studies at Pacific University put out its call for faculty fellowship proposals, and I jumped at the opportunity to gain some level of support for my new undertaking. My proposal [9] outlining the ideas and the motivation for the project was accepted. Beyond benefiting from the general support of the center, the fellowship allowed me to receive a course release during the fall semester of 2011, essentially freeing up 8-9 hours per week for the 14-week term. Rather than walking into my Tuesday/Thursday course on intermediate Web design, I was riding along the rural roads of Washington County with my Canon Powershot SX230HS point-and-shoot camera snapping images of trash. Data collection had begun. After each ride I would return to my home and download the 20-30 images into Apple's iPhoto application, where I weeded out duplicates, made simple edits, and labeled each photo in such a way that it could be easily integrated into the larger project that had yet to take shape.

The Powershot camera uses global positioning technology to embed geographical data into each photo, including its longitude, latitude and altitude. iPhoto has a "locations" feature that taps into Google's mapping technology and plots the geographical position of photos. Seeing my images appear on iPhoto's map-based user interface was proof that I could eventually build my own system for displaying the trash images on a Google map. After the ten rides were complete and the 133 documented items were ready for production, I immersed myself in the world of Google Maps and JavaScript programming.

As I write this, I am halfway through my first class in Web programming that relies entirely on JavaScript and its associated code libraries. The class moves much slower than its Flash/ActionScript predecessors, but it's clear to me and the students that the skills gained will serve them for well for many years. When a new language or technology does come along to supplant JavaScript, as is more than likely, I feel confident that the students will be more adaptable because of having worked within an open source environment directly in the browser.

Also at this moment, Dotted Landscape is online, but is not quite complete. The bedrock coding is done, the user interface is designed and built on HTML 5 and CSS 3, and the mapping functionality is solid. What remains is the final collection of content that will serve as the first few "stories" or "histories" for selected pieces of garbage. When I set out on this project, I knew that I would not be the primary creator of the trash stories. My hope was, and still is, to engage members of the community to "adopt" a piece of trash and submit to me a piece of content that gives the selected item life and, in doing so, make it just a little more beautiful. I look forward to the day that I can share the site without hesitation. In the meantime I am already benefitting from the knowledge gained in the project's design and implementation.

Notes

[1] See: http://www.wetellstories.co.uk/stories/week5/#cover

[2] See: http://www.wetellstories.co.uk/stories/week2/

[3] See: http://www.wetellstories.co.uk/stories/week1/

[4] See: http://thewildernessdowntown.com

[5] See: http://www.adobe.com/products/flashruntimes/statistics.html

[6] See: http://jquery.com

[7] See: http://prototypejs.org

[8] See: http://www.apple.com/hotnews/thoughts-on-flash

[9] See: http://www.dottedlandscape.org/pdf/geraci_fellowship_proposal.pdf

Dotted Landscape: Berglund Center for Internet Studies Fellowship Review and Analysis Part 3

by Michael Geraci

The Technology Behind the Journey

There are a number of online tools and technologies that were combined in the making of the Dotted Landscape project. The planning of the rides themselves relied on a Web service known as Map My Ride. [1] Map My Ride allows cyclists to create and search for cycling routes all over the world. The site provides a wealth of information about cycling routes and produces printable guides. Relying on an innovative modification to Google's mapping system, riders can plot routes based on location, distance, terrain type, and difficulty. I used Map My Ride to create the ten routes that I would cover on my bike for the purposes of this project. You can go to Map My Ride and search on "Dotted Landscape" or "Michael Geraci" to find my

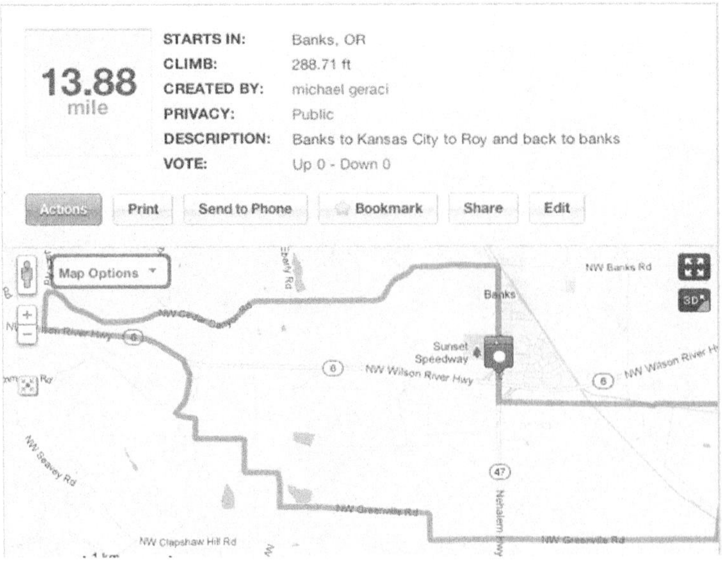

collection.

Figure 5. A screen shot of a cycling route on Map My Ride.

Map My Ride was just the beginning of the useful tools I came to use and appreciate in the making of this project. Another tool that I did not intend to use, but found invaluable, was an online conversion tool for the geographical data produced by my camera. When I started implementing my own mapping system to plot the location of the trash I learned, much to my chagrin, that Google's system relied on the WGS 84 format, which expresses geographical location in decimal format (e.g., 45.50983, -122.991 [1] for latitude and longitude, respectively). My camera, along with many other GPS devices, records location in the more conventional degrees, minutes, and seconds (e.g., 45,30.59N, 122,59.46W). This difference required that every geo-location that I had recorded had to be converted to Google's standard. Luckily, I was able to find numerous online sources for the conversion of this information. I employed a student research assistant to help me in running the conversions, which had to be done one at a time. We used two sites for this task: Computer Support Group, Inc.'s "GPS Latitude and Longitude Converter" [2] and iTouchMap.com's "Latitude and Longitude of a Point" service. [3]

With the data in the correct format, I set about learning how to embed Google maps on a Web page, set their initial view properties, and plot locations within them. The inclusion of Google maps on a site or page is a fairly common and well-documented practice in Web development, but the placement of multiple markers with embedded information that would be included in the markers' info windows necessitated my first in-depth study of JavaScript programming. I had used JavaScript in small amounts throughout my tenure as a Web developer, but this usage was for fairly common practices such as building rollover effects for buttons, and drop-down menus for site navigation. This new endeavor required that I learn to create code "objects" for each marker that contained all of the data used to create the map points for each piece of litter. Early versions of this meant writing code like:

```
var r4i1Marker = {title:"object title",id:49,ride:4,date: "September 27, 2011",location:{lat:45.509833,lng:122.991}, thumbnail:"imgs/thumb/r4i1.jpg",full:"imgs/full/r4i1.jpg", caption:"image caption",url:"item49.html"}
```

This format for encapsulating multiple properties for a single object enabled me (via JavaScript) to not only place markers in the interface, but aso for all aspects of their presentation to be self-contained in a single, portable code element that could be accessed by the browser. After successfully generating all the marker data for the first ride in the project, I felt that this system, while technically appropriate, was not the most efficient way to store and access the information about the 133 trash items I would be featuring on the site. Further research was needed to find a more flexible and scalable system of structuring data. The research quickly yielded the use of AJAX, [4] Asynchronous JavaScript and XML, as the way to write a single function that would serve as the technological backbone of the entire project. But a move towards this efficiency meant more study.

AJAX is a common technology that drives many popular Web sites such as Facebook, Netflix, and just about all major Google services like maps, Gmail, and Google Drive. In a nutshell, it is a system of passing data back and forth between the user's browser and the Web server in real time, thereby eliminating the need for constant page loading. AJAX is not a language, but a mode of JavaScript programming that relies on an external data source written in XML, [5] or other standard data structures like JSON. [6]

I was no stranger to XML, as it is a common format for storing information that needs to be accessed by any application or device that can read it. My first use of XML was in the creation of RSS "feed" files that I created in 2006, when I began exploring the world of Podcasting [7] as an earlier bit of professional development as an educator. I set about stripping all of the object notation (as shown above) out of my JavaScript and converting it to standard XML. The object shown above soon became just a fraction of a growing XML library that I wrote for the project using the free text editing application, TextWrangler [8], which looked like this:

```
<item>
<title>Car Front Bumper</title>
<id>49</id>
<ride>4</ride>
<number>1</number>
<marker>r4i1Marker</marker>
<date>September 27, 2011</date>
<location>
<lat>45.509833</lat>
<lng>-122.991</lng>
<road>Hwy 219 South of Hillsboro</road>
</location>
<category>automotive</category>
<info>
<full>imgs/full/r4i1.jpg</full>
<thumb>imgs/thumb/r4i1.jpg</thumb>
<caption>
A silver bumper from the front of a small car
</caption>
</info>
<nar>
<url>item49.html</url>
```

```
<media>imgs/full/xl/r4i1.jpg</media>
</nar>
</item>
```

Storing the information for the site in this format allowed me to abstract my "back end" data from the site's code and access some or all of it by any number of JavaScript functions.

JavaScript is not a new language; it has been around since 1995. One of the main reasons why it has become so popular in recent years is because a coding eco-system has grown up around it that has made it easier to tap into the vast functionality without having to fully master all aspects of the language. The free jQuery code library [9] sits on top of the JavaScript behemoth and lets developers implement large-scale functionality on their websites in a few short lines of code. JQuery's own motto is "write less, do more" and, faced with the task of writing the engine for Dotted Landscape, this was appealing to me. Similar to my previous experiences with XML, I was no stranger to jQuery as it is the tool of choice for creating slick online photo galleries, animations, and other Web 2.0 experiences. However, in all of these cases, jQuery is easily plugged into a webpage and a few simple additions to HTML markup results in browser "magic" that do not necessarily require an in-depth understanding of what was going on behind the scenes. For the first time, I was faced with using jQuery to simplify the creation of custom site behavior that was not just plugged in. Luckily, jQuery is well documented online [10] and there are numerous sources for writing AJAX that drives functionality in Google maps. [11]

After a few weeks, the AJAX functionality was running and now a single jQuery function (all 132 lines and 3300 characters of it) was bringing my ten maps and their associated pieces of trash to life. Enthused by the successful implementation of this system, I decided to expand the site's core functionality to include the dynamic generation of the sidebar menus on the site that listed all the trash for the current ride (see figure 6). Extracting the titles from the XML file and building a listing of them was a simple matter. However, I wanted the user to be able to click an item in the menu and have the corresponding marker in the map interface open its info window. This small feat required learning how events (like mouse clicks) in one part of the page could be passed from one object to another. This is made slightly more complex by the fact that the map's functionality is being driven by Google's back end programming interface and my menu was driven by its own code library. Adding to this complexity was the fact that everything in the site was now being generated dynamically in code and nothing had a hard-coded existence that would make this a simple task. The solution came down to about ten lines of code that were the result of about four weeks of research and trial and error. It may seem like an exorbitant amount of time to invest in such a simple piece of functionality, but I was pleased by the idea that the site had the potential to scale infinitely. In effect, I could add 10, 100, or 1000 more pages of routes (or pieces of trash) to the site and everything would continue to work without any changes to the underlying technology.

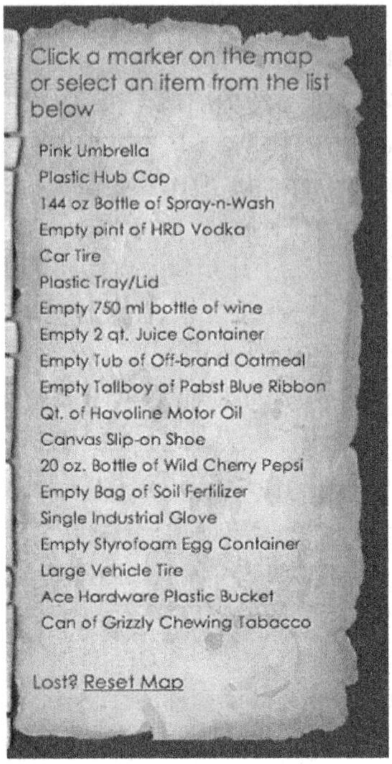

Figure 6. A screen shot of the sidebar menu from www.dottedlandscape.org.

Seeing the code behind the site work so well motivated me to think about a new addition to the site: the thumbnail view of the trash for each route sans the map interface. My students would be the first to accuse me of the sin of adding to my project's scope so late in its development — something I heavily discourage in my upper division courses — and they would be right in this critique. However, I was so encouraged by the technical developments of the project that I had to take my newfound abilities out for a spin in the name of adding a new angle to the display of the garbage. After all, the mapping functionality was the hard part. Adding a thumbnail gallery to the site would be easier to implement and, for the most part, it was.

I began building the thumbnail gallery interface by duplicating all of the site's current files and building a parallel set that simply had no maps in the main content element (an HTML 5 <article> element, in case you're wondering). I then made a copy of the JavaScript/jQuery engine that rendered the maps, markers, and sidebar menu and rewrote it to populate the now empty map area with the thumbnails of all the images that were used in the info windows. This is a good example of how moving to the XML format allowed all the 'guts' of the site to be used in different ways with no alterations or additions to the pool of data.

Once the thumbnails were appearing, I took things one step further and added a "lightbox" effect that allows the user to call up an enlargement of the image in an overlay that floats above the page. There are dozens of code libraries that allow for this effect. However, my jQuery research led me to another add-on: the free Overlay library from jquerytools.org. [12] This particular bit of code has some nice options for styling the presentation of the overlays, including animated fade-ins, drop shadows, and embedded captions. The only downside is that all the assets for the overlay, including the enlarged images, get loaded with the page rather than when requested by the user, so the download time of the thumbnail galleries is noticeably longer than it is for the maps. The last hurdle was adapting the overlay code to the thumbnails that (like the sidebar menu) were generated dynamically in code rather than written right into the HTML, which would have been simple. Since my code engine was writing the HTML on the fly, it just took a few extra lines to embed the overlay functionality into each thumbnail. All in all, this little bit of scope creep took less than four hours to implement and, most importantly, will scale with the rest of the site if ever there is a need to add or subtract any amount of content.

In addition to the overlay plug-in, I chose to pursue another pre-built add-on for my project. The free jQuery library infobubble.js [13] can be added to a site with a Google map and lets you create highly customized info windows that can include a tabbed interface so they contain any number of extra bits of information that is easy to navigate. I used this feature to include a larger photo of each piece of trash inside of the small bit of real estate available in the pop up info window.

Figure 7. A screen shot of the tabbed info windows and custom map marker used on www.dottedlandscape.com.

Beyond the customized info windows, I also decided to create my own map markers to replace Google's default red "pin" markers. My intent was to enhance the overall quality of the site's presentation while learning even more about what was possible with Google's mapping tools. I found an online guide to creating custom markers [14] and learned how to create the markers and their separate semi-transparent shadows in a graphics editor like Photoshop. Adding these two images to the site and appending the required lines of code to the site's main code engine was a relatively simple procedure that delivered the results I was looking for.

When I set out to do this project, I knew that the technological aspects would challenge and introduce me to a new set of tools that I would have ample use for in my personal and professional pursuits. The combined use of Google's mapping programming interface, JavaScript, jQuery, and all the code libraries that complement and enhance the possibilities was indeed a valuable experience that I will continue to learn and use well into the future. With a small amount of development yet to go in the completion of the project, I anticipate even more technical challenges that I look forward to tackling.

Notes

[1] See: http://www.mapmyride.com

[2] See: http://www.csgnetwork.com/gpscoordconv.html

[3] See: http://www.itouchmap.com/latlong.html

[4] Ajax (programming). (n.d.). In *Wikipedia.* Retrieved from http://en.wikipedia.org/wiki/Ajax_(programming)

[5] XML. (n.d.). In *Wikipedia.* Retrieved from http://en.wikipedia.org/wiki/XML

[6] JSON. (n.d.). In *Wikipedia.* Retrieved from http://en.wikipedia.org/wiki/JSON

[7] Podcasting. (n.d.). In *Wikipedia.* Retrieved from http://en.wikipedia.org/wiki/Podcasting

[8] See: http://www.barebones.com/products/textwrangler

[9] See: http://jquery.com

[10] See: http://docs.jquery.com

[11] See: http://code.google.com/edu/ajax/tutorials/ajax-tutorial.html

[12] See: http://jquerytools.org/demos/overlay

[13] See: http://google-maps-utility-library-v3.googlecode.com/svn/trunk/infobubble
[14] See: www.x2tutorials.com

From Where I Came: How Digital Narratives About Place Can Illuminate Everything

by Linda Hunt, Ph.D., FAOTA, OTR/L
School of Occupational Therapy, Pacific University

Back Story

Twelve years ago I read *Everything is Illuminated* by Jonathan Safran Foer. [1] It is the account of one man's experience in his destroyed ancestral homeland. The homeland is a village called Trochenbrod (Trachimbrod in the book) in what is now western Ukaine. Reading this book about visiting one's ancestral country and village fascinated me, especially, since my dad's family came from a similar area in Lithuania. I remember my dad telling me that the film set of Fiddler on the Roof looked just like his village where he grew up. When my dad passed away in 1995, my mother gave me all his legal papers including a passport, birth certificate and my grandparents' wedding certificate. The village listed on all documents was Malot. This launched my search for trying to find Malot on a map. I had a yearning to visit this place, because, for me, it would be magical in some way.

Through many Internet searches, I learned the village called Malot had a name change. It was now Moletai. My dad told me Malot was in Russia, however, it was actually in Lithuania. He thought it was in Russia because Lithuania was ruled by Russia and people around him spoke Russian. So now, I had the place on a map. Then the pieces came together even more. I was invited to speak at a conference in Vilnius, Lithuania, about 40 south of my dad's birthplace. I planned my journey to see this village finally, not knowing if anything still resembled the place as it was in 1917--when my dad left.

Upon returning to the United States, I was so moved by my visit to Moletai that I could not stop talking about it. I, therefore, created a website, (http://fromwhereicame.wordpress.com) [2] and posted my account of the journey. Here begins the project called the Heritage Project.

Before I show you the website posting, I want you to see a model of the original town center that was destroyed by Germany during WWII. The town center has been rebuilt to resemble the original buildings. The second picture shows my family (husband and daughter) in front of a building in the new replicated town center.

Figure 1. A model of the town as it was before WWII.

Figure 2. Hunt's wife and daughter in front of the Moletai town center.

Figure 3. Molat in the early 1900s showing the dense population and a thriving town.

Here is my story posted on the website:

For the first 60 years of my life, I believed that I had Russian heritage. That's what my dad told me. He had always said that his family left Russia to escape persecution. After he died, I came across his passport and learned that he was actually born in Molat, which isn't actually in Russia. It's in Lithuania. Upon this realization I was a little disappointed, as I loved Tolstoy, vodka, Doctor Zhivago, *and beautiful coats. I didn't know what Lithuania was famous for — I didn't even know where exactly it was.*

Once I started exploring it, I was intrigued with the romance of Lithuania, a country taken over by the Russians (while my dad lived there), Poles, Germans, and Soviets. Lithuanians finally achieved national freedom in the 1990s. I had read the book, Everything is Illuminated *and wanted to go see the place of my family's heritage. The first synagogue was built in 1728. In the 1700s, Jews were invited to Lithuania to help bring prosperity to the country. I do not know how many generations back my family lived in Molat. It is one of those questions I wished I had asked.*

I learned that there were 2397 inhabitants in Molat in 1897, the time my grandparents and great grandparents lived there, and eighty percent (80%) of them were Jews. Now, the Jewish population in the renamed village, Moletai is 10 to 100. Currently, residents are not required to give their religion in the census; therefore it is difficult to know the actual Jewish population. When my dad, born in 1911, lived there, Jews and Lithuanians lived side by side, until the Jews were bullied and killed. Later, those that stayed would be murdered due to Nazi influence. My family left in 1917 to save their own lives.

Figure 4. A restored trade house. Moletai, Lithuania.

When we arrived in Moletai, to our surprise and delight, we saw original, small, wood houses still standing and occupied by current residents. The double doors, shown in the picture, are more typical of Jewish homes. Some houses had traces of holes, with layers of paint over them, on the right side of the doorpost where a mezuzah (a scroll with verses of the Old Testament) may have hung at one time. While we were there, the open market was going strong. There were colorful mums (chrysanthemums) for sale. A big cardboard box, on display, was filled with sunflower seeds and visited by birds, swooning down to gather their lunch. There were challahs and dark rye breads. There were more cardboard boxes filled with onions and potatoes. Women in their 70s and 80s were selling goods. Walking up and down the streets, I wondered where my dad had lived. Was his house still standing? Where was my grandfather's blacksmith business? My dad told me that his village looked like the village portrayed in the film, Fiddler on the Roof. Seeing old photos, in the Moletai museum, of the village in the early 1900s, confirmed that it surely did.

Exploring further, I was surprised to find that the Jewish cemetery was still there, located on a hill, overlooking the village, in it maybe 100 tombstones still stood. The stones that were legible were engraved in Hebrew. Many had a Jewish star at the top. Each stone was made of pink or black granite. There is a movement in Eastern Europe to restore Jewish cemeteries.

Figure 4. Jewish cemetery in the town of Moletai.

The Russians and Nazis destroyed many Jewish cemeteries.The Soviets used the tombstones for bricks to build structures. Many cemeteries that remain do not have the Jewish population present to maintain them. Yet, in Moletai, our guide, Simon believed that this cemetery had been restored because the stones were standing erect and the grass had been somewhat cleared. I had brought 30 polished colored rocks to place on the stones, a Jewish tradition marking one's visit. However, in my excitement to visit my father's birthplace, I left the rocks in my suitcase lying on the floor back at the Congress Hotel.

While in Lithuania, I discovered that the foods I love and bring memories of family and Jewish culture were actually Lithuanian foods: boiled potatoes that were then baked in oil (now I have the recipe), kasha, a type of potato pancakes (they actually served us kasha pancakes, delightful), smoked fish, dark rye bread, sunflower seeds, borscht, poppy seeds, farmer's cheese, and Smetana, a type of sour cream. Borscht served with hardboiled eggs and Smetana, hot or cold. All this reminds me of meals with my dad and the joy of reminiscing the heritage he gave me.

The Moletai countryside is beautiful. My family came from a place of rolling hills, dense, tall forests with birch trees, and many lakes. It is now called "the Land of Lakes." Lots of rain in the fall. Is this why I love to walk in rain? Why I sit out on the porch while it is raining? Winters are harsh with cold temperatures and deep snow. I never thought about my dad as a child living in such severe weather. Now, I do. As a child, I dreamed of living in the North Country, somewhere beautiful such as my current home in Montana. My small town in Montana reminds me of Moletai.

As our guide and driver drove us back to the hotel in Vilnius, I sat in silence thinking about my family's life there. I thought about how my grandmother learned to bake all my favorite goodies in this town. When I was a child, my dad would stop by her apartment every Friday. He brought home her baked challah, cookies with colored candies on top, and kamish bread. I learned that crocheted linens were popular in Lithuania, and it was there my grandmother learned to make all those crocheted handkerchiefs she gave me. I always loved my grandmother. Being in the town, where she was born and grew up, really solidified my heritage. Hopefully, it was a week that my own daughter will reminisce about in the future with her children showing them photos of where her grandfather and great grandparents were born. The lesson is to reminisce now with family. There are so many questions I have and no one has the answers. I do have an answer to why I have Marc Chagall's painting, Fiddler, *in my home.*

Background Research

The publication of Robert Butler's seminal article in 1963 regarding life review processes launched a desire to understand and elucidate the role of memories in the lives of older adults. [3] Narrative approaches to understanding the human condition are gaining advocates in the social sciences, mental health, and gerontology. Reminiscence is part of this narrative approach and is defined here as: the recall of personally experienced episodes from one's past. Parker [4] proposed promoting a better understanding of reminiscence processes through a framework that included continuity throughout one's life. Missing history in one's life may diminish one's self-identity. Having continuity with one's ancestral history and experiencing a culture through place may help to strengthen identity. Reminiscence, here, is viewed as cognitive activities across the lifespan of self and ancestors, where the proposed project may enhance the mental and emotional health of others. Currently, reminiscence is investigated and/or applied by several disciplines, including occupational therapy, nursing, recreational therapy, social work, education, theology, gerontology, and several divisions of psychology (e.g., developmental, cognitive, personality), to name only a few. [5] Those reading the website postings may also find mental and emotional health by learning about from where their ancestors came, even though they are not able to travel there themselves.

The development of this website may be helpful in establishing reminiscing groups. It appears that group reminiscence leads to a greater frequency and enjoyment of reminiscing and an interest in continuing further peer group activity. [6] The website may be beneficial to share in group therapy and launch insightful conversations about culture. This has merit for exploration by students for group activities serving older adults in Pacific University's Gerontology and Occupational Therapy programs.

Methods

Equipment

Equipment included the iPad. The iPad also provides a camera, which helped take pictures of interviewees'. Apps were downloaded for recording interviews and other media. [7] Photoshop was used for editing pictures of people, places, and artifacts.

Process

Occupational therapy students sought out ethnic minorities to be interviewed or requested that individuals write their story for submission. Occupational therapy students distributed surveys via e-mail or in person to willing participants within two weeks of interviews or written submissions to the From Where I Came website. IRB was not sought. Agreeing to complete the survey sufficed for participant approval. Four surveys were distributed and all six participants returned each of the surveys with every question answered. Each survey consisted of six questions on a five-point Likert scale that highlighted topics of social connectedness, cultural discovery, and personal identity related to each participant's experience of submitting their story or being an interviewee. Three open-ended questions were included at the end of the survey to capture participant thoughts and suggestions intended for further research.

Results

Six individuals posted their story of going back to an ancestral place. Two were interviewed by the students, who then transcribed the interviews and posted them on the website, with photos provided. The other interviews were turned into stories, as readers seemed to prefer this format better. The quantitative data results showed that sharing an ancestral story was an 87.5% positive experience for the four participants as 21/24 questions were marked "agree" or "highly agree" (see Table 1). Among the responses received from the three open-ended questions, individuals wrote:

1. Question regarding sharing a visit to their ancestral home:

"It made me really think about the thread of where I came from and how that impacts who I am today."

"Makes me more grateful for my ancestors and want to learn more about them and I appreciate them."

"Understanding one's roots helps one understand one self."

"I realized it was nice being able to say out loud what I think and feel about my family, heritage, and just overall culture."

2. Question regarding participating in this project:

"...Has also made me realize that I want to know more about my family's experiences growing up and persevering in communism."

3. Question regarding the interviewing process:

"Maybe have topics ready such as food, transportation, family, landscape, etc. ready because it helps spark observations one had or reflections that don't necessary come up with an open ended question."

"I think having interview questions that were answered and then put in a summary would make more sense than the tedious task of writing out every word that I said during the interview."

Conclusion

In a time when technology is deeply integrated in society, the Internet age may lead to depersonalization, if life stories are not shared. From Where I Came was created to allow people to share experiences of heritage, traditions, and culture, through the medium of a virtual environment. Those reading the website postings may find mental and emotional health by learning about from where their ancestors came, even though they are not able to travel there themselves.

Telling and retelling of significant events often times occurs through the context of social interactions. Sharing self-narratives with peer groups, family, and friends influences one's identity and provides meaning to one's life. Children who know their heritage have a stronger sense of control and an increased self-esteem. [8]

The Occupational Therapy Practice Framework: Domain and Process (OTPF) [9] provides a summary of occupational therapy practice guidelines describing the profession. Specifically, it relates to practitioners, students, educators, researchers, payers, and consumers. Included in the OTPF are domains related to cultural, social, and virtual environments. Leisure participation, leisure exploration, and social participation also contribute to the goal of promoting occupational health and wellbeing and are outlined in the OTPF.

While all individuals may submit stories, this website encourages ethnic minorities to post, as these groups may have fewer opportunities for finding others who relate to their story. Future research will examine how various ethnic groups relate stories; how much information is disclosed; and identify common themes.

Table 1: Survey Results from post-interview/submissions for "From Where I Came" Project (results posted April 2014)

	Highly Disagree	Disagree	Neutral	Agree	Highly Agree
I enjoyed sharing my personal experiences with people.			1		3
I enjoy hearing about other people's personal experiences related their heritage and/or ancestry.				1	3
In the past I have had the chance to talk to family members, friends, or acquaintances about my 'ancestral home.'				4	
Visiting my 'ancestral home' made me think deeper about my own identity.					4
Getting the chance to read other people's stories of visiting their ancestral home is of interest to me.				2	2
Doing this interview has encouraged me to find out more about my own cultural heritage.		1	1		2

Notes

[1] Safran Foer, J. (2002). *Everything is illuminated*. Harper Perennial: New York, NY.

[2] From Where I Came. (n.d.) Retrieved from http://fromwhereicame.wordpress.com

[3] Butler, R. N. (1963). The life-review: An interpretation of reminiscence in the aged. *Psychiatry* 26, 65-76.

[4] Parker, R. G. (1995). Reminiscence: A Continuity Theory Framework. *The Gerontologist*, 35, 4, 515-525.

[5] Webster, J. D., Bohlmeijer, E. T., & Westerhof, G. J. (2010). Mapping the future of reminiscence: A conceptual guide for research and practice. *Research on Aging*, 32, 527-564.

[6] Sherman, R. (1987). Reminiscence groups for community elderly. *The Gerontologist,* 27(5) 569-572.

[7] The app used was MicPro. Retrieved from https://itunes.apple.com/us/app/microphone-+-recording-pro/id475687238?mt=8

[8] Birren, J. E., & Svensson, C. (2013). Reminiscence, life review, and autobiography: Emergence of a new era. *The International Journal of Reminiscence and Life Reivew,* 1(1), 1-6.

[9] American Occupational Therapy Association (2008). Occupational Therapy Practice Framework: Domain & Process (2nd ed.). *American Journal of Occupational Therapy,* 62(6), 625-683.

SOCIAL SCIENCE

Volume 13

Pornography, Space, and the Internet: The Politics of the Seattle Public Library System as Documented by Readers of Vice Magazine

by Matthew Yasuoka
Student Fellow, The Berglund Center for Internet Studies

The Change.org petition entitled, "Seattle Public Library: Stop allowing pornography to be watched on public library computers," claims that it stands "for everyone who does not want to participate in viewing the disenfranchisement of others." [1] The petition represents only a recent development in the Seattle Public Library's ongoing interactions with pornography. In 2012, "A Seattle librarian refused to force a man watching hardcore porn on a computer to move to a more discreet location, even after a woman with two children complained." [2] This was even after in 2010 the Washington Supreme Court in a six to three decision held that the library can block porn if it chooses. [3]

However, the Seattle Public Library has chosen not to block porn, much to the chagrin of certain patrons. Earlier this year, Julie Vanderburg asked a man at the Beacon Hill Library to stop watching porn, which led the librarians to ask her to "stop approaching patrons." [4] The conflict facing the Seattle Public Library system stems from the divergent perceptions of what role libraries play in society. Todd Anten writes in the Texas Journal on Civil Liberties and Rights, "While some view libraries as public spaces with a duty to be 'family-friendly,' others view libraries as research centers obligated to provide constitutionally protected information." [5] The conflict between public and private spaces lies at the core of the Internet.

In this article, I intend to analyze the interactions of individuals in the comments section of Vice magazine. I have chosen to study Vice because the magazine is both a part of "counterculture" and "'trendsetting metropolitans," resulting in its position as "the number-one tastemaker" for the 21- to 34-year-old demographic. [6] Further, the Alexa Rankings, a leading monitor of web traffic, shows that "people who went to college are over-represented" in Vice's readership, there is also an overrepresentation of males and an underrepresentation of females. [7] With Vice's readership in mind, I had a few research questions. First, does the readership of Vice support bourgeois views of sexuality? Second, how do its readers interact with distinctions of class? Third, what does Vice reveal about the relationship between the Internet and special politics?

Literature Review

The core of my interest lies in understanding how individuals interpret specific media artifacts and events. Mass self-communication "is self-generated in content, self-directed in emission, and self-selected in reception by many that communicate with many." [8] I think that comments on news articles serve as a perfect example of this discursive tool, as they are self-sorted, and since media consumption choices are based on individual beliefs [9] and are entirely self-directed. Comments provide immediate responses to a specific cultural artifact in an organic manner that allows for the documentation of interactions between different cultural paradigms.

Public and private spaces form the basis of social interaction. As Zizek notes that "every order of explicit normativeness has to rely on a complex network of informal rules which tells us how we are to relate to explicit norms" including how, when, and to what extent we apply them. [10] Thus, sometimes "the explicit 'no' effectively functions as the implicit injunction to get on with it, but in a discreet way." [11] In effect, society is built off of considerations regarding time, place, and manner, or spacialization. Dr. Jeff Cain asserts that "the Web is now less of a place for information to be provided, searched for, and digested, and more of a dynamic participant within our social landscape." [12] His words allude to the tension at the heart of the Internet, which lies in its function as a social space. Dr. Jim Porter explains, "the Internet is at the same time a public square, a public library, a television, a shopping mall, a newspaper, a movie theater, a game device, a virtual world, a communication medium, etc." [13] This confounds societal norms because the constructed zones of exception collapse online.

At the same time, the Internet plays a critical role in class distinctions. The Pew Research Center found in a September 2013 study that of the fifteen percent of Americans that do not have Internet access nearly twenty percent of Americans cite "the expense of owning a computer or paying for an internet connection" as the reason they cannot connect. At the same time, nine-percent of Americans that use the Internet lack home access. [14] As Vice magazine keenly observes, "Just because you're reading this on your iPad or whatever doesn't change the fact that not everyone has a computer. . . many of the library's patrons don't have access to personal computers, or have had to give up Internet service because of financial challenges." [15]

The advent of the Internet and the class divides it accentuates relate directly back to sexuality. Laura Kipnis traces the interaction between class and sexuality in order to develop a "low-theory" of sexuality. She analyzes Hustler magazine and acknowledges, "control over the body has long been associated with the bourgeois political project," but this in fact allows it to become a discursive tool for the lower class. As Kipnis concludes, "the body is a privileged political trope of the lower social classes. . . through which bodily grossness operates as a critique of dominant ideology." [16] The discourse of the body is one that strips away the manners and tact demanded by middle class life.

Middle class life is dominated by the optic and the aesthetic. As Kipnis put it, "the bourgeois. . . want to remove the distasteful from the sight of society." [17] This visual politic serves to allow for the stabilization and domination of competing worlds. Goldberg-Hiller summarizes it simply, "what makes law legitimate are the frameworks of temporiality, spatiality, speech, and silence that synthetically make law appear enduring, monolithic, and just." [18] Thus, appearances lie at the core of the bourgeois society. The frameworks that Goldberg-Hiller point out often define specific and legitimate contexts for actions. Bakhtin traces the nature of laughter and its various forms observing, "early Christianity. . . condemned laughter. . . this intolerant seriousess. . . made it necessary to legalize the gaiety. . . During the Easter season Laughter and jokes were permitted even in church." [19] He contrasts this sort of specifically sanctioned laughter under the feast with the laughter of the carnival, which existed in a "completely different, non-official, extraecclesiastical and extrapolitical" sense. [20]

Therefore, there is a difference between the sanctioned private, unseen viewership of pornography and viewership that takes place as a spectacle in public. Much in the same way, discourses of the body differ in their message and potential for counterhegemonic existence depending on whether or not they abide by bourgeois control of the body.

Methodology

In this study, I am going to analyze comments on a news article from Vice magazine, [21] responding to the Seattle Public Library's continued efforts to support access to pornography on library computers. I am going to do a content analysis of the various comments in order to understand the ways in which individuals framed their response to the story. I coded for three different themes that I saw in pilot readings of the comments. (1) class; (2) space; and (3) gender. I also coded for two frames: (1) the violation of rights; and (2) the save the children frame, which I coded any time a commenter argued that it was a matter of protecting children. I use a good deal of qualitative analysis to interpret commenters' arguments relating to the library policy, along with the broader social implications of such arguments.

Results

Of the 53 comments 19 were not related to the topic of discussion. Of those, seven were off-topic political statements of the "Liberalism is a mental disorder" variety. Six were about minor details of the story itself. The last six were one word or completely off topic. Of the remaining 34 comments, 16 framed the issue as one of space, 16 focused on the gender aspects, seven employed the save the children frame, four discussed class.

Analysis

Spacialization

Spacialization remains a central part of the middle-class, bourgeois social structure. The location where an act takes place becomes more important than the act itself. This obsession with space lies at the core of many commenters concerns. One commenter suggests a solution to allow individuals to watch porn in the library, without exposing children,

> *What if they had a separate, closed off area for computers? Like one that didn't block anything, and then the ones out in the open blocked porn and other graphic things? Idk, I'm pretty anti-censorship, but I wouldn't want children to be exposed to that sort of thing.*

The subdivision of spaces plays a central role in the modern capitalistic existence. In the same way that specified spaces are created for work and home and play. This in turn leads to the specialization of spaces for specific activities. The department store represents the best visual signifier of this spacialization, with its specific organization and compartmentalization of domestic life for easy consumption. And when I enter a department store I know that I am not allowed to play golf in it or watch porn. The delineation of activities into sanctioned spaces is conveyed by one commenter, who observes,

> *It's okay to look at porn in a place where little kids are running all*

around but you can't smoke in a bar where there is only adults who are all consenting to be there. Fucked.

The commenter compares the act of smoking—a social taboo—to viewing porn—another social taboo—the commenter analyzes the contextual nature of the actions and compares their perceived legitimacy. The commenter then rejects the notion that viewing porn in a library fits with social mores more than smoking in a bar. The discussion of legitimacy in regards to time, place, and manner of an action is central to the notion of capitalism. To do an activity outside of its sanctioned space is considered lacking in manners. One commenter calls the viewing of pornography in a library, "just plain rude behavior." The message is clear: the particular place an act takes place in determines its appropriateness.

The Internet undermines the territorialized spaces of society, by allowing a different space to transpose itself into the carefully organized sphere of conventions. It brings the pornographic crashing into the forefront of the public life. Sex and by extension pornography are both facts of life and yet it is considered tactless to discuss them in public, or for children to glimpse them or discover their existence. However, the Internet allows for two different spaces to exist in the same geographic location. The individual at the computer can view anything they desire, creating their own private space. In a public location this creates a clash between the codified manners of the bourgeois expectations of the place and the individual's constructed space. One commenter arguing in favor of porn in libraries states,

*Yes, because clearly we'd all be *much* better off with your "world view" or that of the US Supremes. Your "SafeLibraries" program reads like just another Gladys Kravitz "social watchdog" program pimped by the conservatives to micromanage the adult lives of US citizens. Let's make a deal: you don't define for me what's appropriate for me, and I won't define for you what's appropriate for you; we'll both make adult decisions to be responsible for our own business, and will mind it thusly.*

In response to him, other commenters emphasize the inappropriateness of the space. One person states:

But I think refusing to tell some dude watching hardcore porn in a public library to knock it off because it might threaten his right to be a creepy motherfucker, is where you officially hit the point of absurdity. Thinking that people should watch porn in places that aren't full of

kid [doesn't equal] being a conservative who wants to "micromanage the adult lives of US citizens."

Thus, it is clear that space is a central issue for the readers of Vice magazine who reaffirm bourgeois notions of spacialization advocating for the continued demarcation of areas for legitimate action. The Internet challenges the appropriate through its ability to challenge territorialized boundaries.

Class

While class is a central issue brought up in the article, and in sexuality, most authors avoid class. Class only appears in four comments, yet they fit with Kipnis' understanding of class distinctions of sexuality. One brazen commenter makes the issue directly economic proclaiming,

> *[P]orn isn't a human right, libraries have full rights to not allow it in a public space... If you can't afford your own computer, or an internet cafe, suck it up and buy a magazine. The world doesn't exist to please your dick.*

The comment directly engages with the notion that access to porn is a privilege, but also that it must be purchased. The commenter conveys a sense that only those that can afford to pay for access to porn deserve to have it. This economic argument relating to porn plays out in the other comments as well. Another commenter emphasizes that allowing porn in the libraries will cause them to collapse:

> *Parents will, of course, simply chose to avoid Public Libraries. And then they will simply chose not to fund Public Libraries. But whatev' At least no one is cramping your sacred adult choices.*

Indeed, many commenters, even those that don't mention class, feel like the ability for individuals to watch porn means an end to the library system, or at the very least their access to it. The issue of class was used in conjunction with concern for the library apocalypse. As one commenter put it,

> *Hurray, the grown up babies have won the right to keep the real babies out of the library. Your space, you won it fair and square, any one who complains is a Bad Person because it's your right to deny children Safe Places. You, however, because you are a special snowflake, have*

the right to whatever you want, no matter what it imposes on other people around you. Congratulations! The only actual, real Small People who are hurt by this are those who's parents are not wealthy. But this isn't about them, after all, it is about YOU.

This individual exemplifies what I like to call the rich man's burden. Their argument is entirely about how the library's porn policy will limit the ability of poor children to access the library due to their parents' fear of porn. Yet, as Kipnis points out, attitudes towards sex and sexuality are different depending on class. Thus the commenter assumes that the parents of the less wealthy have the same views as them but more importantly assumes the mantle of saving them. The commenter also conveniently ignores the part of the article that talks about access to the Internet. It's not about all "not wealthy" people being able to access the Internet or libraries so much as it is about saving babies.

Gender

Gender came up surprisingly often as early commenters thought the article's writer was a man, until one commenter pointed out that the writer was in fact a woman. The issue of gender assumptiveness on the part of the commenters is addressed by one commenter who theorizes,

I wonder what it was that made ppl think a man wrote this? I guess ppl stereotype and think only guys watch porn n jack off. Livin' in the Past... The times have-a-been-a-changin... I remember back in the summer of '98 when I caught my mom, grandma, and aunt watching gay guy porn while sippin' on Rumple Minze and Dr. Pepper. Grown Woman Shit... THEY WERE A LITTLE SWEATY...

This commenter locates the heart of the issue as many of the other gender comments focused on what were normal activities for males and females. After one commenter questioned the writer's taste in pornographic movies, another commenter defended the author's choices, noting, "calling "him" sexually depraved for watching gay porn, and fat porn. . . is neither depraved nor particularly irregular for a female." Another commenter assumed that all women wear certain clothes observing, "The author has no problem with porn in a public library but try playing Rush Limbaugh real loud......bet she pops her spanx over that!" Gender plays a central role in public perceptions of sexuality, a fact the commenters are keenly aware of. One notes, "I'd like to see what might have happened if you had done this while male," which reinforces the figure of the male watching pornography that probably led to the assumption of a male author addressed by an earlier commenter.

At the core of the assumptions and articulations of appropriate performance lies aesthetics. The comments convey how each commenter views the act of porn watching as either gendered or not, in turn separating the subjects "woman" and "porn watcher." The fact that the commenters originally thought the writer was a man plays into the bourgeois desire for visually digestible culture, as the "sight" of the individual portrayed in the article clearly referenced their understanding of the aesthetic masculine subject. The interactions over the internet without face-to-face contact allow for individuals to avoid easy visual cues, forcing them to use the frameworks they've developed for delineating individual subjects, resulting in a fascinating tendency to assume identity based on conformity to actions they've preselected.

Conclusion

I think there is a great deal of room for further study here, especially in regards to how individuals construct and determine gender, when forced to determine it through an individual's actions without seeing them. It is clear that commenters entered the social engagement with centered ideas of the subject of man and woman and then applied this subject to the writer's actions. This article is not the best for determining this, as perceptive readers of the Vice article could check the byline. It would be interesting to see how those same commenters, absent the article author's name, perceived her gender.

I also think that there's a great deal of room for further study in regards to the Internet's role in spacialization. The Internet is broadening the world and personalizing it, but how does it interact with preexisting spaces? I think analyzing other articles to see if the commenters have the same concern about space could be fascinating.

I think that being able to study the instant reaction of individuals to the cultural event/cultural object is fascinating, as it allows for patterns to emerge that showcase the diversity and convergence of opinion. I would like to focus another study on reactions to a pop culture object, such as a song, video, or tv show, through comments or tweets, as I think this could help us to better understand the common interpretations of society's dominant image culture.

While Vice claims to oppose societal norms, it appears that the reason it is so appealing to marketers is because it is a very safe opposition to norms. When Vice questions societal norms, its readers respond in a way that reaffirms the dominant "upper class" view of sexuality. In this, Vice manages to be a safe form of counterculture, as its readers, through the comments, reaffirm their preconceived beliefs about the world. In essence, some of Vice's readers treat counterculture, as a novelty, something to examine and tour, but not a viable belief system. On the other hand, a minority of the commenters demonstrate the countercultural ethos espoused by the magazine. In order to determine which type of reader dominates the publication it would be interesting to do a larger study of the entire site. The comments on this article reveal a fundamental tension between Vice's readership and its supposed countercultural status.

Notes

[1] Mathieson, A. (n.d.) Seattle Public Library: Stop allowing pornography to be watched on public library computers. *Change.org*. Retrieved from http://www.change.org/petitions/seattle-public-library-stop-allowing-pornography-to-be-watched-on-public-library-computers#supporters

[2] Purewal, S. J. (2012). Seattle Library Lets Man Watch Porn in View of Children. *PC World*. Retrieved from http://www.pcworld.com/article/249516/seattle_library_lets_man_watch_porn_in_view_of_children.html

[3] Grygiel, C. (2010). State Supreme Court: Libraries can block Internet porn. *Seattle PI*. http://www.seattlepi.com/local/article/State-Supreme-Court-Libraries-can-block-Internet-883448.php

[4] Ho, V. (2013). Seattle libraries to porn watchers: Come on in. *Seattle PI*. http://blog.seattlepi.com/thebigblog/2013/09/08/seattle-library-to-porn-watchers-come-on-in/#15724101=0

[5] Anten, T. (2005). "Please Disable the Entire Filter": Why Non-Removable Filters on Public Library Computers Violate the First Amendment. *Texas Journal on Civil Liberties and Rights*. Retrieved from *Lexis-Nexis*.

[6] Wilkinson, C. (2008). The Vice Squad. *The Guardian*. http://www.theguardian.com/media/2008/mar/30/pressandpublishing.tvandradioarts?gusrc=rss&feed=media

[7] Alexa. (2013). vice.com. *Alexa*. Retrieved from http://www.alexa.com/siteinfo/vice.com

[8] Castells, M. (2007). Communication, Power and Counter-power in the Network Society. *International Journal of Communication*, 248

[9] Kristof, N. D. (2009). The Daily Me. *The New York Times*. Retrieved from http://www.nytimes.com/2009/03/19/opinion/19kristof.html?_r=0

[10] Zizek, S. (2008). *Violence*. New York: Picador. pp. 157.

[11] Zizek (2008), pp. 158.

[12] Cain, J. (2009). Web 2.0: How the Web got Loose. *Interface*, 9. Retrieved from http://bcis.pacificu.edu/interface/?p=3656

[13] Porter, J. (2011). Is The Internet A Public Space? *Armstrong Institute for Interactive Media*

Studies. Retrieved from http://aims.muohio.edu/2011/02/01/is-the-internet-a-public-space/

[14] Zickuhr, K. (2013). Who's Not Online and Why. The Pew Research Center. Retrieved from http://www.pewinternet.org/Reports/2013/Non-internet-users.aspx

[15] Galvin, S. (2013). Testing Seattle's Porn-Friendly Public Libraries. *Vice*. http://www.vice.com/read/testing-seattles-porn-friendly-public-libaries

[16] Kipnis, L. (1992). (Male) Desire and (Female) Disgust: Reading Hustler. In Grosserberger, L. (eds) *Cultural Studies*. London: Routledge. 226.

[17] Kipnis (1992), pp. 227.

[18] Goldberg-Hiller, J. (2011). Persistance of the Indian: Legal Recognition of Native Hawaiians and the Opportunity of the Other. *New Political Science*. 23-44. pp. 27

[19] Bakhtin, M. (1968). *Rabelais and His World*. Bloomington: Indiana University Press. 72-78

[20] Bakhtin (1968), pp. 6.

[21] All comments analyzed are taken from: Galvin, S. (2013). Testing Seattle's Porn-Friendly Public Libraries. *Vice*. http://www.vice.com/read/testing-seattles-porn-friendly-public-libaries

Web Culture: Using Memes to Spread and Manipulate Ideas on a Massive Scale

by Gavin Brown
Student Fellow, The Berglund Center for Internet Studies

Introduction

"The Internet gives millions access to the truth that many didn't even know existed. Never in the history of man can powerful information travel so fast and so far. I believe that the Internet will begin a chain reaction of racial enlightenment that will shake the world by the speed of its intellectual conquest," said former member of the Louisiana State Representative and former Klu Klux Klan Member, David Duke. [1] The Internet and its uses have grown exponentially since its inception. Through websites, social media, blogs, wiki, and streaming video sites, Internet users are able to use images, text, and audio to create and develop both insightful and outrageous depictions of our culture. The things that people put on the Internet follow trends and include patterns, styles, and characters based on common ideas that people share and propagate. Internet users have assigned these products the same name that Richard Dawkins used in his analogy to genes – memes. Though Dawkins work revolves around genes, the memes on the Internet have very similar characteristics. In the online environment memes can be spread incredibly fast and far on massive scales, regardless of content. They may educate, entertain or potentially discriminate.

The Origins and Functuality of a Meme

Richard Dawkins first adopted the term meme in his book, *The Selfish Gene*, published in 1976. Dawkins described memes as: "tunes, ideas, catch-phrases, clothes, fashions, ways of making pots or of building arches" which evolved into trends that many people follow. Memes are units of information that are transferred from one person to another. [2] The example Dawkins included was "if a scientist hears, or reads about a good idea, he passes it on to his colleagues and students. He mentions it in his articles and his lectures.

If the idea catches on, it can be said to propagate its self, spreading from brain to brain." [2] With the creation of the Internet, and especially with the tools of Web 2.0, the meme has a new outlet in which people are able to spread their ideas from brain to brain. Cultural ideas are represented in images, text, audio, and film. These different formats of memes can now be emailed, tweeted, shared, blogged, YouTubed, and spread among other formats.

Through computers, cell phones, and tablets people can connect to the Internet 24/7. A meme is no longer restricted to word of mouth, or another form of communication that may take a long time to gain traction and popularity. The world now has millions of people spreading many different memes about their culture, politics, and opinions through the Internet. Memes that represents our culture and our values now have the possibility of being viewed by millions upon millions of people of all ages and nationalities, rather than a single classroom of young adults.

Memes have three main characteristics that give them value and sustain their popularity. These characteristics are as applicable in regards to the Internet as they were in the original definition. In *The Selfish Gene*, Dawkins theorized that memes had to have "fidelity, fecundity, and longevity" to stay alive (194). Fidelity referred to a meme's ability to be copied and transferred from person to person. [3] Since everything on the Internet is digital information, memes can be accurately transferred from person to person through audio, video, images, and text without altering their original form. Various websites allow for the easy creation of memes where stock images are prepared and customized text is easily incorporated. Examples of these websites include MemeGenerator, MemeMaker, and QuickMeme. Through the use of social networks, the transferring of memes is as easy as a click of the mouse. In addition to the ease of sharing memes, the rate at which they spread is another defining characteristic. [3] This rate is called fecundity. The more a meme is shared, the longer it can survive and promote its messages or cultural values to viewers. Websites such as Facebook, Twitter, and Tumblr are popular social networks where users have the ability to easily post images and links to memes. The more a meme is posted and shared, the more people will view it, and the longer it will be alive on the Internet. [3] This contributes to longevity, which refers to the length of time that a meme is applicable. The topics of memes vary widely from foods, to advice, to current popular trends. These types of memes tend to have a longer life. Other memes are very specific to a particular point in time. If a meme is only applicable to a certain point in time, then the meme will only last as long as that point of time is relevant to the viewer. [3] An example of this is the JibJab "This Land Is Our Land" video. The video is a 2004 Flash animation that includes then U.S. President George W. Bush exchanging insults with Senator John Kerry in the form of a music video. This meme was only applicable to the 2004 election. The political candidates would be different for every election after that. [4] Politics are a common topic for memes, but once an election has passed, the humor of that particular meme has lost its effect.

Memes are a prime example of creative reproduction and collaboration that exists on the Internet. Unlike music, movies, and software piracy, meme creation is an art form that was created by the users for the users. Memes are a source of intellectual art created by people who have based the art on a part of popular culture. One of the older and most popular forms of memes is the cat-meme commonly known as LOL Cats (Laugh Out Loud Cats). Images will usually show cats in various positions and text will act as titles for the content of the image. A popular website for these images is icanhas.cheezburger.com. [5] I can has Cheezburger evolved over time itself. Originally the title was spelled as "I can haz cheezburger". [5] Websites like "I Can Has" are places where the reproduction of images are not only allowed, but also encouraged. Another popular collaboration meme was "All Your Base Are Belong To Us." "All Your Base Are Belong To Us" is a term from a video sequence in a 1989 Japanese video game known for its poor Japanese to English translation (Duds, 2008). The popularity of this meme, like I Can Has's cat images, used real footage from the video game to spark a collaborative process. Internet users are able to systematically download editable materials from the Internet where each person is able to recreate their own meme that complies with their own ideas and opinions. The "All Your Base Are Belong To Us" was a popular meme that evolved through Photoshop manipulation. People would upload their own images with the phrase, "All Your Base Are Belong To Us," imprinted in some way into the image, such as on a newspaper, or billboard, or a piece of nature. These digitally altered images were then uploaded to collection sites online such as SomethingAweful.com forums. [6] The term "All Your Base Are Belong To Us" evolved enough to become a piece of Internet history and made an appearance in Disney's *Wreck It Ralph* (2012) where the term was spray painted as graffiti on a wall. [7] The popularity also provided inspiration for a Kansas City musical artist to create his own dance song that was based off of the meme. [8] The meme "All Your Base Are Belong To Us," was a highly recognizable trend that prompted others to create additional media to continue the life of that meme.

Humors and Commentary

Memes can be sorted broadly into two categories, either "absurdist humor" or "social commentary." [3] A study of memes in 2007 found that out of nineteen mainstream memes that were published up until that year, seventeen had humor as their key component. [3] There are millions of comedic memes online that poke fun at many different aspects of culture. Memes will take a common image or person of notability, such as Gene Wilder's character, Willy Wonka, from *Willy Wonka & The Chocolate Factory* (1971), together with the topic of college graduates (http://goo.gl/TZpTq). The condescending look that Gene Wilder is giving in the photo can play to many different captions. The captions are satirical of college graduates who finish college with a degree but end up getting a minimum wage job such as working at a coffee shop. [9]

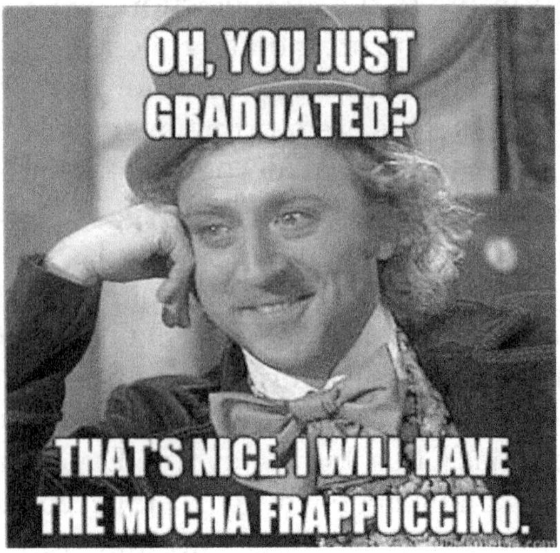

QuickMeme.com (*http://goo.gl/*

On the other hand, "social commentary" can usually depict issues that are currently going on in the world and present viewers with a different perspective. One such example would be the "Pepper Spraying Cop" meme. [10] In November 2011, when Lieutenant John Pike casually pepper sprayed students who were peacefully protesting at University California Davis, the image went viral on the Internet. Immediately after the incident photoshopped images were published and appeared everywhere on the Internet. [10] A common commentary of this incident is the "Modern Warfare 2 Pepper Spraying Cop." [11] The combination of this incident with the cover of the graphically violent video game, *Modern Warfare 2*, illustrates the militaristic tactics that some United States police forces may employ, even against peaceful protesters. [11] The ability to place the image of Pike in a number of other images illustrates the way Western ideologies can be presented. Normal citizens have the ability to mock Pike, as well as anyone else, through the visual power of a meme.

Toxic-Memes

Memes are not only funny cat photos; they are the way people think about their culture. Memes are a product of the culture that people live in. These depictions of our culture can clash with the ideologies of other cultures in dangerous ways. In 2002, Dan Dennett spoke at a TED conference about memes that he termed as "toxic-memes." [12] "Toxic-memes" are memes that are ideas that do not mesh with other ideas and are be dangerous to other cultures. [12] Dennet pointed out Sayyid Qutb as a propagator of fanatical Islamic ideas. Through Sayyid Qutb and his Qutbist followers, Dennet stated that they were able to spread Qutb's fanatical ideologies through their "press films, fashion shows, beauty contests, ballrooms, wine bars, and broadcasting station."

[12] Qutb's ideas later on influenced fanatical groups such as Al-Qaeda and other followers of Osama bin-Laden. The memes, or ideas, created by the fanatical Islamic organizations were spread out in the world through newspapers, radio, television, and eventually the Internet is a convenient mode of communication for "toxic-memes." While Qutb's fanatical ideas were spreading, Westernized memes, or ideas, were also spreading through radio, television, and the Internet. As Western memes spread exponentially around the world, they come in contact with other cultures unfamiliar, unimpressed, or even angered with the memes of the Western Culture. As western memes "spread our education and our technology, [. . .] we're the vectors of memes that are currently viewed by the hosts of many other memes as a dire threat to their favorite memes. The memes that they are prepared to die for." [12] The fundamental ideas spread by Qutb is no longer limited as it was during his lifetime.

As the Internet became one of the fastest growing forms of communication is human history, people with all different types of opinion make use of its capabilities. With the terrorism becoming a rampant activity in many parts of the world, groups such as the Taliban, Lebanese Hezbollah, Afghani Taliban, Palestinian Hamas and the Pakistani Tanzeem-e-Islami all have functional web pages that connect people over large distances and culture barriers. [13] Not only are fundamental websites spread ideology and propaganda to support each organizations cause, web sites such as www.alneda.com was used as "donation" platform which was used to purchase "weapons to be used against [citizens of the U.S.], while there were also "volumes upon volumes of zipped documents outlining specific ways to kill [U.S. citizens]." [14]

Not only Islamic fundamentalism is expanding through the use of the Internet, but White Supremacy has also started created followings. Through long distances, the Internet connects people with similar interests. Jesse Daniels points out in her book, *Cyber Racism: White Supremacy Online and the New Attack on civil Rights,* that there are three main point why people should be concerned about white supremacy online. First, she points out the "easy access and global linkages" that the Internet is capable of having with people around the world. Secondly, she figures that the hatred present on the Internet may create harm in real life. Finally, Daniels assumes that racism on the Internet will present a challenge "to honoring cultural values such as racial equality." [15] Anybody who has a computer can access the Internet and propagate their own ideas and opinions of discrimination if they wish.

Conclusion

Since people have been connecting with each other faster than ever before with the Internet, ideas are shared across far greater distances without the barriers of the past. Since memes first appeared as a trend on the Internet, they've been spread in every format that can be shared with other users. Users are able to create content that examines, mocks, and even discriminate against other people's cultures. The culture of LOLcats and other Internet memes spread virally during the past two decades. The Internet memes contain both comical value and social commentary. Discriminatory content has since appeared on the Internet and is steadily growing in many different forms of hatred. The Internet is a free world without borders and international law reigning over it. Content is shared on a massive scale regardless of its message. Certain groups are trying to take advantage of this ease of transmission to achieve the same level of globalization for discriminatory content. The Internet is not only a place for funny cat photos; there are dangerous ideas that are being spread the same way as other memes.

Notes

[1] Daniels, J. (2009). *Cyber Racism: White Supremacy Online and the New Attack on Civil Rights*. Lanham, Maryland: Rowman & Littlefield Publishers.

[2] Dawkins, R. (1989) The Selfish Gene. Oxford: Oxford UP. 192. Print.

[3] Knobel, M. & Lankshear, C. (2007). Online Memes, Affinities, and Cultural Production. In Lankshear & C., Knobel, M. (eds.) *A New Literacies Sampler* (vol. 29). New York: Peter Lang Publishing. 199-227.

[4] JibJab.com. This Land! YouTube, 16 Nov. 2007. Web. 04 Dec. 2012. Retrieved from http://www.youtube.com/watch?v=z8Q-sRdV7SY.

[5] I Can Has Cheezburger? (n.d.). Retrieved from http://icanhas.cheezburger.com/

[6] Duds, J. (2008). All Your Base Are Belong To Us. Retrieved from http://knowyourmeme.com/memes/all-your-base-are-belong-to-us

[7] McKinney, L. (2012). Leeroy Jenkins Lives! The 6 Best Video Game References In "Wreck-It Ralph." *Movieline.com*. Retrieved from http://movieline.com/2012/11/12/wreck-it-ralph-best-video-game-references-aerith-kano-konami-code/

[8] Taylor, C. (2001) All Your Base Are Belong To Us. *Time*. Retrieved from http://www.time.com/time/magazine/article/0,9171,100525,00.html

[9] QuickMeme.com. (n.d.). Creepy Wonka. Retreived from http://www.quickmeme.com/

meme/3565ys/.

[10] Jardin, X. (2011). The Pepper-spraying Cop Gets Photoshop Justice. *The Guardian*. Retrieved from http://www.guardian.co.uk/commentisfree/2011/nov/23/ pepper-spraying-cop-photoshop-justice.

[11] Charlie, C. (2011). Pepper Spraying Modern Warfare. Best of "Pepper Spraying Cop" Memes. *Smosh.com*. Retrieved from: http://www.smosh.com/smosh-pit/memes/best-pepper-spraying-cop-meme.

[12] Dennet, D. (2007) Dangerous Memes. TED: Ideas Worth Spreading. Re trieved from http://www.ted.com/talks/dan_dennett_on_dangerous_memes.html

[13] Khatib, L. (2003). Communicating Islamic Fundamentalism as Global Citizenship. *Journal of Communication Inquiry*, 27(4), 389-400. pp. 389. doi: 10.1177/0196859903255776

[14] Regis, J. (n.d.). Hacked, tracked, and NOW Owned by the U.S.A. Retreived from www.alneda.com [*Editors note: as of the print publication of this article the site no longer exists*].

[15] Daniels, J. (2009). pp. 6.

Still Anonymous: Guilt by Association and the Official Story in New York Times Coverage of Anonymous

by Matthew Yasuoka
Student fellow, The Berglund Center for Internet Studies

On November 13, 2012, Kylie Kylem tweeted, "I don't know what to do anymore. I can't get out of my room. I can't face the world i don't want to be alive im done [sic]." Within minutes, Internet trolls started goading her to kill herself. Anonymous, the loosely organized collective of online hactivists, immediately responded by attacking the suicide trolls, rebuffing their advances saving Kylie's life.

This type of "op" (the term used by Anonymous to refer to their protest work) is not uncommon within Anonymous, which is part of "the free culture movement—a coalition as varied as Wikipedia contributors, Flickr photographers and online educators, and prominent figures like Julian Assange." [1] The organization, while often criticized, prides itself upon its ideological ethos. In fact, The New York Times argues that hacktivists "differ from mainstream computer criminals in that they claim to be motivated by ideals as opposed to financial gain." [2]

Anonymous' decentralized, disorganized, and diversified nature lead it to protest injustices as far reaching as Internet laws in North Korea [3] to the government cover-up in the Stuebenville rape case [4] to Scientology's efforts to defraud members. [5] While characterizing Anonymous may prove difficult, it is clear that the organization is globally involved, politically motivated, and philosophically defined.

In this study, I seek to gain a greater understanding of media coverage patterns of Anonymous. In particular, how the media industrial complex frames and defines Anonymous.

Literature Review

Media analysis

Media scholars use framing to refer to the process that decides information in news stories. Robert Entman defines framing as "selection and salience." [6] Frames order information, deciding what information is fit to print and what information is unfit. Boykoff and Yasuoka argue, "media frames. . . focus the public's attention on particular events, issues, and ideas." [7] Boykoff observes, "media representations. . . are critical links between people's everyday realities. . . and the ways in which these are discussed at a distance." [8] Overall, journalists pick specific aspects of events to focus on, in order to organize the chaos of current events. These judgments are made at a distance from the events and, thus, can differ from the actuality on the ground.

The concept of indexing refers to another process of information selection in the media. W. Lance Bennett defines "indexing" as the "range of sources and viewpoints" within a story. [9] Althaus, Edy, Entman, and Phalen observe that indexing studies stem from the fear that media coverage could be "so constrained by. . . debate among political elites that the public remains poorly informed." Thus, the "empirical goal of. . . indexing is to chart and explain the closeness. . . between media discourse and debate among political elites." [10] In this paper, I am going to use indexing in a new way. Rather than count the types of sources used by the media. I am going to index the media's coverage of tactics, counting the number of times each tactic used by Anonymous is mentioned. In doing so, I hope to see whether or not the range of tactics is closer to Anonymous' diverse toolbox or to the government's focus on specific tactics, such as vandalism and attacks on credit card companies.

Social movements

Gilham and Noakes differentiate between contained protest groups that are (1) "well known to the police," (2) "employ familiar tactics," and (3) are "hierarchically organized" (i.e. they have a leader); [11] and transgressive protest groups that are (1) "not well known," (2) "use innovative tactics," and (3) have "a flat organizational structure" (i.e. leaderless). [12] In this paper, I will be considering Anonymous a "transgressive protest group" as it is not a known force to the police (such as PETA or the NAACP), but a new and complex force that uses confusing and novel tactics (such as Doxing, trolling, or DDoS attacks), while remaining leaderless. Tactics play a large role in understanding social movements. McCarthy and Zald's argue that for social movements, "dilemmas occur in the choice of tactics, since what may achieve one aim may conflict with behavior aimed at achieving another." [13] Movements must balance their tactics and their objectives in order to be effective.

Media coverage of social movements can both help and hinder the movements' efforts. Boykoff notes that, "most people learn what they know about social movements from the media." [14] In a study of political trials involving activists, Barkan observes that media coverage can be an important resource for movements, acknowledging historical and racial divides of coverage patterns. [15]

Methodology

In this study, I am going to index media coverage of Anonymous by looking at (1) whether sources from Anonymous were interviewed; (2) which ideological motivations appear the most, and (3) which tactics used by anonymous received the most coverage.

I decided to focus on The New York Times because it is the third most circulated newspaper in print and the most popular online paper. [16] I used the search terms "CAPS (anonymous) AND internet" on Lexis-Nexis, from which I removed all irrelevant articles, resulting in a 34-article dataset. The unit of analysis for my study was the article. Thus, I read every article and noted, which tactics, ideological motivation, and frame appeared in individual pieces, counting the number of articles that contained each thing I was measuring. The tactics I will be indexing are: cyber vandalism, hacking social media, stealing secrets, counter media coverage, Doxing, and Distributed Denial of Service (DDoS) attacks. Doxing refers to the practice of releasing personal information about a target. DDoS refers to flooding a target site with so much traffic that it crashes. [17]

The ideological motivations I will be indexing are: anti-capitalist ideals, democracy promotion, transparency, anti-rape efforts, and anti-bullying efforts. I also carried out a standard indexing study. I counted the number of articles that quoted sources from Anonymous. I also counted the total number of different Anonymous sources across all articles. I wanted to compare the number of articles and the number of sources to see if there were few articles that quoted Anonymous, few sources from Anonymous, or both.

I am also going to be looking at how Anonymous was framed by the media. The frames I will be coding for are: the cyberterrorists frame, the guilty by association frame, the hacktivist frame, and the criminality frame. The unit of analysis was the article and multiple frames could be coded for a single article.

Table 1-Tactics

	Cyber Vandalism	Hacking social media sites	Stealing Secrets	Doxing	DDoS	Counter media coverage
Number of articles	8	4	10	5	7	3
Percentage	23.52%	11.76%	29.41%	14.70%	20.59%	8.82%

Table 2-Ideology

	Anti-Capitalism	Democracy promotion	Transparency	Anti-Bullying	Anti-Rape
Number of articles	2	1	7	2	10
Percentage	5.88%	2.94%	20.59%	5.88%	29.41%

I was interested in looking at the intersection between ideology and tactics and how the media coverage changed because of the specific ideological motivation. I created a sub-data set of all the articles that had both a tactic coded and an ideology coded:

Table 3- Correlations between ideology and tactics in media coverage

	Cyber Vandalism	Hacking social media sites	Stealing Secrets	Counter media coverage	Doxing	DDoS
Number of articles	3	0	6	1	5	2
Percentage (n=12)	25.00%	0.00%	50.00%	8.33%	41.67%	16.67%
Percentage (n=35)	23.52%	11.76%	29.41%	8.82%	14.70%	20.59%

I then ran a correlation test and got a 0.82 correlation between the sub-data set and the regular tactics data. This means that 82% of the change is the result of the variable, in this case, the presence of an ideological correlates to the change in the preponderance of the tactics. Doxing's prevalence increased most drastically when paired with tactics, while DDoS attacks and Hacking Social Media Sites both saw a decline in their prevalence.

Table 4-Frames

	Cyberterrorist frame	Hacktivist Frame	Guilt by Association Frame	Criminality Frame
Number of articles	1	8	10	4
Percentage (n=34)	2.94%	23.53%	29.41%	11.76%

It is interesting to note that The New York Times predominantly avoided the cyberterrorist frame, opting instead to imply criminality or extra-legality, by covering Anonymous in the context of other criminal or reprehensible organizations. For example, in coverage about Silk Road, the online bazaar of drugs and other illegal paraphernalia, the author drops in a single Paragraph, at the end, which mentions an Anonymous member and compares them to Dread Pirate Roberts. [18] In another, article a senior security advisor says, "There are three categories of hackers: Russian criminals trying to rob us blind; the Chinese who are trying to steal our secrets; and then there's Anonymous. . . we're treating them all the same." [19] The coverage here insinuates that Anonymous should be considered in the same grouping as Chinese hackers and "Russian criminals." This characterization is a subtler form of defamation than the outright accusation of cyberterrorism, a claim that The New York Times only used once, by and large, the paper allowed its readers to connect the dots about Anonymous and its association, with organizations viewed as our enemies and criminals.

Table 5- Indexing-sources

	Articles	Total
Anonymous Sources	8	12
Percentage (n=34)	23.52%	n/a

Overall, it is clear that The New York Times more often than not chose not to interview Anonymous in its coverage of Anonymous. Of course, this could be an extension of the phenomenon observed by Gilham and Noakes regarding leaderless organizations, the fact that "they have no one for the police to directly negotiate with." [20] By that logic, the lack of organizational structure could also preclude media engagement and interviews, because the mass media lacks clear indicators of whom the authority on the subject is, and, thus, default to other sources that are perceived to have more credibility.

Conclusion

Overall, it is clear that coverage of Anonymous primarily focuses on the transgressive nature of the organization, while emphasizing the ideological aspects of the movement. Further research is needed to understand coverage patterns across publications. Studying the coverage of Anonymous could help media scholars to understand how the prestige press approaches digital activism and new social movements using new tactics. It is worth noting that the theft of government and corporate secrets was the most covered tactic, which could potentially be a reflection of the current political zeitgeist. However, coverage of ideology and tactics in tandem placed a greater emphasis on Doxing indicating a difference between the paper's perceptions and the tactics used by Anonymous to achieve its goals.

Notes

[1] Cohen, N. (2013). A Data Crusader, a Defendant and Now, a Cause. *The New York Times.*

[2] Siegel, M. (2013). Australia Arrests the Professed Head of LulzSec, Which Claims a C.I.A. Hacking. *The New York Times*

[3] Sang-Hun, C. (2013). North Korea Moves Missile to Coast, but Little Threat Is Seen. *The New York Times.*

[4] See: http://www.rollingstone.com/culture/news/anonymous-vs-steubenville-20131127

[5] See: http://www.salon.com/2013/10/02/anonymous_vs_scientology_partner/

[6] Entman, R. (1993). Framing: Toward Clarification of a Fractured Paradigm. *Journal of Communication* 43(4). p. 51-58. Quote at 52.

[7] Boykoff, J. and Yasuoka, M. (2013). Gender and politics at the 2012 Olympics: media coverage and its implications. *Sport in Society*. 1-15. pp. 5.

[8] Boykoff, M. (2012) *Who Speaks for the Climate?* Loc. 164.

[9] Bennet, W., Lawrence, R., & Livingston, S. (2006). None Dare Call It Torture: Indexing and the Limits of Press Independence in the Abu Ghraib Scandal. *Journal of Communication* 56. 467-485. pp. 468.

[10] Althaus, S., Edy, J., Entman, R., & Phalen, P. (1996). Revising the Indexing Hypothesis: Officials, Media, and the Libya Crisis. *Political Communication* 13. 407-421. pp. 408.

[11] Gilham, P. & Noakes, J. (2007). "More than a March in a Circle": Transgressive Protests and the Limits of Negotiated Management. *Mobilization: An International Quarterly* 12.4. pp. 343-344.

[12] Gilham and Noakes (2007). pp. 343, 346.

[13] McCarthy, J. & Zald, M. (1977). Resource Mobilization and Social Movements: A Partial Theory. *American Journal of Sociology* 82(6). 1212-1241. p. 1217.

[14] Boykoff, J. (2007). *Beyond Bullets*. Oakland, CA: AK Press. p. 16.

[15] Barkan, S. E. "

[16] See: http://stateofthemedia.org/2013/newspapers-stabilizing-but-still-threatened/newspapers-by-the-numbers/

[17] See: https://whyweprotest.net/community/threads/welcome-to-whyweprotest.111548/

[18] Bilton, Nick. (2013). "A Digital Underworld Cloaked in Anonymity." The New York Times

[19] Chozick, Amy and Savage, Charlie. (2013). "Hacker Case Leads to Calls For Better Law." The New York Times.

[20] Gilham and Noakes. "'More than a March in a Circle': Transgressive Protests and the Limits of Negotiated Management." Mobilization. 341-357. pp. 349

ENGLISH

Volume 13

Reading Across the Pond: Attempts at a US-British Cyber Exchange Literature Course

by Brently Johnson
English Department, Pacific University

"England and America are two countries separated by a common language"
— George Bernard Shaw

Ricky Gervais, the British actor and comedian, raised the hackles of many Americans a few years back for his "disrespectful" and "mean-spirited" sense of humor as host of the Golden Globe Awards. He took jabs at Hollywood, poked at producers, and was bleeped a healthy number of times. Michael Russnow, despite claims that he is "not a prude", went on to write for the Huffington Post that it was Gervais' "lapses in judgment that resulted in so-called jokes that were in severely bad taste." [1] Russnow spoke for many American critics it seemed ("the opposite of dull and deferential is not snotty and abusive"—LA Times; [2] "Are we at war with England? If not, then why have we been subjected to two years of Gervais hosting the Golden Globe Awards?"—Washington Post [3]) appalled at how shock standup might pass for primetime humor. In the UK, The Telegraph ran these headlines on Gervais' act: "Golden Globes 2012: Ricky Gervais Falls Flat." At first glance, it might have appeared that the Brits, too, were equally dismayed, but, reading on, the article faulted Gervais not so much for his ability to insult, but for the "missed open goals" to lampoon poorly made films and the actors receiving awards for them, Madonna being a particularly glaring oversight. [4]

Granted, Gervais was invited back two more times as host, perhaps because many Americans "got" his sense of humor after all, or perhaps, as I am more prone to believe, shock and abuse are synonyms for better ratings. Gervais upset both the US protocol for humor as well as our protocol for imagined Brits: eloquent, demure, deferential, i.e. Colin Firth's elegant acceptance for his award for the King's Speech.

When I polled my students on which version of The Office they found more humorous—Ricky Gervais' British original versus the American adaptation with Steve Carrell—they generally resisted ranking one over the other, but smartly compared how they processed the varying ways humor was presented. Gervais' character, David Brent, was "angry" and "vindictive," which was "guiltily funny," while Carrell's Michael Scott was "awkward" and "slightly dim," just as misguided as Brent's character but in a more doltish, loveable way. While they resisted claiming one was superior to the other, a majority of them remarked that they preferred Carrell's adaptation because he was more relatable in his fallibility and childishness, that "he was easier to forgive and attach to." Gervais, similar to his Golden Globe routine, turned out to be "mean" more than funny, resulting in the lack of a "need to root for him."

Ultimately, what was missing from Gervais and his British version was a cultural value system that my students could relate to and cheer for. As one particularly astute student put it, "Regardless of how funny I find the British Office, ultimately I do want to walk away feeling better; I could watch several episodes in a row and guffaw with the best of them but eventually I would want to see some triumph, some salvation, some redemption."

I found it interesting that my students resisted commenting on humor per se, but more on the results of that humor on their well-being. It seemed from their comments that they sought a humor that served them positively, not one that might compromise a more optimistic outlook on life. Their responses mirrored a review from The Atlantic comparing the two versions of The Office: whereas both were commentaries on the existence of modern office life, ultimately, "where the British found despair, the Americans found hope. Where the British saw pain, the Americans saw joy." [5]

How great of an influence does our culture hold over how we respond and interpret language and its meanings—whether in the form of a joke or a serious work of extended literature? Depending on where and when a person is born, how much will their understanding of the same written work differ? This relationship between writer and reader and the cultures they hail from, particularly those from Britain and the United States, formed the basis of a literature course I taught at Pacific University in the spring of 2013 in which I asked and examined the question: "How is literature understood as a cultural product?" The course attempted to answer this question through both cross-cultural and blended classroom strategies, crossing the Atlantic via information technology and web-based tools. In conjunction with a faculty member and her students attending York St. John University in York, England, we read and shared viewpoints on common texts though video conferences, online forums, and group chat rooms. The course was divided topically, ranging from humor to nature, nationalism, class and the American Dream, with the hope of engaging cultural consciousness towards why we interpret a text in the ways we do. And once we more actively engage the process of reading a text through a cultural lens, how do we begin to understand ourselves as cultural texts as well? If I, for instance, relate to a certain character's motives and another student does not, how much of that relationship is borne out of a national identity unbeknownst to me? Furthermore, once I begin to recognize where my opinions and connections stem from, how do I move closer to a keener awareness of how I am a cultural product too? The goal of the course, then, was to gauge the influence culture holds over the construction of literature, as well as our individually constructed selves.

While the primary investigation of the course peered into the relationships between reader and text via cultural placement, a secondary aim focused on how technology might enhance this relationship. By its very nature, this type of course would be extremely limited if not for web-based tools, which allow for immediate correspondence and reaction across great distances. Our first order of business was to establish a common platform for students to communicate through, and since both institutions used Moodle as their course management system, it became our virtual learning environment. Here we could post announcements, readings, surveys, forum questions, chat rooms, and web conference tools. With the purpose of self-expression through various mediums, groups consisting of three to four students from both classes could pose questions to one another, both within their classes and with those abroad, through a weekly online forum. Additionally, every other week, these groups would meet using webcam technologies for more informal discussions of culture and daily life. Finally, at the end of each major unit, class would be held simultaneously as a web conference, meeting at 10am PST and 5pm GMT. Here, students from both sides of the pond would share their perspectives on that unit's topic and readings with the instructors acting as guides.

Given the constraints of time zone differences, diversity in educational models and student experiences, the flexibility of a blending learning curriculum worked to dissolve some of the traditional frameworks of pedagogical culture. Partially based in Elbow's "decentering" theory, online forums and chat rooms were meant to allow students to teach one another. [6] I found it important to step into the discussions occasionally, not only to encourage complexity of thought but also to let the students know I was listening.

The first forum post asked students to comment on a text and reply to one another. We quickly realized this format was too open ended, resulting in an overwhelming string of individual posts, a room of many mouths but no ears. Borrowing from Caroline Persell's work in "Using Focused Web-based Discussions to Enhance Student Engagement and Deep Understanding" we assigned roles to the group members, and asked them to post and reply by a certain hour.[7] Tweaking Persell's categories, one student was designated the "Poser" and by 5pm had to pose a question to the group, at which time everyone would type a reply. The "Contrarian" had to propose, by 8pm, a counter viewpoint that had not been raised, and everyone had to post a second reply to this new point. Finally, two other group members were appointed as "Reporter" and "Spy," charged with summarizing and reporting back to the class their own group's general discussion (reporter) as well as doing the same but for another group's discussion (spy). While these two roles held a certain sex appeal (who doesn't want to be a spy?), the students found summarizing the conversation confusing and tedious. It felt like busy work to them and I never fully established its parameters before we dropped these roles in favor of more responders.

With such variation of viewpoints on display, students were encouraged to see one another as "texts," viable sources they could refer to when grappling with their own interpretation of more formal works. In order to assess how students put these various perspectives into a formulated whole, they were asked to write a mini-essay of 500 words for every longer piece of work we read, interpreting it from a cultural point of view. As a 200 level literature course, these essays, the daily readings and postings on line, as well as a reflective final project represented the bulk of their intellectual and written work.

Raymond Williams' work Resources of Hope: Culture, Democracy, Socialism chants the mantra, "Culture is ordinary." His thoughts and writings influenced the formations of cultural studies, insisting on a more complicated relationship between high and low culture. "A culture is common meanings, the product of a whole people, and offered individual meanings, the product of a man's whole committed personal and social experiences." [8] As he wished to dismantle the walls placed around various groups within a culture, he worked towards a more inclusive view on culture, where local and individual culture mingled with national identity as well. The question of "what is culture?" became a mantra in my course similarly, with students curious as to where their individual choices were part and parcel of a culture at large. It wasn't my intention to answer this question (if one exists) but to encourage exploration of its varieties through face-to-face and digital exchange. I touted the course as "study abroad," (without the exorbitant costs) where, in fact, it was just as much about "study within."

Using Williams as an initiating text, we applied his theories to contemporary novels that inferred an interchange between individual and national identities. Chuck Palahniuk's Fight Club, Jon Krakauer's Into the Wild, Zadie Smith's On Beauty, and Tony Harrison's extended poem "V" commented directly and indirectly on how the individual self might be understood through a broader culture. Initially, students in my classroom were resistant to seeing themselves as cultural products, an interesting cultural point in itself—is this resistance particularly American, where we pride ourselves on individuality? But, as we examined Fight Club's protagonist, a figure so consumed by a material culture that packages identities for sale that he has literally and figuratively created an alter-ego or self in response, students grappled with the book's commentary on modernism's effects of creating the "other" within ourselves. The point of the class was to measure various reactions to narrative events, characters, and themes in order to better understand how we bring to a text a priori value systems and assumptions on truth. One resultant point that surfaced from our discussions on Fight Club, first within our own class then with our British counterparts, was the mixed interpretations of the American Dream. Because the novel parodies an apocalyptic fallout from a capitalist regime, certain students recognized Palahniuk's intentions while others truly wondered, "Why is the narrator so unhappy?" Of course, each student came to the text with different experiences. One student was clearly proud that her parents were the epitome of the American Dream, having started out with little means or education and "made something out of themselves," proven by sending three children to college. Conversely, another student, an African-American female, seemed genuinely confused by the concept of a communal dream, both for what it stood for, and for whom. On a forum post, she wrote, "Whose dream is this? This is not my dream. This was never my dream to have." As students dissected the novel's commentary on the authentic self's struggle against the influences of culture, they simultaneously analyzed themselves and the cultural narratives they had been told, asking, "How much am I the author of my own life's story?"

Another crucial theme raised by Fight Club revolves around the sacredness of the individual and promotion of self against the various "clubs" to which one belongs. In this case, cross-examining the self against British notions of community helped bring about more complexity on how we understand ourselves within national cultures. For instance, when our classes met jointly for our web conference, the British students voiced an identification with the narrator's struggle for identity, but deferred more often to the sacrifice of self if for the greater good. (This paralleled discussions of place and space later in the semester, particularly to what extent the physical landscape determined emotional horizons, but more on this later.) Students from Britain were less likely to consider moving away from their communities to pursue a life on their own; American students were nearly the opposite, seeing hometowns as oppressive and stilting. Of course, there were exceptions from both sides of the pond, but, overall, a clear divide existed between the two groups.

After forum posts and in-class discussions as well as our cross-cultural web conferencing, the essay assignment asked students to put it all together, seeing a specific theme in Fight Club through a cultural lens. Students were encouraged to include discussions into their essays where appropriate, linking the processes of reading to a more thorough interpretation of a text. Several students claimed they came into a greater awareness of how they assumed a set of values based on the American Dream as soon as the question was asked, "Is there no equivalent British Dream?" They understood how a national story had been scripted more clearly, and how they were defined by it or in opposition to it.

At this point in the semester, headway was being made towards a blended learning, cross-cultural literary exchange, but would be slowed by several factors. First, coordinating technologies was proving difficult. My colleague had difficulty locating the proper equipment and, sometimes space, on her end, resulting in a scenario where I literally asked her if she would "translate" for us what her students were saying. Looking back through my notes from our first webconference, I wrote, "It was as if we were trying to communicate underwater." Unless we were seated next to the laptop's built-in microphone, the voice came through as garbled; thus, a great deal of a fluid discussion was symbolically "lost in translation," as we struggled to summarize our students' thoughts and questions and maintain any semblance of a conversation.

So, while we dealt with technological issues, a more serious setback occurred when I was made aware, three weeks in, that the British students were not actually receiving credit for the course. The international webcam groups we had assembled, the forum groups as well, eventually dissolved completely, as the British students became busier during their term, and lacked the motivation to communicate with any consistency.

These developments changed my approach and expectations for the course. I eventually became content with knowing the majority of our shared experience would come through the various webconference class sessions only, which were still well attended. My colleague was active in joining in forum postings, but I knew that it would be necessary to drive the course inward, examining each unit more from the various American perspectives available in the class, revising, in my mind, our aim to "literature as a micro-cultural product."

With a revised methodology in place, we continued the blended learning applications of online forums within groups of students from our class only. I surveyed my students six weeks into the course on where their learning was taking place and both the in-class discussions as well as online forums ranked high, although class discussions consistently scored better than online forums. While one student claimed that "once you sit and stare at a screen and expect someone to discuss a topic it won't happen easily," another student remarked that s/he "liked how we can each say what we need or want to say if we didn't get the chance or courage to share in class." In terms of the international group exchange, more ambitious members connected with one another via Facebook. One student was active with a Youtube international group exchange outside of class. We even investigated the idea of joining an online pen pal site as well, but it never came to fruition. These revisions in approach with the resulting feedback suggest to me that an online learning component enriches a course, but cannot replace face-to-face class time; likewise, an international perspective enhances how we comprehend a text more fully, but that diverse positions abound in a typical class alone.

As we did with Fight Club, the question of cultural consciousness and its impact on how we make meaning informed our discussions with Jon Krakauer's Into the Wild, a journalistic investigation into the life and death of a young man, Chris McCandless, who similarly rejected notions of upward mobility and contentment through material accumulation. With this text, though, we aimed our lenses more on place and its influences on McCandless. As evidenced in this work, to what degree does the spatial relationship between external landscapes determine the interior paths we take?

Barry Lopez's ruminations on landscape enforce the power our physical environment holds over our identities. In his essay, "Landscape and Narrative," he writes, "I think of two landscapes—one outside the self, the other within." The relationship they share, according to Lopez, greatly determines who we are and how we participate with land. "The interior landscape responds to the character and subtlety of an exterior landscape: the shape of the individual mind is affected by land as it is by genes." [9]

Take the weather, for example. How much influence does a temperate British climate exact on its population's demeanor, values, and outlook, its archetypal polite and reserved individual? How much influence does the extreme weather of the western United States exact on its inhabitants, the archetypal individual who is rugged, resilient, innovative, and hard working? In the case of weather, perhaps more than anything, it isn't so much whether a mild versus wild climate reflects one's true nature, but that an awareness of a perceived relationship does, indeed, exist. As our peers in Britain would later point out, certain characters, ironically, were their truest selves when they were "performing identity."

The unit focused on McCandless's physical journey, a familiar one to Americans, as he hit the road, seeking the mystical landscape of the open West. His Thoreauvian quest to shuck all material holdings and to embrace the romantic appeals of nature and simplicity flowed out of a long current in American nature writing and national mythos, from Manifest Destiny to the modern environmental cathedral in the woods. William Cronon's essay, "The Trouble with Wilderness," provided a frame from which to view McCandless's journey, especially in terms of our notions of nature as culturally constructed. As Cronon claims, "we too easily imagine that what we behold is Nature when in fact we see the reflection of our own unexamined longings and desires." His essay sets out to deconstruct how our nation has utilized nature as metaphor for renewal, progress, and independence. That pioneer spirit, then, is held up to wilderness and mirrored back to us as evidence of its existence. From the days of westward expansion to the hallowed aisles of REI today, we see the American values of freedom, trailblazing, risk taking, and hard work operating still.

The argument can be made that McCandless embodied these ideals. His longings and desires centered on independence, renewal, reinvention of the self (he even takes on the moniker Alexander Supertramp), and spiritual freedom that arrived through empty spaces, such as Alaska, no less ironically named, the last frontier. Tragically, his journey ended in his death, which called into question his associations with nature as romanticized and misguided, as false constructions of reality he knew little of. Regardless of whether one deems McCandless a hero or fool, his narrative speaks to an American sensibility, one where we have subconsciously sought a wildness within through a wilderness outside.

While I anticipated a greater awareness of how space affects identity through our cross-cultural discussions (the mere fact that England is a small island tipped me off) I was not expecting the variety of attitudes towards nature within my own class. As several students expressed distaste and distance from all things nature—from deep woods hikes to flies in the park—I began to question the assumption I held that Americans define themselves by a wilderness credo: go west, young man, that is where the future lies. Initially, I suspected the learning moments would stem from students' growing awareness of the cultural influences on their perceptions of nature and wilderness. But, quickly, I realized I had been guilty of holding my own assumptions, particularly in terms of how the class defined nature in American terms to begin with. While McCandless is a flawed character in many ways, I was surprised by the number of students who did not identify with his desires to seek a certain brand of authenticity from nature. Why would someone seek answers from a place as frightening and as lonely as Alaska and not their own community instead? Why would someone think that giving up material possessions would provide enlightenment in the first place? He wasn't testing out his independence, he was being selfish and rude. I was not expecting these reactions and was delighted by what I was learning too: while this course focused on comparative national culture to provide a deeper understanding of literary and real lives, the lines of culture within one country are nearly limitless, drawn across gender, age, class, race, and the like. Circling back to what we had learned from Fight Club, to claim there is a national Dream or Destiny risked appropriation, and failed to see that nature as recreation and re-creation (as in reinvention of the self) is just as dependent on race, class, and history as it is on reality.

In addition to meeting with my colleague in York the summer prior to the course, I took a week long hike through the North York Moors National

Park. Showing pictures of the countryside to my class, the villages and farms operating within the park's boundaries, challenged American notions of wilderness as separate from civilization. Again, this worked to show how our notions of space are dependent on place. Despite the diminished participation from our British collaborators, the webcam class sessions proved useful, even as we were still challenged by audio equipment. It amused me to watch my students from rural areas of the Northwest puff with pride when they considered how "removed" they were from "civilization," especially compared to our British peers. When the YSJU students did not understand camping in a tent far removed from a car or a hike where you might not come across another human being, my students embraced the Western persona that McCandless had sought as well. They had left themselves open for deconstruction: how might their pride be reflected in the American legacy of landscape and identity? Our British peers, conversely, did not seem ashamed of their notions of space, nor their lack of need to explore it. Traveling home on weekends, returning to their hometowns after graduation, seemed desirable; returning to one's hometown in America after college would be often perceived, however, as a step backwards in the individual's attempt to better him or herself. One student in my class put it this way, "When I learned that English people don't have the drive to better their positions in life--that they're content to just have what is allotted to someone of their station--that was a cultural shock to me. I wonder if that explains their acceptance of their physical environment, too?" Regardless of the problematic generalizations, what is inherent in her assumptions is that not wanting to "get out" of one's home place in the name of self-improvement is seen as worsening one's condition. Her comment strikes me as both restless and ambitious; the thought of staying put as a possibility to betterment is nearly impossible to see because of a deeply entrenched American value that equates movement with upward mobility, that likens an unlimited landscape with unlimited opportunities. Thus, the intent of the course is primed for realization: through a text, we increasingly become more conscious of the cultural influences on a literary narrative, which, in turn, leads to greater examination of how our individual narratives are shaped by culture too.

Considering place through a historical consciousness dovetailed with our final unit and text by Ian McEwan's book Atonement. Because the novel contemplates the distinctions between fiction and reality, especially during WWII, through metanarrative techniques, it provoked discussion on the accuracy of historical interpretations we see our national identities within. What past events define our nations and what values of identity are to be learned from their infusion into the culture? Here, collaboration with my colleague was essential, as we utilized Moodle to post historical interpretations relevant to our countries. She gathered comparative national symbols culled from history—John Bull v Uncle Sam, Britannia v Columbia, The Statue of Liberty v The Angel of the North—and asked, "What national stories are told by these symbols? Who tells the story and who is the speaker's audience?" Naturally, we could then begin to deliberate notions of patriotism and nationalism, how they define both collective and individual selves.

The novel calls into question historical truth through its protagonist Briony Tallis, a precocious young girl who claims she has witnessed a crime when, in fact, she has not. The repercussions of her misperceptions—her inability to detect that truth might exist beyond her myopic interpretation—speaks thematically to perspective and how the accuracy of events depends greatly on one's point of view. Without giving the ending away, the book's entire narrative itself is rendered suspect, and we are left wondering what is fact and what is fiction and where do the two cross paths. Or, as one student wrote in her mini-essay, "To end the book in this way was a further example of how our lives and environment shape us to hope and want to believe in certain things. It goes to show that even our sincerest attempts to understand the truth can be misconstrued in the haze of our cultural blindness and that the smallest misconception can have dire consequences."

Thematically, Atonement became summative for the objectives of the course: when we consider the exactitude of our interpretations of a text, how often do we fail to see it through multiple lenses? The more perspectives we can imagine while viewing a text, however, the closer we come to understanding that the meaning we make of it is one of many. Once this awareness is achieved, we become better readers of literature, while deconstructing ourselves as well.

Notes

[1] Russnow, M. (2012). The 2012 Golden Globes: The Taming of Ricky Gervais. *Huffington Post*. Retrieved from http://www.huffingtonpost.com/michael-russnow/the-2012-golden-globes-th_b_1208358.html.

[2] McNamara, Mary. (2011). Golden Globes: Host Ricky Gervais was just too nasty. *The Los Angeles Times*. Retrieved from http://articles.latimes.com/2011/jan/17/entertainment/la- et-globes-review-20110117.

[3] Steuver, Hank. (2011). TV review: Golden Globes-bring us the head of Ricky Gervais. *The Washington Post*. Retrieved from http://www.washingtonpost.com/wp-dyn/content/article/2011/01/16/AR2011011604722.htm

[4] Collin, R. (2012). Ricky Gervais falls flat. *The Telegraph*. Retrieved from http://www.telegraph.co.uk/culture/film/film-news/9017140/Golden-Globes-2012-Ricky-Gervais-falls-flat.html.

[5] Thier, D. (2011). "The Office": Why the American Remake Beats the British Original. *The Atlantic*. Retrieved from http://www.theatlantic.com/entertainment/archive/2011/04/the-office-why-the-american-remake-beats-the-british-original/237958/

[6] Elbow, P. (1973). *Writing Without Teachers*. New York: Oxford University Publishing.

[7] Persell, C. (2004). Using Focused Web-based Discussions to Enhance Student Engagement and Deep Understanding. *Teaching Sociology*, 32(1), 61-78.

[8] Williams, R. (1989) *Resources of Hope: Culture, Democracy, Socialism*. London: Verso. pp. 96.

[9] Lopez, B. (1989). Landscape and Narrative. *Crossing Open Ground*. New York: Vintage, 61-72.

Don't Forget To Be Awesome: An In-Depth Exploration of Nerdfighteria

by Brianna Castellini
Student Fellow, The Berglund Center for Internet Studies

I have never been considered "popular" by any definition, nor have been the type of person to be comfortable around, well, other people. Thankfully, having literally grown up with the Internet, I was not entirely alone, and had a social outlet in some form or other. Even social psychology would agree that I had a legitimate support system, because a group is merely "a collection of people who are perceived to be bonded together in a coherent unit to some degree." [1] But even I, so comfortable on the Internet from such a young age, couldn't have predicted the importance of a particular online community in my personal life. The community to which I'm specifically referring is that of Nerdfighteria, or the social group that arose from fans of the popular YouTube "vlogging" duo, brothers Hank and John Green.

Though they were only a few years apart, Hank and John didn't have much in common, but when "video blogging," or "vlogging" became popular on YouTube, they decided it might be interesting to give this new style of communication–and their waning relationship–a chance. And so started Brotherhood 2.0, a vlogging project the brothers used to keep in touch and get to know each other better. They signed up on YouTube under the channel name "VlogBrothers" and agreed that for the entire year of 2007 they would not exchange any textual communication; everything they had to say to each other had to be said during their videos, which they took turns posting every weekday. At first, it was just for fun, for the two grown brothers to reconnect via a growing internet trend. But as the year went on, the brothers created something completely unintentional that has been going strong for the past seven years: a community known as Nerdfighteria.

The term "nerdfighter" originated while Hank and John were still doing Brotherhood 2.0 (after 2007 they ceased with daily uploads, but continue to post on a regular weekly schedule), as a name for the people who considered themselves fans of the original video project. Urban Dictionary defines them as, "People who instead of being made up of cells and organs and stuff are actually made out of awesome." I became a nerdfighter in late 2008, during my junior year of high school, and have been proud to contribute and participate in the community ever since. The greatest part about being a nerdfighter isn't knowing that there are other fans of the Vlogbrothers out there, but knowing what those other fans can do, when they come together, under the responsible leadership of John and Hank. Today, we're going to look at a variety of nerdfighter contributions to society, from the charity event Project for Awesome and the Emmy-winning web series The Lizzie Bennet Diaries, to the sex positive YouTube channel Sexplanations and the international nerdfighter collaboration channel TheseFolk, among many other examples.

A Brief History

Ten years ago, neither John nor Hank would have been able to predict their future job as vloggers, partially because YouTube didn't exist ten years ago, and partially because they both already had careers. John Green, the elder sibling, is a New York Times bestselling young adult novelist, whose latest work The Fault in Our Stars and his 2008 novel Paper Towns are currently being adapted into film. In total, he has written four novels himself and collaborated on several others. In addition, John "was [the] 2006 recipient of the Michael L. Printz Award, a 2009 Edgar Award winner, and has twice been a finalist for the Los Angeles Times Book Prize."[2] He graduated from Kenyon College with a double-degree in English Literature and Religious Studies.

Hank, full name William, was definitely a more traditional "nerd" at a much younger age. He has a bachelor's degree in biochemistry and a masters in environmental studies, and his first career was running the website EcoGeek straight out of graduate school. "Within a year, EcoGeek was my full time job. There were plenty of other people who were excited about how technology could positively impact the environment." [3]

Education, Charity, and Jane Austen

As the nerdfighter community began with "a new kind of brotherhood," it makes sense to start our journey into "Nerdfighteria" by examining the projects spearheaded by John and Hank themselves to fully understand what a wide net this community has cast. A good first example would be Crash Course, an educational YouTube channel starring both brothers "consisting of five video series: Literature, World History, US History, Biology and Ecology." [4] Since that article was published, they've added series about English literature, chemistry, and psychology. The channel was started with help from YouTube, who back in late 2011 funded 100 new channels to create original programming that could, in theory, rival television. According to the USA Today in 2011,

> *YouTube is shelling out $100 million to producers, according to people familiar with the matter, who spoke on condition of anonymity. The money is an advance on advertising money the videos will bring in, and Google will recoup its portion first before splitting the proceeds. [5]*

Today, three years since the channel's launch, the brothers have over 1.4 million subscribers and 79 million video views. [6] Plus, their videos have been used in classrooms across the world. For a channel focusing on education with an average video length of ten minutes, that's pretty impressive.

Staying with the online video theme for a moment, we can move to what, in my opinion, is the most significant contribution of the nerdfighter community: the Project for Awesome. Green and Green write,

> *The very first Project for Awesome was organized in 2007, and has been held annually on December 17-18 every year since. During Project for Awesome, thousands of people post videos about and advocating for charities that decrease the overall level of world suck. As a community, we promote these videos and raise money for the charities. [7]*

In 2013, for example, nerdfighters raised over $800,000 for charity in 48 hours, which was split amongst the top-voted charities promoted by community videos.

The day before the 2013 event, John Green, in a brief phone interview with The Indianapolis Star, said, "This is my favorite two days of the year because it's when I'm reminded of how great the community that's built up around our videos is." [8]

In 2013, the top-voted charities included: The Harry Potter Alliance, a charity often working closely with the nerdfighter community; This Star Won't Go Out, a charity started by the parents of a teenage nerdfighter, who passed away from cancer in 2010; Save the Children; The Office of Letters and Light; To Write Love On Her Arms; and water.org, among several others. [9] During 2012, I made a Project for Awesome video about The Office of Letters and Light, the nonprofit that runs National Novel Writing Month, an event that tasks authors with writing an entire novel within the span of a single month, which I have participated in twice. I wrote my senior thesis novel during "NaNoWriMo," and wanted to give back, even though my own bank account wasn't sufficient for donations. 2012 was also the first year the "OLL" charity won a portion of donations, which I would like to think is related, in some part, to my efforts.

Before 2012, John and Hank would collect the donations during the Project for Awesome, through sites like Indiegogo, and donate directly from their own bank accounts. However, since 2012, all donations go to the brothers' 501(c)3 nonprofit: The Foundation to Decrease World Suck. The foundation "is 100% volunteer operated and exists solely for the purpose of raising funds to be donated to other non-profit organizations. The majority of fundraising is through and during the annual Project for Awesome." Having a nonprofit has made the Project for Awesome run much more smoothly, and also allows all donations made during that event to be tax deductible. These donations would not be possible without the engagement and dedication of the nerdfighter community.

Before we more deeply explore the community itself and the YouTube channels that have sprung from the Vlogbrothers' influence, I would be remiss to ignore mentioning The Lizzie Bennet Diaries. The Jane Austen Society of North America explains this project best,

> *One of the latest adaptations of this story is the Emmy Award-winning YouTube Series The Lizzie Bennet Diaries, produced by Hank Green and Bernie Su, which has become a social media phenomenon as it uses transmedia storytelling by presenting a modernized adaptation of Jane Austen's Pride and Prejudice through several YouTube channels as well as Twitter and Tumblr accounts (and even Pinterest and Lookbook accounts). [10]*

The idea came from Hank and his wife Kathrine's obsession with Austen's original novel, and also his extensive understanding of video-blogging and social media platforms, both of which were essential to telling the story. The characters in Lizzie's main video blog all had their own Twitter and Facebook accounts and would interact with one another as the story required, as well as with fans. For instance, an important milestone was Darcy following Lizzie on Twitter, right as the video blog showed them starting to get along. Though one could still easily follow the story if he or she only watched the videos, the multimedia elements served to deepen the immersion into Lizzie's world. I could go on to discuss how wildly popular and critically acclaimed the series was, but the Emmy (for Original Interactive Program) speaks for itself.

The Community at Large

Now that we understand the incredible influence of John and Hank, we have to discuss how that influence has translated to the nerdfighter community, through looking at various related YouTube channels such as TheseFolk and

Sexplanations, and various inspired projects like the novel "This Star Won't Go Out".

First, related YouTube channels. Though the Vlogbrothers certainly weren't the first to post jump-cut video blogs, they are arguably the most influential. A myriad of similar "collaborations" sprung from Brotherhood 2.0, beginning with the similarly yearlong projects like FiveAwesomeGirls and, later, FiveAwesomeGuys. Many of the individual members of those collab channels, short for collaborative channels or channels where multiple individuals post content, went on to become YouTube celebrities in their own rights, like Kristina Horner, who has produced and acted in a YouTube dystopian web series and holds over 120,000 subscribers, and Charlie McDonnell, a music, short film, and vlogging sensation with over 2.2 million subscribers.

And then there's TheseFolk, a collaboration channel of like-minded nerdfighters who met on an online forum in early 2011. Myself and thirteen other people started talking and decided to embark on a pair of sister collab channels, "TheseFolk" and "ThoseFolk." Seven members each, one video a day. I was chosen as the Sunday video-poster for TheseFolk, and so began one of the most interesting two and a half years of my Internet life.

Our sister channel ThoseFolk stopped posting consistently by the first summer, a mere four months after we began, but TheseFolk was still going strong. We had some lineup changes, going through three different "Mondays" and two "Fridays," but eventually we settled on seven consistent, passionate nerdfighters.

Each week we decided on a theme for our videos. At first, it was things like all answering the same questions to get to know each other a bit, but from there it descended into everything from "lip-sync week" to "make up your own exercise routine," the latter of which I used to film a Harry Potter-themed exercise regiment, using inside jokes from the novels to design different workouts.

Our long-distance friendships occasionally coalesced into real-life meet ups. First, our Monday and Saturday posters, both from the midwest, met up within the first couple months of our channel. The year after that, RJ, our Welsh Friday, and Laia, our Spanish Wednesday, met up while the Barcelona native was traveling in the UK. And during the summer of 2013, I visited Spain with my travel writing class and spent a day in Barcelona with Laia, seeing her city through her eyes.

After about a year and a half of posting impressively regularly, members started missing uploads on a more consistent basis. At the beginning of the project, we were mostly kids, with no real responsibilities, but by the end many of us were in serious relationships, entering or leaving college, and getting full-time jobs. It no longer made sense to stick to regular uploads, so on

October 28th, 2013, I uploaded the final video to our channel, entitled "Goodbye, TheseFolk," and we put the project to rest. However, though the channel itself has been retired, our friendships have not, and, to this day, we all stay in touch via Facebook and via our own personal YouTube channels, where many of us still post videos. I essentially grew up with TheseFolk, and to a more general degree, Nerdfighteria. Though I may not have initially sought out this group for self-knowledge as many do, I almost accidentally learned the type of person I wanted to and could be. [11]

Some of these inspired channels aren't meant to pay homage to the Vlogbrothers' style, however, and instead were simply made possible by the support and encouragement from the brothers and the community. One such channel would be Sexplanations, a sex-positive video series hosted by clinical sexoligist Dr. Lindsey Doe. Dr. Doe posts one to two videos a week, sometimes answering community questions about sex, relationships, and sexuality, and sometimes discussing a broader topic relating to those themes. The goal of Sexplanation is "to give the universe comprehensive sex education in an engaging fashion. We invest in this goal with many hours, skills, and kreplits–organizing knowledge of sexuality and making it beautifully accessible through YouTube." [12]

The channel has been active less than a year at the time of writing this article, but has already accrued over 95,000 subscribers and many dedicated followers. Dr. Doe's open, frank discussion of sexuality is welcoming for many people, who would otherwise be too embarrassed to discuss these issues with friends or family. Personally, it has been a great comfort for me to have easy access to these videos, considering the largely underwhelming nature of my own sex education in my public middle and high schools.

The final community project I want to discuss in relationship with Nerdfighteria is the novel "This Star Won't Go Out: The Life and Words of Esther Grace Earl." Esther Earl was a dedicated teenage member of the nerdfighter community, who passed away from thyroid cancer in 2010. She and John became friends in 2009, after they met at a Harry Potter convention, where Hank, a singer-songwriter, in addition to a science geek, was performing. Earl was a fan of John's books and helped other online friends maintain one of the largest nerdfighter fan websites. She was also the inspiration for John's protagonist in his novel The Fault in Our Stars, a young adult love story about teens with cancer.

According to her parents, Earl had wanted to be a published author since she was in third grade. [13] Unfortunately, her battle with cancer got in the way. After she died, her father collected her writings and diary entries, intending to print a few copies for friends and family. He sent it to John, who sent it to his editor, seeing the potential. From there, the small idea grew into a

431 page book, complete with diary entries, emails, and blogs by Earl, with an introduction penned by John, all exploring a young woman's battle with cancer and how the internet comforted her in her darkest hours. "The Internet is what you make of it," John said. "It can be used for distraction and dishonesty. Or you can choose to use it to extend and enrich our friendships and conversations, the way Esther did." The book was published in late January 2014, just four years after the primary author passed away. Earl also inspired a charity, This Star Won't Go Out, run by her parents for families with children living through cancer, which has given away more than $130,000 dollars since its inception and is also a consistent beneficiary of the Project for Awesome funds. [14]

I didn't know Esther, but a few weeks before she died I had subscribed to her YouTube channel, endeared to her perky attitude. Though I only got to see a few uploads before she passed away, her positivity through the most unfair of circumstances continues to inspire both myself and nerdfighters like me.

Feminist Analysis

Now that we fully understand the complexity and breadth of this community, we unfortunately have to look to a less fun facet of it: the recent sexual abuse scandal. Over the course of late 2013 and early 2014, several 20-something male YouTubers popular in Nerdfighteria were outed as sexually and emotionally abusive, [15] necessitating a response from John and Hank, as well as their DFTBA Records business partner, Alan Lastufka. It would have been easy, in this situation, for any of these adult men to support their long-time male friends from the community, especially, when the cases brought against them cited abuses from several years ago. It would have also been easy to downplay the seriousness of the accusations, since several didn't use the word "rape" or imply it, speaking more about non-penetrative abuse. Finally, it would have been incredibly easy to use slut shaming rhetoric to blame the young women victims for not being safe. However, in keeping with the pattern of remembering to be awesome, the community leaders stuck to progressive, third-wave-feminist rhetoric to discuss the issue.

First, some context for third-wave, also called sex-positive, feminism. "It might seem intuitively that the pro-sex position tends to encourage us to stake our political project on the liberatory value of sex per se, whereas the radical feminist position reads 'sexual freedom' as freedom from oppressive sexual relations." [16] Sex-positive feminism is the reclaiming of female sexuality, forcing it away from alignment with the opinions and perceptions of the patriarchy and, most unfortunately, of other women and feminists. Third-wave feminist rhetoric, then, can be defined as rhetoric that accepts sex, heterosexual or otherwise, for procreation or otherwise, but rejects abuses of it.

However, sometimes the definition of "sexual abuse" gets murky, leading otherwise third-wave feminists to slut shame women into blaming themselves for their "alleged" abuses, and to feel bad about how much sex they're having. Reynold and Ringrose observe, "Often a thinly veiled attack at the attractive 'assets' of the girl or women in question, slut shaming is of course a deeply classed discourse, whereby associating 'sluts' with 'prostitutes' and 'whores' her sexual value is to be diminished and kept in check." [17] Essentially, even third-wavers can fall into the trap of defining sex as bad, if it doesn't happen the way that a particular third-wave feminist belives sexual relations should happen. So when approaching situations of sexual abuse, it's important to keep rhetoric sex-positive, without trying to pigeonhole what types of sex we're being positive about, and the Green brothers, as well as Lastufka, have absolutely done that.

"I won't comment on the specifics of this relationship because that isn't my place." Hank wrote on his Tumblr, when the first of many male nerdfighters, in this particular case musician Tom Milsom, was revealed to have engaged in a sexual relationship with an underage fan. "But the mere fact that [the sexual relationship] existed infuriates me...sexual relationships need to be equitable and they can't be when people are in dramatically different life stages or when one person enters the relationship as a fan of another." [18]

Notice how Hank doesn't say that the underage fan should have known better, or that they shouldn't have been having sex at such a young age in the first place. Instead, he ignores the issue of sex entirely, and instead focuses on the context of the sex, which was a much older person taking advantage of a fan of his work, a person, whom he had intrinsic (being older) and extrinsic (being a musical idol of hers) control over. The fan was not shamed for having sex, but the abuser was.

John's response was much shorter than Hank's, as he mostly mirrored his brother's words, but it was just as important, as he's also a community leader.

> *I've written and deleted thousands of words about this today, and I'm grateful to Hank for saying most of what I wanted to say. Consenting adults: Go forth and do all the things! But the abuse of power we seem to see regularly in these manipulative fan/creator relationships is reprehensible and unacceptable. [19]*

Once gain, having a sexual relationship is not shameful, according to John, but manipulating someone into a relationship, especially when that someone is a younger fan, absolutely is.

Finally, we can look at Lastufka's response, another nerdfighter community leader, and how it continued the trend of not shaming the girl. In fact, Lastufka was the first to acknowledge his previous friendship with Milsom in his statement:

> *I am making no attempt to hide the fact Tom and I were once friends. He spent a weekend at my house, we worked on numerous songs and other musical projects together back in 2009. But hearing about some of the things he's done, and was doing back then, has hurt, and I no longer wish to make another dollar off his fame or name. [20]*

The latter sentence of this response referred to Lastufka taking Milsom's CDs and merchandise off of the DFTBA records website. Once again, an adult-male, in a position of power in this community did not try to excuse the actions of his former friend, did not shame the teenaged girl for being sexually active, and did not decry the act of sex as a whole.

As a final thought, Hank had this to say about the whole troubling situation:

> *My only consolation is that I honestly believe these issues are coming to light in this community not because they are more common, but because we are more empowered to speak out and not hide from or cover them up. And that's excellent, because you cannot fix a problem if you do not face a problem.*

Conclusion

I don't know why I didn't become a part of the nerdfighter community earlier. It wasn't for a lack of web access or time spent online. I, actually, don't even remember how I finally came to stumble upon this pot o' gold at the end of the cat-GIFs-and-porn rainbow that is the Internet. All I know is: I'm glad I did. Since becoming acquainted with this community, I attended VidCon, an in-person, three-day conference that the Vlogbrothers organize each year (since 2010) for content creators and industry professionals to discuss online video, where I met both Hank and John. I have made a Project for Awesome video in support of my favorite literary non-profit, donated to the Foundation to Decrease World Suck, bought nerdfighter teeshirts, started a nerdfighter collab channel with people from all around the world, and began my final semester in college. I have loved, lost, traveled around the world, started calling myself a feminist, and read a lot of books, many of them written by John Green. Above all, though, I have continued to deepen my involvement in and appreciation for one of the most massive, impressive, and giving communities on the Internet.

Interested in becoming a nerdfighter? Then you are one. Welcome friend, and DFTBA (Don't Forget To Be Awesome).

Notes

[1] Baron, R. A., Branscombe, N. R., & Byrne, D. (2008). *Social Psychology*. Allyn & Bacon (eds.), p. 380.

[2] Green, J. (2014). John Green's biography. Retrieved from http://johngreenbooks.com/bio-contact/

[3] Green, H. (2014). Hank Green, Internet Guy. Retrieved from http://hankgreen.com

[4] Lee, D. (2013). Romeo + Juliet + Chipotle = crash course. *Tampa Bay Times*. Retrieved from http://web1.sptimes.com/tb-two/blog/2013/2/14/romeo-juliet-chipotle-crash-course/

[5] Nakashima, R. (2011). YouTube launching 100 new channels. *USA Today*. Retrieved from http://usatoday30.usatoday.com/tech/news/story/2011-10-29/youtube-original-programming/50997002/1

[6] Green, J., & Green, H. (2014). Crashcourse youtube channel. Retrieved from http://www.youtube.com/user/crashcourse

[7] Green, J., & Green, H. (2013). About:: Project for awesome. Retrieved from http://www.projectforawesome.com/about

[8] Lindquist, D. (2013, December 16). John Green is fired up for 'Project for Awesome'. Indy Star. Retrieved from http://www.indystar.com/story/entertainment/arts/2013/12/16/john-green- youtube-vlogbrothers-hank-the-fault-in-our-stars/4041719/

[9] Green, J. (2014). Giving Away Over $700,000 [Web Video]. Retrieved from http://www.youtube.com/watch?v=8Yml2xJdooA/

[10] Halvorsen Zerne, L. (2013). Ideology in the Lizzie Bennet Diaries. *Persuasions On-Line*, 34(1).

[11] Tajfel, H., & Turner, J. C. (1986). The social identity theory of intergroup behavior. In S. Worchel & W. G. Austin (Eds.), *The social psychology of intergroup relations* (2nd ed., pp. 7-24. Monterrey, CA: Brooks-Cole.

[12] Doe, L. (2014). Sexplanations-subbable. Retrieved from https://subbable.com/sexplanations

[13] Minzesheimer, B. (2014). "nerdfighter" Esther Earl becomes an author. *USA Today*. Retrieved from http://www.usatoday.com/story/life/books/2014/01/27/this-star-

wont-go-out-by-esther-earl/4800107

[14] Earl, L. (2013). This star won't go out foundation: Our mission. Retrieved from http://tswgo.org/our-mission.html

[15] Baker-Whitelaw, G. (2014). The Tom Milsom abuse scandal and YouTube's troubling cult of worship. Retrieved from http://www.dailydot.com/fandom/tom-milsom-underage-sexscandal/

[16] Glick, E. (2000) Sex positive: Feminism, queer theory, and the politics of transgression. *Feminist Review*. 19-45.

[17] Renold, E., & Ringrose, J. (2011) Slut-shaming, girl power and 'sexualisation': Thinking through the politics of the international slutwalks with teen girls. *Gender and Education*. 333-43.

Book Reviews

Volume 13

Diane Duane's *Omnitopia Dawn*

A Review by Jenn Ngo

Duane, Diane (2010). *Omnitopia Dawn*. New York, NY: DAW Books, Inc.

The Berglund Center always offered me great opportunities to learn more about the Internet around me, so when they suggested Diane Duane's Omnitopia Dawn, I only had to read the synopsis to be once again enchanted. I was not familiar with Duane's many science fiction and fantasy novels, but my interest in the Internet and related technology's impact on the way we conduct our 21st century lives made Omnitopia seem like something I'd be very interested in reading about.

One passage in particular stood out to me as an apt summary of the Omnitopia experience: "Any kind of game you could think of was here somewhere, either as a Macrocosm built by the game company's in-house staff, or as Microcosms built by favored gamers. Endless possibilities, endless challenges were here...." [1]

Omnitopia is an online gaming experience, much akin to our world's World of Warcraft [2] or Second Life [3], in which players can assume an identity and choose an in-game world to play in. Omnitopia is a truly "massively multiplayer" experience containing 121 worlds, or Macrocosms, for players to travel throughout and explore. There are also countless Microcosms, smaller-scale worlds designed and maintained by an elite group of users, which is where we meet one of our players, Rik Maliani, or Arnulf the Manyfaced, as he is known in-game.

First, we are led through a sneak peek of Omnitopia from the perspective of an average-Joe player, Rik Miliani. He takes the reader through Telekil, the singular original game world of Omnitopia, to the Ring of Elich, the gateway to new worlds—"the discovery of this gigantic game within a game... had turned the massively multiplayer online gaming world on its ear. No one had ever dreamed that such a number of gaming worlds, or such complexity and magnitude, could or would ever be staged inside the same platform." [4] Throughout Omnitopia Dawn, Duane takes the opportunity to paint a picture of a place of infinite possibilities, literally from the ground up.

A particularly interesting concept in Omnitopia is the coveted opportunity some players receive to create their own Microcosms. Duane's descriptions of what goes into a Microcosm (starting, of course, with a dark empty space and an illuminated neon "FOR RENT" sign) are intriguing: "bright wirelike outlines of light...described where everything—table, trees, flowers, upside-down pterodactyl—had been...a visual expression of the framework that the virtual textures and other sensory information are hung on." [5] I also appreciated Duane's descriptions of various areas of Omnitopia which characters travel through, whether for business or pleasure. Her attention to detail, building fantastic worlds, is where Omnitopia shines.

Moving on to the story, most of the focus is placed on the conflict between Omnitopia's First Player, Creator, and CEO, Dev Logan, and his rival and former business partner, Phil Sorenson. Other side characters' stories support the main conflict between the two, as Phil sets in motion a plan to bring the Omnitopia's expansion rollout to a screeching halt, and his former business partner to his knees.

My one issue with Omnitopia is that the story moves much too slowly, roving between too many points of view, sometimes to the point of incoherence. While I appreciate that it may have been a stylistic choice to mirror the experience of a more adventurous player spending time travelling through various Omnitopian Macrocosms, I tend to prefer a more straight-and-to-the-point narrative. I found it easy to not really care what was happening in the insignificant tales of the magazine reporter or the hacker, until they began to join into what I thought was the most exciting event of the story: about a day before the rollout. Then it wasn't until a surprising twist in the plot was revealed about a quarter from the end of the book, that things got really interesting.

Upon finishing the book, I was a little disappointed, because I felt that the storyline with the most intrigue and potential only began to be revealed in the last quarter. After finding out that Omnitopia Dawn is the first in a series, however, I felt better about the way the book ends. That said, I am looking forward to this story's further development, now that the groundwork for the story has been laid.

Notes

[1] Duane, Diane (2010). *Omnitopia Dawn*. New York, NY: DAW Books. pp. 9.

[2] See: http://us.battle.net/wow/en/

[3] See: http://secondlife.com/

[4] Duane (2010), pp. 13.

[5] Duane (2010), pp. 53.

Birgit Bräuchler *Cyberidentities at War*

A Review by Aaron Greer
Department of Anthropology, Pacific University

Brauchler, Birgit (2013) *Cyberidentities at War: The Moluccan Conflict on the Internet.* (J. Gaines, Trans.). New York, New York: Berghan (Original work Published 2003).

Violent conflict, sadly, is not new to human interaction. But violent conflict continued on the Internet is new, as anthropologist Birgit Bräuchler demonstrates in her recently translated book, Cyberidentities at War: The Moluccan Conflict on the Internet. Bräuchler aims to get anthropology up to speed with current studies of the Internet, by conducting an ethnography of the clash between Muslims and Christians in the Moluccas that took place both on the ground and in cyberspace. Bräuchler's dual-sited ethnography challenges anthropologists to look beyond terrestrial field sites for studies of cultural change, conflict, and identity politics. What Bräuchler offers in her cyberanthropological study is an investigation of how geographically situated conflicts can be extended online. In Bräuchler's terms, Internet identities are expanded domains of socio-spatial contexts, [1] thus, offering anthropologists insight into the means and media of how territorialized subjects expand identities in deterritorialized spaces. [2]

Violent conflict erupted in 1999 in the Moluccas after long simmering tensions between Muslims and Christians boiled over after a seemingly minor and, not surprisingly, contested event involving a bus driver and a passenger. [3] What precisely happened is not clear, but the aftermath certainly is. Hundreds of mosques and churches were torched and thousands of lives were claimed, mostly in horrific massacres. Each act of destruction touched off a new episode in a blood feud that took four years to settle. Making matters worse, the conflict was exacerbated by outside actors, including the Indonesian government, who had vested interests (mostly monetary) in prolonging the feud. Within weeks of the outbreak of violence, several websites emerged that aimed to organize followers, garner support from around the world, and broadcast details of the conflict as the writers saw it.

Bräuchler's aim was to sort through the many websites, join mailing lists hosted by Christian and Muslim groups, and follow online discussions. In addition, Bräuchler spent a year in the Moluccas from 1996-97, two years before the outbreak of violence. Her customary year of territorialized fieldwork provided her with the lived context necessary to make links between the emergent discourses online and the lives of the Internet actors offline. Through this method, Bräuchler distinguishes her work from other online ethnographic projects that make no attempt to document and analyze offline contexts. [4] The dual-sited approach allowed her to analyze the ways in which identity politics in the Moluccas were transferred to the Internet, thus intensifying the conflict.

The content Bräuchler discovered on several of the busiest websites is hardly surprising. The first and most prolific Christian site to emerge, the Masariku Mailing List (MML), at first attempted a somewhat even-handed account of the conflict. This soon gave way to fear mongering, slander, and outraged reports of the "cruelty of the Muslim attackers, their superiority with regard to weapons, and the involvement of the military and jihad fighters." [5] The Muslim websites hardly differed. Here Muslims cast the conflict as one not simply between Moluccan Christians and Muslims, but one of a global conflict between Judeo-Christian imperialists (of which the US is a key actor) and Islam. In this conspiratorial accounting, the US, in collusion with Israel, is attempting to Christianize and Zionize the world, starting with (where else) the Moluccas. [6] The rhetoric of one Muslim website states emphatically that, "We are prepared to destroy the American troops!!!...America has never won [a war, presumably] apart from Rambo!" [7]

Bräuchler ultimately concludes from her exhaustive study of online material that a pattern of action/reaction emerged, just as conflicts offline do. [8] Both sides feared "religious cleansing" and sought to remedy that possibility by using the Internet to control their identities, representation, and accounts of the offline events. [9] The Internet offered Christian and Muslim cyberactors a medium to promote a sense of authenticity and provide evidence to support their arguments. Additionally, each side could enlist the support of distant communities and keep them updated, often by the minute, on the conflict.

Bräuchler's ethnography offers anthropologists valuable insight into uses of new technologies to expand offline realities. Indeed, her biggest contribution to anthropological theory is this very point. That said, such a conclusion offers little insight into the ways in which technologies shape, transform, or contour interpretive logics or discursive frameworks. While the ethnography does alert readers to uses of the Internet in violent conflict, it reads like a protracted accounting (354 pages) of, as the great anthropologist Clifford Geertz would put it, "one damn thing after the next." Bräuchler's analytical framework only illuminates how the Internet continues offline hostilities online. Beyond that, there is virtually no analysis of Internet technology's effect on performative logics. This problem is compounded by the simple problem of rapid obsolescence. Bräuchler's book was published in German in 2003. English readers couldn't get their hands on it until 2011, well after the advent of YouTube, Facebook, Twitter, Tumblr, and countless other networking sites. Bräuchler addresses this problem in an epilogue from 2011, which attempts to bring the ethnography up to date. The problem however is that the 340 pages previous to it read like a 1950s account of space travel. As a snapshot in the early life of the Internet and its role in a regional conflict, the book is rather unique. But beyond that, it fails to say anything surprising about the Internet and modernity.

Notes

[1] Brauchler, B. (2013). *Cyberidentities at War: The Moluccan Conflict on the Internet.* (Jeremy Gaines, Trans). New York, NY: Berghan. pp. 17-18.

[2] Brauchler (2013), p. 43

[3] Brauchler (2013), p. 64

[4] Brauchler, (2013), p. 43

[5] Brauchler, (2013), p. 103

[6] Brauchler, (2013), p. 182

[7] Brauchler, (2013), p. 180

[8] Brauchler, (2013), p. 260

[9] Brauchler, p. 314

EDITORIAL

Volume 13

NSA Surveillance: How it's happening and why you should care

Editor's Note: The opinions expressed here are those of a student fellow and do not necessarily represent the opinion of Interface or the Berglund Center for Internet Studies.

By Paul O'Day
Student Fellow, The Berglund Center for Internet Studies

The government has been monitoring Internet traffic for nearly as long as the Internet has existed. By tapping Internet service providers (ISPs), they can tap the data stream before it reaches your computer. This means they have access to everything that's unencrypted, and even if the connection is encrypted, they'll still be able to tell what sites you visit. ISP monitoring can only give the government so much, however; after all, some traffic is encrypted, which is why the government also cooperates with the tech companies on the other end, like Facebook or Google, meaning they still have access to much of the encrypted data by asking the company you sent it to.

Of course, most of the details about these activities are secret—the significant information we have comes from leaks. Until recently, the fact that the NSA has programs to gather data directly from Internet companies was pure speculation, and the full extent of government monitoring is still secret. However, what information we have shows a clear disregard for the privacy of Internet users by the government. The judicial system has intervened to uphold the law on at least one occasion, and NSA officials have repeatedly lied to the public about the existence and scope of these programs, as well as about any abuses of these systems. Personnel have abused these systems, which is to be expected—every system is abused—but far too many abuses were due to a lack of proper safeguards.

Abuse and secrecy aren't the only problems with these programs. They certainly violate implied protections under the fourth amendment against unreasonable search and seizure. The government is gathering and saving a massive amount of information about its citizens' Internet habits, and it would be possible for them to put together a file on the interests, political leanings, connections, and browsing history of any citizen that regularly uses the Internet. This would be illegal and time-consuming, and while there's no indication that the government is doing this, the capability exists.

The main law being used to justify most of this surveillance is the Foreign Intelligence Surveillance Act (FISA). Enacted in 1978 in response to illegal spying by the FBI and CIA, FISA defines who the government is allowed to spy on, under what circumstances, and the procedures for doing so. Specifically, it prevents the government from intentionally targeting US citizens in surveillance, and limits targeting foreign citizens for more than 24 hours, without acquiring a warrant. Despite this, the NSA still monitors US traffic. In fact, in 2011, the FISA court ruled that the NSA was illegally collecting US emails and had to stop. Instead, the NSA now separates US emails into separate database [1], the justification for which is that the DOD guidelines don't count data as "collected" unless it is "received for use by a DOD intelligence component [including NSA agents] in the course of their official duties." [2] Thus, according to the DOD guidelines, it's ok for the NSA to store US emails without a warrant, but they need a warrant if they want to read them.

The most rudimentary form of monitoring the government conducts is at the ISP level. There have been various programs to do this, but the most successful (and as far as we know, the one currently in use) was revealed in 2003, by AT&T technician Mark Klien. Klien reported that there was a room in the SBC communications building in San Francisco called Room 641A that was being used to monitor Internet traffic. Former senior NSA analyst William Binney claims that there are "10 or 20" of these as of 2006; Room 641A is simply part of the main system in place to monitor traffic at the ISP level. [3]

Internet traffic consists of chunks of data called packets. A packet can be thought of as a letter, consisting of: the header, which is like the envelope with the recipient's and senders addresses; and the data, which is the letter's contents. Room 641A contains equipment used for Deep Packet Inspection (DPI), which filters traffic by both the header and the data. This means that the NSA can filter traffic according to who sent it, where it's going, and what it contains. However, The spread of encryption is making DPI less useful. Encrypted traffic consists of packets where the data part can be read only by the sender and the recipient, meaning that the NSA can see only who is communicating, but not what they're communicating about.

One of the ways the NSA addresses this weakness is with a program called PRISM. PRISM involves the cooperation of as many as 100 US tech companies. [4] Instead of monitoring Internet traffic directly, the NSA gets the data from tech companies the data was sent to. Former NSA contractor Edward Snowden revealed it in July of 2013. The exact details of how the government gathers the data is unclear, but leaked NSA slides show that PRISM involves "collection [of data] directly from the servers from these US data providers: Microsoft, Yahoo, Google, Facebook, PalTalk, AOL, Skype, YouTube, Apple." [5] The slide says the NSA gets data "directly from the server", which could mean a couple of things: either the NSA has direct access to the server or the company takes the data directly from their server and gives it to the NSA. Google has denied allowing the NSA direct access to its servers, saying that they "disclose user data to government in accordance with the law, and we review all such requests carefully." [6] Apple has denied ever hearing about PRISM. [6]

The NSA claims it only gathers data under PRISM and related programs on a case by case basis – a fact sheet put out by Director of National Intelligence James Clapper, in response to the leaks, claims that "Under Section 702 of FISA, the United States Government does not unilaterally obtain information from the servers of US electronic communication service providers." [7] Note that Clapper only says the NSA does not unilaterally obtain information from the servers of US electronic communication service providers. Outside the US, the NSA is much less restricted, because they are allowed to assume that traffic going in and out of foreign servers is foreign, which gives rise to another program meant to gather data directly from Internet companies, called MUSCULAR, which was also revealed in the Snowden leaks. MUSCULAR involves tapping the private international networks of these large Internet companies. Since the tapping happens overseas, there are much fewer restrictions on it, allowing the NSA to freely gather data that would be encrypted when sent to the end user – before it's encrypted. [8] Like room 641A, MUSCULAR is becoming less and less useful as tech companies start encrypting their internal communication: Google started encrypting their internal communications in November 2013, and Yahoo plans to do so by early 2014. [9]

Even though we don't have all the details, it's pretty clear the NSA is heavily invested in monitoring Internet traffic; even if they don't look at it, having the capability to gather this much data is a clear violation of our right to privacy. The right to privacy is one of the most important. It's also one of the most underappreciated – after all, why would a law-abiding citizen care if the government monitors their Internet traffic, especially, if it's in the name of stopping terrorism? Systemic encroachments on the privacy of civilians are a key aspect of oppressive governments. A government that is comfortable abusing its technical advantages to gather a complete profile of all of its citizens effectively has the ability to blackmail any of its citizens. On a less extreme scale, if the NSA has access to the private Internet history and emails of government officials, they have leverage to blackmail those officials—especially those up for election. Imagine if a the NSA threatened to publicly release embarrassing emails or browsing habits of any congressman who tried to cut their funding, hurting their reelection chances. It's impossible to know if the NSA does this, but at this point, the NSA enforces the only regulations on the NSA. Losing the right to privacy also means losing protection for whistleblowers like Edward Snowden, who is now a fugitive from the US government. If the NSA had access to his email records, he almost certainly would have been stopped, before his leaks reached the public, only serving to further cover-up a fundamental flaw of the system as a whole.

Even if we trusted the government to protect our right to privacy in the face of growing surveillance, the government is made up of flawed individuals. The Snowden leaks detail "thousands of abuses", from mistyped search terms (one incident caused the NSA to gather thousands of phone calls from Washington DC because of a software glitch) to agents spying on love interests. [10] Officially, the NSA admits to an average of one abuse a year over the past decade. [11] These abuses are happening on a relatively small scale, but they serve to highlight an important point: the apparatus that this data is flowing into is not a perfect machine of justice, but a complex collection of people, some good, some bad, some competent, others incompetent.

Over the past decade or so, the NSA has successfully set up a very extensive Internet monitoring system. They can monitor nearly anything a person does on the Internet. They have access to browsing history through programs like room 641a, and they have direct access to emails and other data through programs like PRISM and MUSCULAR. These monitoring capabilities are not in and of themselves a problem, being able to intercept criminal's communications has always been an important part of law enforcement, and it's becoming more important with the rise of ubiquitous communication devices like cellphones and laptops, as well as the rise of virtual crime. The strategies employed by the NSA to monitor Internet traffic are troubling. The NSA has shown a clear disregard for our right to privacy and the law. Unfortunately, they did not do this alone. Congress has been complacent at best, and the judicial branch has been slow to challenge violations of the law. Now that the full extent of this surveillance is becoming clear, it's more important than ever to write your elected officials, raise awareness, and support companies that respect individual privacy.

Notes

[1] CNET News. (2013). Facts on the Collection of Intelligence Pursuant to Section 702. Retrieved October 10, 2013 from http://www.scribd.com/doc/146570400/PRISM-Facts-on-the-Collection-of-Intelligence-Pursuant-to-Section-702

[2] Department of Defense. (1982). *Procedures Governing the Activities of DOD Intelligence Components that affect United States Persons.* (DoD 5240 1-R). Retrieved December 13, 2013 from http://www.fas.org/irp/doddir/dod/d5240_1_r.pdf

[3] Bamford, J. (2012). The NSA Is Building the Country's Biggest Spy Center (Watch What You Say) . *Wired.* Retrieved October 9, 2013 from http://www.wired.com/threatlevel/2012/03/ff_nsadatacenter/all/1

[4] Gellman, B., & Poitras, L. (2013). U.S., British intelligence mining data from nine U.S. Internet companies in broad secret program – The Washington Post.The Washington Post. Retrieved October 10, 2013 from http://www.washingtonpost.com/investigations/us-intelligence-mining-data-from-nine-us-Internet-companies-in-broad-secret-program/2013/06/06/3a0c0da8-cebf-11e2-8845-d970ccb04497_story.html

[5] Ball, J. (2013). NSA's Prism surveillance program: how it works and what it can do. *The Guardian* . Retrieved October 10, 2013 from http://www.theguardian.com/world/2013/jun/08/nsa-prism-server-collection-facebook-google

[6] Greenwald, G., & MacAskill, E. (2013). NSA Prism program taps in to user data of Apple, Google and others. *The Guardian*. Retrieved October 10, 2013 from http://www.theguardian.com/world/2013/jun/06/us-tech-giants-nsa-data

[7] CNET News (2013).

[8] Gellman, B., & Soltani, A. (2013). NSA infiltrates links to Yahoo, Google data centers worldwide, Snowden documents say. *The Washington Post*. Retrieved December 15, 2013 from http://www.washingtonpost.com/world/national-security/nsa-infiltrates-links-to-yahoo-google-data-centers-worldwide-snowden-documents-say/2013/10/30/e51d661e-4166-11e3-8b74-d89d714ca4dd_story.html

[9] Brandon, R. (2013). The Verge. *The Verge*. Retrieved December 15, 2013 from http://www.theverge.com/2013/11/18/5118150/yahoo-ceo-marissa-mayer-plans-to-encrypt-data-against-nsa-by-2014

[10] Gellman, B. (2013). NSA broke privacy rules thousands of times per year, audit finds. *The Washington Post*. Retrieved December 14, 2013 from http://articles.washingtonpost.com/2013-08-15/world/41431831_1_washingtonpost-national-security-agency-docments

[11] Dozier, K. (2013). NSA admits rare willful surveillance violations. *Yahoo! News*. Retrieved December 15, 2013 from http://news.yahoo.com/nsa-admits-rare-willful-surveillance-violations-211422017.html

Director's Message

The Berglund Center for Internet Studies has been involved in the analysis and dissemination of the impacts of the Internet on the world since 2000. As the web turned 25 this year, we have lived the influence that the Internet has had on our lives, from giving us to access vast amounts of information, creating new and exciting platforms for communication, education, social interactions and the development of new business platforms, services and products. As the Internet evolves, so does our own Berglund Center, and its Journal *Interface*, which over the past 13 years, has served as an open source publication to share our collective voice on the Internet and its impacts.

The Internet has stopped being a "thing" such as electricity stopped being a thing we speak of with awe. We have evolved our thinking and adjusted our mission and vision to reflect the new opportunities that creativity presents in the current state of technology, and have chosen to support multi-disciplinary scholarship, entrepreneurship, and the development of leadership skills through the incubation of ideas, products, and services at the Center. This mission expands on the Center's original intention to be a source of information about the disruptive technology that was the Internet, adding a new focus on finding and defining disruptive and innovative ideas, products, and services. In essence, we are broadening our horizons beyond the Internet and engage in scholastic and creative endeavors that will shape the direction and future of our Center and that of *Interface*.

This new direction is an exciting and challenging opportunity to allow *Interface* to evolve into a peer-reviewed, special topics publication that would highlight areas of creativity and innovation within all areas of scholarship, not just education or computing, and open the doors to publish new papers with a broader impact. We intend on increasing the rigor and scope of Interface by reducing the number of issues and accepting papers that have a common theme, in order to create a topic-specific, special issue focused, open source online publication.

This new direction will require time to establish the new infrastructure for Interface, to set-up the publishing staff, editors and reviewers, and to launch the new publication. The volume of Interface in front of you will, therefore, be the last one published under the current format and content guidelines. Special thanks and acknowledgements are needed for the wonderful staff, in particular Spencer and Matt, the Berglund Fellows and authors, as well as the Berglund Board of Advisors, who have been instrumental in providing and maintaining direction to the Center and Interface for all these years.

Special acknowledgements are due to Nicole Nowlin, Program Coordinator of the Berglund Center (2013-2014), and to Theresa Floyd, Program Coordinator (Floyd started working at Pacific in 1994 and retired from the Center in fall 2013) for their work and leadership, ensuring that the Center and Interface ran smoothly and on schedule for all those years. They both performed tasks above and beyond the expectations of the position and the success of the fellows and students over all those years is a reflection of their devotion to the mission and to the continued education of the future generation of leaders.

J. Andy Soria, Ph.D.
Director of the Berglund Center

APPENDICES

Volume 13

Contributors

Gavin Brown, Student Fellow

Gavin Brown is a student at Pacific University studying Film and Video Production with a minor in Comparative Religion. He is originally from Seaside, Oregon. At Pacific he is heavily involved in activities such as Film Club, Handball Club, and freshman outdoor orientation programs. After college, Gavin plans on pursuing a career in animation and visual effects in Portland, Oregon.

Gavin currently works at the Berglund Center for Internet Studies as an assistant video editor, and writes for Interface as a student fellow. Some of the topics he has written about include: Ebooks as a tool for free education, the use of Twitter as a campaigning tool for presidential elections, and the spead of Internet memes and their effects, good and bad, on the Internet.

Leonard D. Duboff, J.D.

Leonard D. DuBoff is an attorney specializing in business and intellectual property law. Leonard was a professor of law at Northwestern School of Law of Lewis & Clark College for 23 years and has pioneered the field of art law, written extensively on the subject, and lectured all over the world on business and intellectual property. His two-volume text entitled The Deskbook of Art Law is frequently referred to by judges, lawyers, legal commentators and others who are interested in finding out about this important field of law, and it has also been adopted by several law schools as the basis for their courses on art law.

Taylor Farris, Student Fellow

Taylor Farris is a sophomore from Grants Pass, Oregon. She is a candidate for a self-designed major in Communication Studies on top of her major in Creative Writing. After leaving Pacific, Taylor looks towards a two-year commitment with Teach for America to teach high school English. She is an active member of Pacific Speech, and works with both the undergraduate admissions team as well as the new student Orientation program; she also worked with the Pacific Index, the Boxercast morning news show at Pacific, and volunteered with students from a local elementary school.

During her time with the Berglund Center, Taylor enjoys researching topics relating to innovation in education—particularly in conjunction with social media. However, she is also invested in topics concerning global betterment such as clean water, human rights, and advancement in the medical fields.

Forest Grove Conversations Contest 2013

Monique Ramberg, Lewis Beckett, Sydney Weber, Stephanie Fachiol, Noah Drewrey, Rachel Martins, Joelle Bruckert-Frisk

In 2013, the Berglund Center sponsored the Forest Grove Conversations Contest, which tasked elementary and middle school students, with writing about the Internet. The winners of the contest received publication in *Interface.* These young women and men, attend Forest Grove area schools between the first grade and the ninth grade.

Michael Geraci, M.F.A.

Michael Geraci is an associate professor in Pacific University's Integrated Media program. Mike also teaches online courses for the University of Oregon's Applied Information Management Masters program, where he received his Master of Science degree in 2002. Prior to teaching, Mike spent eight years managing Pacific's department of Educational Technologies. In addition, he has experience working as an independent web developer, graphic designer and video production specialist. Mike's scholarly interests center upon the continued evolution of the Web, user experience, and typographic design.

Aaron Greer, Ph.D., Assistant Professor

Aaron Greer is an assistant professor of Anthropology at Pacific University. He is too post-structural to believe in biographies.

Brently Johnson, Associate Professor

Brent Johnson is an Associate Professor of English at Pacific University. He has published creative nonfiction essays and poetry in journals ranging from Ascent and RiverTeeth to Gray's Sporting Journal and North American Review. He is currently working on a memoir based on his travels in an RV with his family through Montana as well as a chapbook of flyfishing poems.

He and his wife, with their two sons, live in Hillsboro.

Julia Naumes, Senior Project Award Winner

Julia is a 2013 graduate from Pacific University and a former member of the Berglund Center, where she helped develop and stage the G2CS summer camp.

Nancy Neudauer, Ph.D.

Nancy Ann Neudauer received her MA and PhD in Mathematics, with a minor in Business and Law, and her BBA in Actuarial Science and Risk Management from the University of Wisconsin. She is the Director of the MAA Dolciani Mathematics Enrichment Grant Program, which funds projects for mathematically talented middle and high school students. As Associate Director of Pacific Northwest Project NExT, a faculty-development program for those interested in innovative pedagogy, she plays an instrumental role in program activities and organising workshops and conferences. Actively involved with the Mathematical Association of America for as long as she can remember (she gave her first talk at an MAA meeting while still a high school student), she has more recently served on the Board of Governors, on several committees, and will be the Visiting Mathematician at the national offices for the autumn of 2014. Nancy is the recipient of the MAA PNW Distinguished Teaching Award. Beyond her primary mathematical research in matroid theory, graph theory, combinatorics, and enumeration, she has applied mathematics to several projects in industry and science. A prolific researcher, Nancy has published peer-reviewed articles on all of these topics. Nancy's passion to teach and desire to communicate mathematics while encouraging students to become independent learners prompted her to develop Directed Reading, a strategy for teaching students to read mathematics. She recently taught a graduate course at the African Institute for Mathematical Sciences, has been a Visiting Scholar at several universities, is Program Chair for the Combinatorial Potlatch, and has organised many conferences. Speaking on her mathematical and pedagogical research, Nancy organizes sessions and presentations around the world to diverse audiences. When not sharing the beauty of mathematics with her students, she races sailboats and travels wherever she can, rarely leaving the house without her passport and a packed bag, just in case.

Jenn Ngo

Jenn Ngo graduated from Pacific University with a major in studio arts with an emphasis in photography and a minor in integrated media. During her time at Pacific, Jenn worked as a graphic designer, designing various posters to promote theatre and band productions. At the Berglund Center, Jenn worked as a publisher and copy editor, putting together Interface. Jenn hopes to continue her writing, photography, and to find work in a field that interests her, such as publishing, design, or photography. She currently works as a photographer/designer at Striking Image photography. She travels to local martial arts, dance, and gymanstics schools to take portraits of the students.

Nicole Nowlin, Program Coordinator, Berglund Center for Internet Studies

Nicole is a graduate of Pacific University who has a degree in Business Administration (International Business) and Japanese with a special interest in international relations. She was a Fullbright finalist for a research grant to Japan in 2011/2012 and was an active member of Pacific's Speech and Debate Team. In her spare time, she caters to her voracious appetite for fiction through novels, comics, movies, and writing. Her interest in comics, particularly Japanese manga, led her to her Student Fellowship in the Berglund Center for Internet Studies and her articles on scanlations and e-manga.

Justin Redona, Student Fellow

Justin Redona is currently a senior at Pacific University working towards a Bachelor's of Science, double majoring in biology and music. As a person of Filipino descent, Justin is heavily rooted in his personal goals and values, always determined to accomplish and achieve his life's dreams. He is very thankful for making it far in his journey through life as he looks back at what he has managed to gain at Pacific University. Aside from his role as a Berglund Student Fellow, Justin also served as a Resident Assistant, Student Ambassador, and music student-teacher of the String Project at Pacific University. Justin plans to attend medical school after graduation.

Steve Rhine, Ph.D.

Steve Rhine, Ed. D. is a Professor of Education in the School of Education at Willamette University in Salem, Oregon. Dr. Rhine began as a high school mathematics teacher for eleven years. Upon completing his doctorate at UCLA, he began a career in teacher education that now spans 17 years. He has been awarded numerous federal and other grants focusing on uses of educational technology that total over $3.5 million. He directed the Oregon Technology in Education Network (OTEN), from 2001-04 that was then funded by the Preparing Tomorrow's Teachers to Use Technology (PT3) program.

He has also been instrumental in a Teacher Quality Enhancement Partnership grant that funded OTEN 2004-09. He is currently working on a $740,000 Fund for the Improvement of Post-Secondary Education (FIPSE) grant that will make use of research on algebraic thinking to help prepare pre-service teachers with understanding of how students struggle as well as technological tools to help develop understanding of challenging topics in algebra. In 2000, he participated on the writing team for ISTE's National Educational

Technology Standards (NETS) for Teachers. He has presented at multiple educational technology conferences. Dr. Rhine has taught courses in Educational Technology, Educational Psychology, Action Research, Multicultural Education, and Mathematics Education.

His current research includes work on conducting online dialogue with student teachers based on digital video clips of their teaching, the role of Web 2.0 in classrooms, and the transition of Mexican and Ukrainian im/migrant students into Oregon schools. He has recently published two books. The first, "A Brilliant Teacher", an engaging account of his year-long trip around the world with his wife and three children. The second, "Integrated Technologies, Innovative Learning: Insights from the PT3 Program", an edited book of stories of efforts by institutions to integrate technology in the development of preservice teachers.

Matthew Yasuoka, Student Fellow

Matthew Yasuoka is a junior double major in Political Science and Creative Writing. He is an active participant in speech and debate. During his free time, Matthew enjoys writing poetry and runs the slam poetry club on campus. He works at the Berglund Center as an editor/publisher and writes for Interface as a Berglund Student Fellow.

Authority System: Evaluating Trust and Authority in Electronic Materials

by Jeffrey Barlow

At the Berglund Center for Internet Studies [1] and the Matsushita Center for Electronic Learning [2] at Pacific University we have long searched for a means to indicate the level of authority of the electronic materials we post. We are well-established centers with well over five million hits per year into our servers. We publish several journals of significance and influence, such as Interface on the *Internet* and *E-AsPac*. [3] However, we also publish many projects done by graduate and undergraduate students. Between these two poles we publish conference papers and occasional papers done by members of our audiences. These materials, then, are created for different purposes and to different review standards.

We know that our audience often selects these materials indiscriminately, based more on their immediate research needs than on the reliability or authority of the materials. In an effort to further educate our audiences, and out of our desire to help establish standards and practices for electronic materials, we have decided to begin "stamping" our materials posted from fall of 2004 with seals indicating their Authority Level.

By Authority Level we do not mean to indicate "good" and "bad" but rather authoritative and non-authoritative or those with higher levels of trust and those with lower levels. Many important works have been created by writers who did not undergo peer-review, did not possess a terminal degree in the field, and who wrote badly with scant attention to scholarly niceties. However, such materials should best be judged by other scholars, or by the test of proving useful or provocative over time. They cannot be trusted at the first reading; they do not speak with great authority.

By applying a seal attesting to Authority Level, we are stating that insofar as we can determine, the reader can "trust" the conclusions of the pieces posted with the indicated level of confidence. In short, pieces at lower levels may be excellent, but we can't determine that they are, and the reader should have a lower initial level of confidence in them.

---

1 http://bcis.pacificu.edu/
2 http://mcel.pacificu.edu/
3 http://mcel.pacificu.edu/easpac/

These levels are explained below, but it should be noted that invariably some materials are in grey areas between categories.

Level 5 materials have to pass a number of tests and represent the highest possible level of trust or authority. They are equivalent to materials published in paper form by scholarly journals or presses. They could be placed in a library and should prove useful for some length of time.

They have the following characteristics, but no piece, of course, will necessarily have all of them:

- Materials certified as Authority Level 5 have been reviewed by scholars in the appropriate field following practices long utilized in scholarly journals and other refereed publications. That is, they have been read closely by one or more established professionals comfortable with the topic area of the piece. The review process was "double-blind." That is, neither the authors nor the reviewers were aware of each other's identities.
- In the judgments of these readers, the piece makes a contribution to the topic being discussed; that is, they are not merely a restatement of existing scholarly opinions.
- The materials have both citations and bibliographies sufficient to permit readers to retrace the author's research steps so as to form their own opinion as to the strength and weaknesses of the pieces when measured against the set of evidence on which they were constructed.
- The author should discuss methodology as well as evidence: how do they know what they know?
- The articles show an awareness of the current state of the topic by referencing or discussing recent scholarship in both important books and articles. The author should probably indicate areas where there are differences of opinion among authorities.
- The author of the piece is known, can be contacted to discuss or defend his or her positions, and themselves have some specialized education, training, or experience relative to their topic.
- The piece is well written and organized and has a minimum of spelling, grammatical or formatting errors, showing the qualities of mind necessary to good research, thought, and writing.

- Such publications would usually include research done in the language(s) of the subject field as appropriate.
- Limitations of Level 5 materials: Despite these strict standards, even the best research and writing has areas of relative weakness, and scholars in the field will often disagree about each others' positions. The more "cutting edge" a piece, the more likely it is to be controversial. For the average reader, however, these controversies are likely to be unimportant ones.

Materials certified as Level 4 are not different so much in quality as in degree from Level 5 materials. They might have the following characteristics:

- The level of authority of the writer may not be the highest possible in the field of study and the process of review may be less thorough.
- The pieces have been read by somebody with some expertise in the field and in effect are certified as free from egregious errors of fact or important omissions.
- The authors are known, can be contacted, and have some relative level of expertise in the field about which they are writing.
- The materials used in the research are obvious if not always strictly cited. A reader should be able, then, to roughly reconstruct the author's research paths.
- The author's methodology should be at least strongly implied if not obvious.
- The pieces should be based on at least some original materials (those written by eyewitnesses or participants with direct knowledge of the events or issues discussed) rather than entirely in secondary materials (those written from analyses of original materials).
- There should be a bibliography.
- The author should demonstrate some expertise in dealing with scholarly controversies and materials.
- Limitations of Level 4 materials: These materials can be used with confidence, but it may well be that there are better materials to be found on these same topics.

Level 3 materials are often the result of research projects done by inexperienced authors, but guided by experienced ones. These might include extensive undergraduate research projects. They have the following characteristics:

- Level 3 materials should be free from errors of fact. If some of their conclusions are controversial ones, these should be held by at least some authorities in the field of study.
- Level 3 materials should depend to a considerable extent upon published and easily available materials so that readers can themselves explore the topic further with some confidence.
- The basis of conclusions drawn in level 3 materials should be clear and rooted in research, not in mere opinion or prejudice.
- Level 3 authors should be known, and can be contacted to discuss their works.
- The works are dated as to time of origin and any updates that occurred.
- Limitations of level 3 materials: Level 3 materials may provide an adequate beginning for serious research, but should not be the sole foundation of such research. They might well provide a good orientation to the topic and suggest additional research paths, but this is their major strength.

Authority Level 2 materials have serious limitations and it is our intention not to publish such materials. For our purposes, however, they might be known by the following characteristics:

- Writing is poorly organized, there are spelling and grammatical errors, all indicators of superficial thinking and research.
- Materials are inadequately cited and there is no useful bibliography so that it is impossible to retrace the author's steps.
- The nature of the evidence relied upon is not clear.

- The author in no way relies upon any obvious authoritative sources or materials.
- The author is not known or cannot be contacted.
- The materials are not dated.
- Utility of Level 2 materials: It may be that serious scholars or researchers could utilize such materials, but most often as the raw material of their own studies. For example, scholars studying popular culture might find blog entries on current films or music or politics useful but would be unlikely to cite them to support their own positions.

Authority Level 1 materials: Again, we will never post such materials, but for analytical purposes we would define them as having the following characteristics:

- A hypothetical "reasonable reader" would find them indicative of non-logical thought processes.
- Writing would be confusing or ambiguous.
- Organization would be so poor as to leave the reader lost and confused; we do not know why paragraphs are arranged as they are.
- There would be no indication of author and no attempt to establish authority.
- Utility of Level 1 materials: Like Level 2 materials, they might be useful for some scholarly projects, but not to convey information or analysis.
- Please note that the standards for Level of Trust for posted pieces vary from those appropriate to electronic sites or clusters per se.

Index

A

B

C

D

E

F

Made in the USA
Monee, IL
08 November 2026

68085079R00155